Hugh Reginald Haweis

My Musical Memories

Hugh Reginald Haweis

My Musical Memories

ISBN/EAN: 9783337084455

Printed in Europe, USA, Canada, Australia, Japan

Cover: Foto ©Thomas Meinert / pixelio.de

More available books at **www.hansebooks.com**

MY MUSICAL MEMORIES

BY

H. R. HAWEIS

AUTHOR OF "MUSIC AND MORALS," "AMERICAN HUMORISTS," ETC.

NEW YORK
FUNK & WAGNALLS, Publishers
10 AND 12 DEY STREET
1884

PUBLISHERS' NOTE.

This book is published from advance sheets, simultaneously with its appearance in England. With the aid of the author, it has been revised for publication in this country, portions being omitted which were deemed of less interest to American readers.

Entered, according to Act of Congress, in the year 1884, by
FUNK & WAGNALLS,
In the Office of the Librarian of Congress at Washington, D. C

CONTENTS.

CHAPTER I.
EARLY LIFE AND RECOLLECTIONS.......................... 5

CHAPTER II.
HEARING MUSIC.. 49

CHAPTER III.
OLD VIOLINS... 85

CHAPTER IV.
PAGANINI... 105

CHAPTER V.
WAGNER... 144

CHAPTER VI.
PARSIFAL... 200

CHAPTER VII.
THE NIEBELUNG'S RING.
   I.—Rheingold 225
   II.—Walküre.. 230
   III.—Siegfried.. 236
   IV.—The Götterdämmerung........................ 242

CHAPTER VIII.
LISZT.. 251

MY MUSICAL MEMORIES.

CHAPTER I.

EARLY LIFE AND RECOLLECTIONS.

I THINK it was Lord Beaconsfield who said that a man is usually interesting in proportion as his talk runs upon what he is familiar with; and that as a man usually knows more about himself than about anything else, he seldom fails to be tolerable if his self-centred talk turns out to be unaffected and sincere. To talk about one's self and to be dull is nevertheless possible. In the early pages of this volume I shall have to do the first to a considerable extent; let me hope to avoid the second.

Music is not the business of my life, but it remains its sweetest recreation; and there is one opinion which used to be widely held by my friends in the old days, and to which I subscribed for many years. Nature, they often said, intended me for a violinist. In fact, my musical life starts from the violin; and, "Stradivario duce"—Stradivarius leading the way—I feel inspired, "after long years," to retrace with a certain keen pleasure these labyrinthine passages of Musical Memory.

There is something about the shape of a violin—its curves, its physiognomy, its smiling and genial ʃƷ's—which seems to invite and welcome inspection and handling.

Tarisio, the Italian carpenter, came under this fascination to good purpose. He began by mending old fiddles; he himself played a little; he grew more enamored of these mysterious, lifeless, yet living companions of his solitude, until he began to "trade in fiddles."

At the beginning of this century, hidden away in old Italian convents and wayside inns, lay the masterpieces of the Amati, Stradivarius, the Guarnerii, and Bergonzi, almost unknown and little valued. But Tarisio's eye was getting cultivated. He was learning to know a fiddle when he saw it.

"Your violin, signor, requires mending?" says the itinerant peddler, as he salutes some monk or padre known to be connected with the sacristy or choir of Pisa, Florence, Milan. "I can mend it."

Out comes the Stradivarius, with a loose bar or a split rib, and sounding abominably.

"Dio mio!" says Tarisio, "and all the blessed saints! but your violin is in a bad way. My respected father is prayed to try one that I have, in perfect and beautiful accord and repair; and permit me to mend this worn-out machine."

And Tarisio, whipping a shining, clean instrument out of his bag, hands it to the monk, who eyes it and is for trying it. He tries it; it goes soft and sweet, though not loud and wheezy, like the battered old Strad. Tarisio clutches his treasure.

The next day back comes the peddler to the cloister, is shown up to the padre, whom he finds scraping away on his loan fiddle.

"But," he exclaims, "you have lent me a beautiful violin, and in perfect order."

"Ah! if the father would accept from me a small favor," says the cunning Tarisio.

"And what is that?"

"To keep the violin that suits him so well, and I will take in exchange the old machine which is worn out, but with my skill I shall still make something of it!"

A glass of good wine, or a lemonade, or black coffee, clinches the bargain. Off goes Tarisio, having parted with a characterless German fiddle—sweet and easy-going and "looking nice," and worth now about £5—in perfect order, no doubt—and having secured one of those gems of Cremona which now run into £300. Violin-collecting became the passion of Tarisio's life. The story has been told by Mr. Charles Reade, and all the fiddle-world knows how Tarisio came to Paris with a batch of old instruments, and was taken up by Chanot and Vuillaume, through whose hands passed nearly every one of those *chefs-d'œuvre* recovered by Tarisio in his wanderings, which now are so eagerly contended for by English and American millionaires, whenever they happen to get into the market.

I have heard of a mania for snuff-boxes—it was old Lablache's hobby. There are your china-maniacs, and your picture-maniacs, and your old-print connoisseurs who only look at the margin, and your old-book hunters who only glance at the title-page and edition, and your coin-collectors, and your gem-collectors, who are always being taken in; but for downright fanaticism and "gone-cooniness," if I may invent the word, commend me to your violin-maniac. He who once comes under that spell, goes down to the grave with a disordered mind.

I said that I was, perhaps, intended for a violinist by nature. I can understand Tarisio's passion, though I never followed out that particular branch of it which led him to collect, repair, and sell. I could not buy violins—the prices have risen since the days of the Italian peddler. I could not cheat people out of them; the world was too knowing for that—and then I was too virtuous. I could not "travel" in violins; it was not my vocation, and one may in these days go far and get little—for it is now about as easy to find a Stradivarius as a Correggio. But long before I had ever touched a violin I was fascinated with its appearance. In driving up to town as a child—when, standing up in the carriage, I could just look out of the window—certain fiddle-shops hung with mighty rows of violoncellos attracted my attention. I had dreams of these large editions—these patriarchs of the violin, as they seemed to me. I compared them in my mind with the smaller tenors and violins. I dreamed about their brown, big, dusty bodies and affable good-natured-looking heads and grinning ʃʅ's. These violin shops were the great points watched for on each journey up to London from Norwood, where I spent my early days.

Youth is the great season of surprises, as it certainly is of delights. There never were such buttercup fields and strawberry ices as in the days of my childhood. Men try to make hay now, but it is poor work; and as for modern ices, they are either frozen amiss or ill-mixed. They are not good enough for me, who can remember what they were in the Exhibition of 1851. One of my keenest musical impressions is connected with that marvellous show. I shall never see such another. As I stood in the gallery of the great crystal transept and looked down upon a spectacle such as has been witnessed since, but had never before been seen, a feeling of intoxication—there is no other word for it—came over me.

I remember perfectly well falling into a kind of dream

as I leaned over the painted iron balcony and looked down on the splendid vista. The silver-bell-like tones of an Erard—it was the 1000-guinea piano—pierced through the human hum and noise of splashing waters, but it was a long way off. Suddenly, in the adjoining gallery, the large organ broke out with a blare of trumpets that thrilled and riveted me with an inconceivable emotion. I knew not then what those opening bars were. Evidently something martial, festal, jubilant, and full of triumph. I listened and held my breath to hear Mendelssohn's "Wedding March" for the first time, and not know it! To hear it when half the people present had never heard of Mendelssohn, three years after his death, and when not one in a hundred could have told me what was being played—that is an experience I shall never forget. As successive waves of fresh inexhaustible inspiration flowed on, vibrating through the building without a check or a pause, the peculiar Mendelssohnian spaces of cantabile melody alternating as they do in that march with the passionate and almost fierce decision of the chief processional theme, I stood riveted, bathed in the sound as in an element. I felt ready to melt into those harmonious yet turbulent waves and float away upon the tides of "Music's golden sea setting toward Eternity." The angel of Tennyson's Vision might have stood by me whispering,

And thou listenest the lordly music flowing from the illimitable years.

Some one called me, so I was told afterward, but I did not hear. They supposed that I was following; they went on, and were soon lost in the crowd. Presently one came back and touched me, but I did not feel. I could not be roused, my soul was living apart from my body. When the music ceased the spell slowly dissolved, and I was led away still half in dreamland. For long years afterward the "Wedding March," which is now considered *banale* and clap-trap by the advanced school, affected me strangely. Its power over me has almost entirely ceased. It is a memory now more than a realization—

eheu! fugaces, Posthume,
Posthume, labuntur anni—

This was in 1851; but it must have been about the year 1846 that I was taken up to a concert at Exeter Hall, and heard there for the first time what seemed to me to be music of unearthly sweetness.

The room was crowded. I was far behind. I could only see the fiddlesticks of the band in the distance. Four long-drawn-out tender wails on the wind rising, rising; then a soft, rapid, flickering kind of sound, high up in the treble clef, broke from a multitude of fiddles, ever growing in complexity as the two fiddles at each desk divided the harmonies among them, pausing as the deep melodious breathing of wind instruments suspended in heavy slumbrous sighs their restless agitation, then recommencing till a climax was reached, and the whole band broke in with that magnificent subject which marks the first complete and satisfying period of musical solution in the overture to the "Midsummer Night's Dream!"

I was at once affected as I had never before been. I did not know then that it was the Mendelssohn mania that had come upon me. It seized upon the whole musical world of forty years ago, and discolored the taste and judgment of those affected, for every other composer. The epidemic lasted for about twenty years at its height; declined rather suddenly with the growing appreciation of Schumann, the tardy recognition of

Spohr, and the revival of Schubert, receiving its *quietus* of course with the triumph of Wagner. People *now* "place" Mendelssohn; *then* they worshipped him.

As my ideas group themselves most naturally about my favorite instrument — the violin — I may as well follow the thread of my narrative in connection with my earliest violin recollections. I became possessed, at the age of six years, of a small red eighteen-penny fiddle and stick, with that flimsy bow and those thready strings, which are made apparently only to snap, even as the fiddle is made only to smash. I thus early became familiar with the idol of my youth. But familiarity did not breed contempt. I proceeded to elicit from the red eighteen-penny all it had to give; and when I had done with it, my nurse removed the belly, and found it made an admirable dustpan or wooden shovel for cinders, and, finally, excellent firewood. Many went that way, without my passion for toy fiddles suffering the least decline; nay, it rather grew by what it (and the fire) fed on. It may not be superfluous to add that I had by this time found means to make the flimsiest strings yield up sounds which I need not here characterize, and to such purpose that it became a question of some interest how long such sounds could be endured by the human ear. I do not mean my own. All violinists, including infants on eighteen-pennies, admit that to their own ear the sounds produced are nothing but delightful; it is only those who do not make them who complain. As it seemed unlikely that my studies on the violin would stop, it became expedient that they should be directed. A full-sized violin was procured me. I have every reason to believe it was one of the worst fiddles I ever saw.

I had played many times with much applause, holding

a full-sized violin between my knees. I was about eight years old when the services of the local organist—a Mr. Ingram, of Norwood—were called in. His skill on the violin was not great, but it was enough for me; too much, indeed, for he insisted on my holding the violin up to my chin. The fact is, he could not play it in any other position himself, so how could he teach me? Of course the instrument was a great deal too large; but I strained and stretched until I got it up; for as it would not grow down to me, I had to grow up to it. And here I glance at the crucial question, Ought young children to begin upon small-sized violins? All makers say " Yes ;" naturally, for they supply the new violins of all sizes. But I emphatically say "No." The sooner the child is accustomed to the right violin intervals the better; the small violins merely present him with a series of wrong distances, which he has successively to unlearn. It is bad enough if in after years he learns the violoncello or tenor. Few violinists survive that ordeal, and most people who take to the tenor or 'cello after playing the violin keep to it. Either they have not been successful on the violin, or they hope to become so on its larger though less brilliant relation; but they have a perfectly true instinct that it is difficult to excel on both, *because of the intervals.* Yet, in the face of this, you put a series of violins of different sizes into the pupil's hand, on the ground that, as his hand enlarges with years, the enlarged key-board will suit his fingers better; but that is not the way the brain works—*the brain learns intervals.* It does not trouble itself about the size of the fingers that have to stretch them.

A child of seven or eight can stretch most of the ordinary intervals on a full-sized violin finger-board. He may not be able to hold the violin to his chin; but he can learn his scales and pick out tunes, sitting on a stool and holding his instrument like a violoncello. Before the age of eight I found no difficulty in doing this. But the greater the difficulty the better the practice. The tendons cannot be too much stretched short of spraining and breaking. Mere aching is to be made no account of; the muscles can hardly be too much worked. A child will soon gain surprising agility, even on a large finger-board. Avoid the hateful figured slip of paper that used to be pasted on violin finger-boards in my youth, with round dots for the fingers. I remember tearing mine off in a fit of uncontrollable irritation. I found it very difficult, with the use of my eyes, to put my fingers on the dots, and even then the note was not always in tune, for of course the dot might be covered in a dozen ways by the finger-tips, and a hair's breadth one way or the other would vary the note. But the principle is vicious. A violin player's eyes have no more business with his fingers than a billiard player's eyes have with his cue. He looks at the ball; and the musician, if he looks at anything, should look at the notes, or at his audience, or he can shut his eyes if he likes. It is his ears, not his eyes, have to do with the fingers.

I was about eight years old. My musical studies were systematic, if not well directed. Every morning for two hours I practised scales and various tunes at a double desk, my father on one side and I on the other. We played the most deplorable arrangements, and we made the most detestable noise. We played Beethoven's overture to "Prometheus," arranged for two fiddles, Callcott's German melodies with piano-forte accompaniment, and without the violoncello part, and Corelli's trios—also without the third instrument. I had somehow ceased to take lessons now. My father's knowledge of violin playing was exactly on a level with my own. His skill, he modestly owned, was even less; but had it not been for him I never should have played at all. Our method was simple. We sat for two hours after breakfast and scraped. In the evening, with the addition of the piano, we scraped again—anything we could get hold of—and we did get hold of odd things: Locke's music to "Macbeth," old quadrilles, the "Battle of Prague," "God save the Emperor," and the "Huntsman's Chorus." I confess I hated the practising; it was simple drudgery—and put it in what way you will, the early stage of violin playing *is* drudgery; but it must be gone through with. And then I had my hours of relaxation. I used to walk up and down the lawn in our garden playing tunes in my own fashion. I got very much at home on the finger-board, and that is the grand thing after all. No one ever gets at home there who has not begun young—not so young as I began, but at least under the age of twelve. I was soon considered an infant phenomenon on the violin, stood on tables, and was trotted out at parties, and I thus early got over all shyness at playing in public.

At this time Jenny Lind and Ernst were both in London; and Liszt, I believe, passed through like a meteor. I never heard any of them in their prime, though I did hear Madame Lind-Goldschmidt sing the "Ravens" at a concert years afterward, and it was my privilege to hear Ernst before he had lost his cunning, nor shall I ever hear his like again. He played once at Her Majesty's Opera House, when the whole assembly seemed to dream through a performance of the "Hungarian Airs." The lightest whisper of the violin controlled the house; the magician hardly stirred his wand at times, and no one could tell from the sound when he passed from the *up* to the *down* bow in those long cantabile notes which had such power to entrance me.

I heard Ernst later at Brighton. He played out of tune, and I was told that he was so shaken in nerve, that, playing a Beethoven quartet in private, and coming to a passage of no great difficulty, which I have often scrambled through with impunity, the great master laid down his fiddle and declared himself unequal to the effort.

Great, deep-souled, weird magician of the Cremona! I can see thy pale, gaunt face even now! those dark, haggard-looking eyes, with the strange veiled fires, semi-mesmeric, the wasted hands, so expressive and sensitive, the thin, lank hair and emaciated form, yet with nothing demoniac about thee like Paganini, from whom thou wast absolutely distinct. No copy thou—thyself all thyself—tender, sympathetic, gentle as a child, suffering, always suffering; full of an excessive sensibility; full of charm; irresistible and fascinating beyond words! Thy Cremona should have been buried with thee. It has fallen into other hands. I see it every season in the concert-room: Madame Norman-Néruda plays it. I know she is an admirable artist. I do not hear thy Cremona; its voice has gone out with thee, its soul has passed with thine.

* * * * * *

In the night I hear it under the stars, when the moon is low, and I see the dark ridges of the clover hills, and rabbits and hares, black against the paler sky, pausing to feed or crouching to listen to the voices of the night.

* * * * * *

Alone in the autumn woods, when through the shivering trees I see the angry yellow streaks of the sunset, and the dead leaves fall across a sky that threatens storm.

* * * * * *

By the sea, when the cold mists rise, and hollow murmurs, like the low wail of lost spirits, rush along the beach.

* * * * * *

In some still valley in the South, in midsummer, the slate-colored moth on the rock flashes suddenly into crimson and takes wing; the bright-eyed lizard darts timorously, and the singing of the grasshopper never ceases in the long grass; the air is heavy and slumbrous with insect life and the breath of flowers. I can see the blue sky—intense blue, mirrored in the lake—and a bird floats mirrored in the blue, and over the shining water comes the sound, breaking the singing silences of nature: such things are in our dreams!

* * * * * *

It is thus only I can hear again the spirit voice of thy Cremona, dead master; but not at St. James's Hall, no longer in the crowded haunts of men as once. Its body only is there: its soul was the very soul of the master who has passed to where the chiming is "after the chiming of the eternal spheres."

I heard other great players: Sivori, delicate, refined, with a perfect command of his instrument—a pupil of Paganini's, playing all his pieces, and probably no more like him than a Roman candle is like a meteor; Chatterton on the harp, a thankless instrument, without variety and never in tune, whose depths are quickly sounded—an *arpeggio*, a few *harmonics*, a few full glorious chords, an ethereal whispering, and *da capo!* Piatti on the violoncello—a truly disembodied violoncello—so pure and free from catgut and rosin came the sound; and pianists innumerable in later days. But if, looking back and up to the present hour, I am asked to name off-hand the greatest players—the very greatest I have heard—I say at once Ernst, Liszt, Rubinstein.

From such heights I am loath to return to my own insignificant doings, but they happen to supply me with the framework for my present meditations: they are, in fact, the pegs on which I have chosen to hang my thoughts. I was at a complete standstill: I sorely needed instruction. I went to the seaside for my health. One day, in the morning, I entered the concert room of the town hall at Margate. It was empty, but on a platform at the farther end, half a dozen musicians were rehearsing. One sat up at a front desk and seemed to be leading on the violin. As they paused, I walked straight up to him. I was about twelve then.

"Please sir," I began rather nervously, "do you teach the violin?"

He looked round rather surprised, but in another moment he smiled kindly, and said:

"Why, yes—at least," he added, "that depends. Do you mean you want to learn?"

"That's it," I said; "I have learned a little. Will you teach me?"

"Wait a bit. I must finish here first, and then I'll come down to you. Can you wait?" he added, cheerily.

I had been terribly nervous when I began to ask him, but now I felt my heart beating with joy.

"Oh yes," I said, "I can wait!" and I waited and heard them play, and watched every motion of one whom I already looked upon as my master.

And he became my master—my first *real* master. Good, patient Mr. Devonport! I took to him, and he took to me at once. He got me to unlearn all my slovenly ways, taught me how to hold my fiddle and how to finger and how to bow. It seems I did everything wrong. He used to write out Kreutzer's early exercises, over his breakfast, and bring them to me all blotted, in pen and ink, and actually got into disgrace, so he said, with his landlady, for inking the table-cloth! That seemed to me heroic; but who would not have mastered the crabbed bowing, the ups and downs and staccatos, and slur two and bow one, and slur three and bow one, and slur two and two, after that! And I did my best, though not to his satisfaction; but he never measured his time with me, and he had an indefinitely sweet way with him which won me greatly, and made me love my violin—a five-pound Vuilhaume copy of Stradivarius, crude in tone—more than ever.

When I left the sea, I lost my master. I never saw him again. If he is alive now, and these lines should chance to meet his eye, I will join hands with him across the years. Why should he not be alive? Hullah and Sainton and Piatti and Mme. Dolby and Mme. Lind-Goldschmidt, and I know not how many more of his contemporaries, and my elders, are alive. Only there was a sadness and delicacy about that pale diaphanous face, its hectic flush, its light hair, and slight fringe of mustache; I can remember it so well; and I must own, too, there was a little cough, which makes me fear that Devonport was not destined to live long. Some one remarked it at the time, but I thought nothing of it then.

I made a great stride under Devonport, and my next master, whom I disliked exceedingly, was a young Pole, Lapinski, who could not speak a word of English. Our lessons were very dull. He taught me little, but he taught me something—the *art of making my fingers ache*—the great art, according to Joachim. My time with him was pure drudgery, unrelieved by a single glow of pleasure or gleam of recreation; he was a dogged and hard taskmaster, knew exactly what he meant, and was utterly indifferent to the likes and dislikes of his pupil—the very opposite to Devonport, whom in six weeks I got positively to love. In music, you learn more in a week from a sympathetic teacher, or at least from some one who is so to you, than from another, however excellent, in a month. You will make no progress if he can give you no impulse.

What a mystery lies in that word "teaching"! One will constrain you irresistibly, and another shall not be able to persuade you. One will kindle you with an ambition that aspires to what the day before seemed inaccessible heights, while another will labor in vain to stir your sluggish mood to cope with the smallest obstacle. The reciprocal relation is too often forgotten. It is assumed that any good master or mistress will suit any willing pupil. Not at all—any more than A can mesmerize B, who goes into a trance immediately on the appearance of C. All personal relations, and teaching relations are intensely personal, have to do with subtle conditions—unexplored, but inexorable and instantly perceived. The soul puts out, as it were, its invisible antennæ, knowing the soul that is kindred to itself. I do *not* want to be told whether you can teach me anything. I *know* you cannot. I will not learn from you what I *must* learn from another; what he will be bound to teach me. All you may have to say may be good and true, but it is a little impertinent and out of place. You spoil the truth. You mar the beauty. I will not hear these things from you; you spoil nature; you

wither art; you are not for me, and I am not for you—
"Let us go hence, my songs—she will not hear."

My next master was Oury. I fell in with him at Brighton when I was about sixteen. He had travelled with Paganini and was a consummate violinist himself. He was a short, angry-looking, stoutly-built little man. Genial with those who were sympathetic to him, and sharp, savage, and sarcastic with others—he made many enemies, and was unscrupulous in his language. I found he had been unlucky, and I hardly wonder at it; for a man more uncertain, unstable, and capricious in temper I never met—but he was an exquisite player. His fingers were thick and plump, his hand was fat and short, not unlike that of poor Jaell, the late pianist. How he could stop his intervals in tune and execute passages of exceeding delicacy with such hands was a mystery to me; but Jaell did things even more amazing with his—stretching the most impossible intervals, and bowling his fat hands up and down the key-board like a couple of galvanized balls.

I was at this time about sixteen, and a member of the Brighton Symphony Society. We played the symphonies of the old masters to not very critical audiences in the Pavilion, and I have also played in the Brighton Town Hall. It was at these meetings I first fell in with Oury.

I noticed a little group in the anteroom on one of the rehearsal nights; they were chattering round a thickset, crotchety-looking little man and trying to persuade him to do something. He held his fiddle, but would not easily yield to their entreaties. They were asking him to play. At last he raised his Cremona to his chin and began to improvise. What fancy and delicacy and execution! what refinement! His peculiar gift lay not only in a full round tone, but in the musical "embroideries"—the long flourishes, the torrents of multitudinous notes ranging all over the instrument. I can liken those astonishing violin passages to nothing but the elaborate embroidery of little notes which in Chopin's music are spangled in tiny type all round the subject, which is in large type. When Oury was in good humor he would gratify us in this way, and then stop abruptly, and nothing after that would induce him to play another note. He had the fine large style of the De Beriot school, combined with a dash of the brilliant and romantic Paganini, and the most exquisite taste of his own. In those days De Beriot's music reigned supreme in the concert-room until the appearance of Paganini. It had not yet gone out of fashion, and I remember hearing Oury play De Beriot's showy first concerto with a full orchestra, at the Pavilion, in a way which reminded me of some conqueror traversing a battle-field; the enthusiasm he aroused was quite remarkable, in that languid and ignorant crowd of loitering triflers. He certainly brought the house down. He was a great player, though past his prime, and he knew how to score point after point without ever sacrificing his musical honor by stooping to clap-trap.

From Oury I received, between the ages of fifteen and seventeen, my last definite violin instruction. After that I studied for myself and heard assiduously the best players, but I was never taught anything. Oury had been trained himself in the old and new schools of Rode, Baillot, and De Beriot, and only grafted on the sensational discoveries, methods, and tricks of Paganini, Ernst, and Sivori. But he was artist enough to absorb without corruption and appropriate without mimicry. He always treated me with a semi-humorous, though kindly, indulgence. He was extremely impatient, and got quite bitter and angry with my ways; stormed at my self-will; said I had such a terrible second finger that he believed the devil was in it. I had a habit of playing whole tunes with my second finger on the fourth string. It seemed more muscular than the rest, and from this point of view quite upset the equilibrium of the hand. He had a habit of sighing deeply over the lessons.

"You should have been in the profession. What's the use of teaching you? Bah! you will never do anything. I shall teach you no more."

Then he would listen, as I played some bravura passage in my own way, half-amused, half-surprised, half-satirical; my method was clearly wrong, but how had I got through the passage at all? Then taking the violin from me he would play it himself, without explanation, and then play on and say:

"Listen to me; that is your best lesson, you rascal! I believe you never practise at all. Nature has given you too much facility. Your playing will never be worth anything. You do not deserve the gifts God has given you."

At times poor Oury took quite a serious and desponding view of me. He would sit long over his hour, playing away and playing to me, telling me stories about Paganini's loosening the horsehair of his bow and passing the whole violin between the stick and the horsehair, thus allowing the loosened horsehair to scrape all four strings together, and producing the effect of a quartet. He described the great magician's playing of harmonic passages, and showed me how it was done, and told me how the fiddlers when Paganini played sat open-mouthed, unable to make out how he got at all his consecutive harmonics.

In his lighter moods he taught me the farmyard on the violin; how to make the donkey bray, the hen chuckle, the cuckoo sing, the cow moo. He taught me Paganini's "Carnival de Venise" variations; some of them —especially the canary variation—so absurdly easy to any fingers at home on the violin, yet apparently so miraculous to the uninitiated. But it remained his bitterest reflection that amateur I was, and amateur I was destined to be; otherwise, I believe, I should have been a pupil after his heart, for he spent hour after hour with me, and never seemed to reckon his time or his toil by money.

If I did not acquire the right method, it was not Oury's fault. He taught me how to hold the violin; to spread my fingers instead of crumpling up those I was not using; to bow without sawing round my shoulder.

"In position," he used often to say, "nothing is right unless all is right. Hold your wrist right, the bow must go right; hold your fiddle well up, or you cannot get the tone."

Above all, he taught me how to *whip* instead of *scraping* the sound out. This springing, elastic bowing he contrasted with the grinding of badly-taught fiddlers, who checked the vibration. Some violinists of repute have been "grinders," but I could never bear to listen to them. Oury poisoned me early against the grinders, and all short of the men of perfect method. He instilled into me principles rather than rules. I caught from him what I was to do, and how I was to do it. He did not lecture at me like some masters; he took the violin out of my hands without speaking, or with merely an impatient expletive, of which, I regret to say, he was rather too free, and played the passage for me. His explanations I might have forgotten; this I could never forget, and I could tell at once whether what I did sounded like what he did.

Oury taught me the secret of *cantabile* playing on the violin—how to treat a simple melody with rare phrasing, until it was transfigured by the mood of the player. He taught me Rode's Air in G—that beautiful melody which has been, with its well-known variations, the *pièce de résistance* of so many generations of violinists and soprani. I was drilled in every note, the bowing was rigidly fixed for me, the whole piece was marked, bar by bar, with *slur*, *p* and *f*, *rall* and *crescendo*. I was not allowed to depart a hair's breadth from rule. When I could do this easily and accurately, Oury surprised me one day by saying,

"Now you can play it as you like, you need not attend to a single mark!"

"How so?" I said.

"Don't you see," he said, "the marks don't signify: that is only one way of playing it. If you have any music in you, you can play it in a dozen other ways. Now, I will make it equally good," and he took the violin and played it through, reversing as nearly as possible all the *p's* and *f's*, "bowing" the slur and slurring the "bow," and it sounded just as well. I never forgot that lesson. At other times Oury was most punctilious about what he called "correct" bowing. He complained of my habit of beginning a *forte* "attaque" with an *up* bow—an unusual perversity, I admit—but I replied, in my conceit, I had observed Richard Blagrove do the same thing. Oury said, as sharply as wisely, "When you play like Blagrove, you may do it too; until then, oblige me, sir, by minding your up and down bow, or I cease to be your violin tutor."

I used about this time to hear some very good quartet-playing at Captain Newberry's, Brunswick Square. The captain had some fine violins; one I specially coveted; he held it to be a genuine Stradivarius; it was labelled 1712, quite in the finest period, and of the grand pattern—the back a magnificently ribbed slice of maple in one piece; the front hardly so fine; the head strong, though not so fine as I have seen—more like a Bergonzi; but the fiddle itself could never be mistaken for a Bergonzi. It had a tone like a trumpet on the fourth string; the third was full, but the second puzzled me for years, it being weak by comparison; but the violin was petulant, and after having it in my possession for thirty years, I know what to do with it if I can ever again take the time and trouble to bring it into perfect order and keep it so, as it was once my pride to do.

On Captain Newberry's death that fiddle was sent me by his widow, who did not survive him long. She said she believed it was his wish.

This violin was my faithful companion for years. I now look at it under a glass case occasionally, where it lies unstrung from one end of the year to the other. It belonged to the captain's uncle; he had set his heart on it, and having a very fine pair of carriage horses, for which he had given £180, he one day made them over to his uncle and obtained the Strad. in exchange. This was the last price paid for my violin, some fifty years ago. It came into the hands of Newberry's relative early in the present century—how, I know not. Many years ago I took this fiddle down to Bath and played it a good deal there in a band conducted by the well-known Mr. Salmon. I found he recognized it immediately. I there made acquaintance with the score of Mendelssohn's "Athalie," playing it in the orchestra. I studied the Scotch and Italian symphonies in the same way.

No amateur should omit an opportunity of orchestral or chorus work. In this way you get a more living acquaintance with the internal structure of the great masterpieces than in any other. I first made acquaintance with the "Elijah" and "St. Paul" in this way. What writing for the violin there is in the chorus parts! what telling passages are those in "Be not afraid," where the first violins lift the phrases, rise after rise, until the shrill climax is reached and the aspiring passage is closed with a long drawn-out *ff*.

When the violins pealed louder and louder, mounting upward, it was always a delight to me to hear my own powerful first string thrilling through all the others. The conductor used to know this passage and the way in which it told on my Strad., and invariably gave me a knowing nod as he heard my violin at the first fiddle-desk through all the others. I may add that, as a rule, when any particular violin in a band is heard above the rest, it usually belongs to a bungler; but there are passages where the leading violins have *carte blanche* to play up, and then, if you can, you may be allowed to sing through the rest; and, if this be anywhere allowable, it is of course so at the first violin desk.

Most boys find it difficult to keep up their music at school; with me it was the reverse; my ill health was the making of my music. I had been an invalid on and off up to the age of seventeen. I remember Sir Benjamin Brodie, the great doctor, a thin, wizen, little old man, coming and staring at me, about the year 1848, at No. 2 Spanish Place, my grandfather's house in London. I was then suffering from hip disease. They asked him whether I should be taken to Brighton. He mumbled something to himself and turned away to speak to my father aside. I merely noticed an expression of great pain and anxiety on my father's face as he listened. Afterward I knew the great doctor had said it did not matter where I went, for in any case I could not live. He thought it was a question of weeks. He little knew how much it would take to kill me. People are born long-lived. It runs in families. It has little to do with health and disease. If you are long-lived you will weather disease, and if you are short-lived you will drop suddenly in full health, or be blown out like a candle, with a whiff of fever or bronchitis. Sir Benjamin pocketed his fee and departed. In great perplexity what to do, we cast lots; I think it was at my suggestion. The lot came out in favor of Brighton. To Brighton I was taken, apparently in a dying state, but at my grandmother's house in Brunswick Square I began rapidly to amend.

My violin was my solace, when I grew strong enough to hold it again. The time that should have been spent upon mathematics, Latin, and Greek was spent in my case upon French, German, and music—I may add novels, for between the ages of twelve and sixteen I read all Bulwer, Walter Scott, G. P. R. James, Fenimore Cooper, and, in certain visits to Bath and Bognor, I took care to exhaust the ancient stores of fiction which I found secreted in the antiquated lending libraries of those privileged resorts.

When I was sixteen it became evident that I was not going to die; my health was still feeble, and my general education defective. I was sent to an excellent tutor at the Isle of Wight, the Rev. John Bicknell, now incumbent of St. Saviour's, Highbury. That good man never overcame my dislike to mathematics, but he got me on in Latin, and he was kind enough to tolerate my violin.

I could no longer play cricket, or climb trees, the chief delights of my earlier days—nor could I take long walks with the boys. I was left entirely alone in play hours—*i.e.*, almost every afternoon. I think I was perfectly happy by myself. And there was such utter solitude for me, in the silent lanes, the summer woodlands, and by the lovely sea-shore, that—well—I had plenty of time to think. I sat on stiles and thought; I tasted almost every kind of berry and herb that grew in the hedges. I watched the butterflies and the teeming insect life, and I would lie down in the woody recesses and leafy coverts like one dead, until the birds, the rabbits, and even the weasels and stoats came close enough for me to see their exquisitely clean soft fur, bright eyes, or radiant plumage. I have surprised a wild hawk on her nest in the gorse, and she has never moved.

About this time I wrote quantities of the most dismal poetry, which appeared at intervals in the columns of the Brighton papers. It was naturally a mixture of Bryant and Longfellow; later on it became a jumble of Tennyson and Browning—but such matters belong more to literature than to music.

Oury had already begun to direct my violin studies. I had ample time at school in the Isle of Wight for practising, and I practised steadily nearly every day. I had a faculty for practising. I knew what to do, and I did it. I always remembered what Joachim had said about tiring out the hand; and with some abominable torture passages, invented for me by that morose Pole, Lapinski, I took a vicious pleasure in making my fingers ache, and an intense delight in discovering the magical effects of the torture upon my execution.

I put my chief trust in Kreutzer's exercises—admirable in invention and most attractive as musical studies—

the more difficult ones in chords being little violin solos in themselves. I perfected myself in certain solos at this time. I had no one to play my accompaniments, and no one cared to hear me play at school, except some of the boys who liked to hear me imitate the donkey and give the farmyard entertainment—including the groans of a chronic invalid and a great fight of cats on the roof—which never failed to be greeted with rapturous applause.

I said no one cared to hear me play at Freshwater. Yes, some people did. One autumn while I was at Freshwater, an old house, Farringford, with a rambling garden at the back of the downs, was let to Baron A.—an eminent light of the Bench—and his charming family. I forget how they discovered my existence, but I dare say Lady A. and the young ladies found the place rather dull, and they were not the people to neglect their opportunities.

I received an invitation to dinner; my violin was also asked. I did not reply like Sivori when similarly invited to bring his violin with him: "Merci! mon violonne ne dine pas!" I saw to my strings and screws, put together my solos, and went.

Soon after the A.'s left Farringford it was taken by the Poet Laureate. At that time I was rapidly outgrowing Longfellow, and my enthusiasm for Mr. Tennyson amounted to a mania: he was to me in poetry what Mendelssohn was in music. I can now place him. I can now see how great he is. I can now understand his relation to other poets. Then I could not. He confused and dazzled me. He took possession of my imagination. He taught me to see and to feel for the first time the heights and depths of life; to discern dimly what I could then have had little knowledge of—" The world with all its lights and shadows, all the wealth and all the woe." In fact, Tennyson was then doing for the rising generation of that age what Byron and Shelley, Wordsworth and Coleridge, had done for theirs; only he united in himself more representative qualities than any one of the poets who preceded him, and in this respect he seems to me still a greater poet, and certainly as subtle a thinker, as any one of them, Wordsworth and Coleridge not excepted.

All this is an after-thought. Then I did not analyze or compare. The Brighton papers received elaborate prose effusions from my pen upon the subject, at the time, of a frothy and rhetorical character. Sometimes I look at them in my old scrap-books, and marvel at the bombast, inflation, and prodigious inanity of the matter and the style. No doubt I was not quite right in my head about Tennyson, and this accounts for my wending my steps toward Farringford one autumn afternoon, soon after he had come there. The poet never went to church, so the poet could never be seen. The man who, in the "In Memoriam," had recently reformulated the religion of the nineteenth century, might, one would have thought, be excused the dismal routine that went on at the parish church, and the patristic theology doled out by the worthy rector. But no! Mr. Tennyson's soul was freely despaired of in the neighborhood, and many of the people about Freshwater would have been "very faithful" with him if they could only have got at him—but they could not get at him. Under these circumstances I got at him.

I suppose the continued play of one idea upon my brain was too much for me. To live so close to the man who filled the whole of my poetic and imaginative horizon, without ever seeing him, was more than I could bear.

I walked over the neglected grass-grown gravel between the tall trees yellowing in the autumn, and up to the glass-panelled doors, as bold as fate.

"Mr. Tennyson," said the maid, "sees no one." I was aware of that. Was Mrs. Tennyson at home? Perhaps she would see me? The servant looked dubious. I was a shabby-looking student, sure enough, but there was something about me which could not be said nay! I evidently meant to get in, and in I got.

In another moment I found myself in the drawing-room lately tenanted by the Baron and Lady A.

There was the arm-chair where Lady A. had sat reclining, with her head resting on a little cushion, as she sang "Auld Robin Gray."

There was the piano beside which Miss M. stood and sang very shyly and under protest in her simple white muslin dress and a rose in her hair; there—but the door opened, and a quiet, gentle lady appeared, and bowed silently to me. I had to begin then.

I had no excuse to make, and so I offered no apology. I had called desiring to see Mr. Tennyson, that was all.

The lady looked surprised, and sat down by a little work-table with a little work-basket on it. She asked me very kindly to sit down too. So I sat down. What next? Now I grew clumsy with a vengeance. All my wits forsook me. I looked out at the tangled garden—everything was allowed to grow wild. I had to say something. I looked at the kind lady, who had already taken up her work and begun plying her needle. I said that my admiration for Mr. Tennyson's poems was so great that, as I was living in the neighborhood, I had called with an earnest desire to see him. I then began to repeat that I considered his poems so exquisite that—a smile was on the kind lady's face as she listened for the thousand and first time to such large and general praises of the Laureate's genius. But the smile somehow paralyzed me. She evidently considered me a harmless lunatic, not an impertinent intruder.

This was fortunate, for had I been summarily shown the door I should not have been surprised. I should not have gone, for I was desperate and prepared to show fight, and be kicked out, if needful, by the Laureate alone; but the Fates were propitious.

Said Mrs. Tennyson, "My husband is always very busy, and I do not at all think it likely he can see you."

"Do you think he would if you ask him?" I stammered out.

Said Mrs. Tennyson, a little taken aback, "I don't know."

"Then," said I, pursuing my advantage with, if any calm at all, the calmness of a calm despair, "would you object to asking him to see me, if only for an instant?"

What passed in that indulgent lady's mind I shall never know; the uppermost thought was probably not flattering to me, and her chief desire was, no doubt, to get rid of me:—He won't go till he has seen my husband—he ought never to have got in; but as he is here, I'll manage it and have done with him. Or she might have reflected thus: The poor fellow is not right in his head; it would be a charity to meet him half-way, and not much trouble.

At any rate at this juncture Mrs. Tennyson rose and left the room. She was gone about four minutes by the clock. It seemed to me four hours. What I went through in those four minutes no words can utter. "Will he come? I almost hope he won't. *If* he won't come, I shall have done all I could to see him, without experiencing a shock to which my nervous system is quite unequal." At that moment, indeed, I was trembling with excitement from top to toe. I thought I would try and recollect some of his own sublime verse; it might steady me a little. I knew volumes of it by heart—couldn't recollect a line anywhere, except—

> Wrinkled ostler grim and thin,
> Here is custom come your way,
> Take my brute and lead him in,
> Stuff his ribs with mouldy hay.

I believe I was muttering this mechanically when I heard a man's voice close outside the door.

"Who is it? Is it an impostor?"

Ah, verily, the word smote me to the heart. What right had I to be there? Conscience said, "Thou art the man!" I would have willingly disappeared into my boots, like the genie in the fairy tale. "O, that this too, too solid flesh would melt;" but I remained palpable and motionless—glued to the spot.

In another moment the door opened. The man whose voice I had heard—in other words, Mr. Tennyson—entered.

He was not in Court-dress; he had not a laurel wreath on his head, nor a lily in his hand—not even a harp.

It was in the days when he shaved. I have two portraits of him without a beard. I believe they are very rare now.

I thought it would be inappropriate to prostrate myself, so I remained standing and stupefied. He advanced toward me and shook hands without cordiality. Why should he be cordial? I began desperately to say that I had the greatest admiration for his poetry; that I could not bear to leave the island without seeing him. He soon stopped me, and taking a card of Captain Crozier's which lay on the table, asked me if I knew him. I said I did, and described his house and grounds in the neighborhood of Freshwater.

I have no recollection of anything else, but I believe some allusion was made to Baron A——, when the poet observed abruptly, "Now I must go; good-by!" and he went. And that was all I saw of Mr. Tennyson for nearly thirty years. The next time I set eyes on him was one Sunday morning, about twenty-eight years later. He came up the side aisle of my church, St. James, Westmoreland Street, Marylebone, and, with his son Hallam, sat near the pulpit, almost in the very spot that had been pointed out to me when I was appointed incumbent as the pew occupied by Hallam the historian and his son Arthur—the Arthur of the "In Memoriam."

But I have not quite done with the interview at Freshwater. As the poet retired, Mrs. Tennyson re-entered and sat down again at her work-table. To her surprise, no doubt, I also sat down. The fact is, I had crossed the Rubicon, and was now in a state of considerable elation and perfectly reckless. I thanked her effusively for the privilege I had had—I believe I made several tender and irrelevant inquiries after the poet's health, and wound up with earnestly requesting her to give me a bit of his handwriting.

This was perhaps going a little too far—but I had now nothing to lose—no character for sanity, or prudence, or propriety; so I went in steadily for some of the poet's handwriting.

The forbearing lady pointed out that she treasured it so much herself that she never gave it away. This would not do. I said I should treasure it to my dying day, any little scrap—by which I suppose I meant that I did not require the whole manuscript of "Maud," which the poet was then writing, and which is full of Freshwater scenery. I might be induced to leave the house with something short of that.

With infinite charity and without a sign of irritation she at last drew from her work-basket an envelope in Mr. Tennyson's handwriting, directed to herself, and gave it to me.

It was not his signature, but it contained his name.

Then, and then only, I rose. I returned to my school, and at tea-time related to my tutor with some little pride and self-conceit the nature of my exploit that afternoon. He administered to me a well-merited rebuke, which, as it came after my indiscretion, and in no way interfered with my long-coveted joy, I took patiently enough and with all meekness.

There is a strange link between these two old memories of Farringford, Isle of Wight. I may call it the link of a common oblivion. Years afterward I tried to recall to Lady A., who frequented my church in her later days, the, to me, delicious evenings I had spent with her and her daughters at Farringford. She had not the slightest recollection of ever having received me there, or sung to me there, or heard me play. She re-introduced me to her eldest daughter, the Marchioness of S., then Viscountess C., one night at her house in Portland Place, who was probably not aware of ever having seen me before, although I remembered her well at Farringford. Years afterward I tried to recall to Mr. and Mrs. Tennyson that preposterous visit of mine, which I have detailed, but neither of them could recall it in the slightest degree.

So strange is it that events which upon some of the actors leave such an indelible impression pass entirely away from the memories of the others—and what a sermon might be preached on that text! The very same scene in which you and I are the only ones concerned, is nothing to you, everything to me.

O ye tidal years that roll over us all—be kind! Wash out the memory of our pain and the dark blots of sin and grief, but leave, oh leave us bright, the burnished gold of joy, and the rainbow colors of our youth!

I have been a martyr to bad accompanists. All young ladies think they can accompany themselves—so why not you or any other man? The truth is that very few ladies can accompany at all. If they sing they will probably try, in the absence of any musical friend, to make shift with a few chords in order that the assembly may not be deprived of a song. But also if they sing they will probably have forgotten the little they once knew about pianoforte playing. To accompany yourself properly you must do it with ease and accuracy: nothing is so charming and nothing is so rare.

Singing ladies, especially amateurs, are pitiably unscrupulous, and moderately unconscious of the wild effect produced by that fitful and inaccurate dabbling with the keyboard which they palm off upon their listeners as an accompaniment. Now and then a Scotch ballad may survive such treatment—a Scotch ballad seems always grateful for any accompaniment at all; but to attempt Gounod or Schubert in this style is conduct indicative of a weak intellect and a feeble conscience.

To accompany well you must not only be a good musician, but you must be mesmeric, sympathetic, intuitive. You must know what I want before I tell you; you must feel which way my spirit sets, for the motions of the soul are swift as an angel's flight. I cannot pause in those quick and subtle transitions of emotion, fancy, passion, to tell you a secret; if it is not yours already, you are unworthy of it. What! when I had played three bars thus, you could not guess that I should hurry the fourth and droop with a melodious sigh upon the fifth! You dared to strike in at the end of a note which my intention would have stretched out into at least another semibreve! You are untrue to the rhythm of my soul. Get up from the piano, my conceited, self-satisfied young lady. Your finishing lessons in music can do nothing for you. Your case is hopeless. You have not enough music in you to know that you are a failure.

But you may be even a good musician and yet not be able to accompany. If you cannot, be passive for a while. You are of no use to me. You want to take the initiative; you must always be creating; you think you know best; you impose your "reading" upon me. What! you will do this when I am the soloist or the singer! You are professional—'tis the vice of professionals—and I am but an amateur. No matter; if I know not best, that is my affair; for better for worse you have to follow me, or you will mar me. The art of true accompanying lies in a willing self-immolation. An excess of sensibility, but a passive excess. Yet must your collaboration be strong. You must not desert me or fail me in the moment of my need or expectancy. You must cover me with thunder, you must buoy me up as a bark is buoyed up on the bosom of a great flood. You must be still anon and wait, dream with my spirit, as the winds that droop fitfully when the sea grows calm and the white sails flap idly, sighing for the breeze. I sleep, but my heart waketh! Every mood of mine must be thine as soon as it is mine, and when all is finished my soul shall bless thee, and thou too shalt feel a deep content.

As from the age of seven I have always played the violin more or less publicly, I entered upon my amateur career at Brighton without the smallest nervousness. My facility was very great, but my execution, although showy (and, I blush to add, tricky), was never as finished as I could have desired. My tone, however, was considered by Oury remarkable, and except when drilling me with a purpose, he would never interfere with my reading of a solo. It was the only point in which he gave in to me.

"I never taught you that," he would say sharply.

"Shall I alter it?" I would ask.

"No, no, let it alone; follow your own inspiration; you must do as you will; the effect is good."

Indeed no one ever taught me the art of drawing tears from the eyes of my listeners. Moments came to me when I was playing—I seemed far away from the world. I was not scheming for effect—there was no trick about it. I could give no reason for the *rall*, the *p*, the *pp*, the *f*. Something in my soul ordered it so, and my fingers followed, communicating every inner vibration through their tips to the vibrating string until the mighty heart of the Cremona pealed out like a clarion, or whispered tremblingly in response. But those moments did not come to me in mixed, buzzing audiences; then I merely waged impatient war with a mob.

They came in still rooms where a few were met, and the lights were low, and the windows open toward the sea.

They came in brilliantly lighted halls, what time I had full command from some platform of an attentive crowd gathered to listen, not to chatter.

They came when some one or other sat and played with me, whose spirit-pulses rose and fell with mine—in a world of sound where the morning stars seemed always singing together.

I was such a thorn in the side of my accompanists that at last they came to have a wholesome dread of me. In this way I often was rid of playing at houses where people asked me to bring my violin *impromptu*, because I happened to be the fashion.

I went up to Trinity College in 1856. I was completely alone. I had an introduction to Dr. Whewell, the Master of Trinity. Soon after passing my entrance examination, I was summoned into the great man's presence. The Master questioned me as to my aims and ambitions. I had none—I told him so very simply: I played the fiddle. He seemed surprised; but from the first moment of seeing him I took a liking to him, and I believe he did to me.

When he married, the Master did a very graceful thing. He sent for me one morning, brought Lady Affleck into the drawing-room, and said in his bluff way, "Mr. Haweis, I wish you to know Lady Affleck, my wife. She is musical; she wishes to hear your violin." The Master then left me with her, and she induced me to arrange to come and play at the Lodge on the following night at a great party. I was to bring my own accompanist. I had played at Dr. Whewell's before that night, but that night the Master paid me special attention. It was part of his greatness and of his true humility to recognize any sort of merit, even when most different in kind from his own.

Whewell's ability was of a truly cosmic and universal character, but nature had denied him one gift—the gift of music. He always beat time in chapel, and generally sang atrociously out of tune. I do not think he had any ear; music to him was something marvellous and fascinating; he could talk learnedly on music, admire music, go to concerts, have music at his house, worry over it, insist upon silence when it was going on; and yet I knew, and he knew that I knew, that he knew nothing about it. It was a closed world to him, a riddle, yet one he was incessantly bent upon solving; and he felt that I had the key to it and he had not.

On that night I played Ernst's "Elégie," not quite so hackneyed then as it is now, and some other occasional pieces by Ernst, in which I gave the full rein to my fancy. The Master left his company, and taking a chair in front of where I stood, remained in absorbed meditation during the performance.

I was naturally a little elated at this mark of respect shown to an unknown freshman in the presence of so many "Heads" of Houses and the *élite* of the University. I played my best and indulged rather freely in a few more or less illegitimate dodges, which I thought calculated to bewilder the great man. I was rewarded, for at the close Dr. Whewell laid his hand upon my arm. "Tell me one thing; how do you produce that rapid passage, ascending and descending notes of fixed intervals?" I had simply as a *tour de force* glided my whole hand up and down the fourth open string, taking, of course, the complete series of harmonics up and down several times and producing thus the effect of a rapid cadenza with the utmost ease; the trick only requires a certain lightness of touch, and a knowledge of where and when to stop with effect. I replied that I had only used the series of open harmonics which are yielded, according to the well-known mathematical law, by every stretched string when the vibration is interrupted at the fixed harmonic nodes. The artistic application of a law which, perhaps, he had never realized but in theory, seemed to delight him intensely, and he listened whilst I repeated the cadenza, and again and again showed him the various intervals on the finger-board, where the open harmonics might be made to speak; a hair's-breadth one way or the other producing a horrid scratch instead of the sweet flute-like ring. It struck him as marvellous how a violinist could hit upon the various intervals to such a nicety, as to evoke the harmonic notes. I replied that this was easy enough when the hand was simply swept up and down the string as I had done; but that to hit upon the lesser nodes for single harmonics was one of the recognized violin difficulties. I then showed him a series of *stopped* harmonics, and played, much to his surprise, a tune in stopped harmonics. He was interested to hear that Paganini had been the first to introduce this practice, which has since become common property. But I have somewhat anticipated.

After the anxiety of my entrance examination at Trinity College, which I passed without glory, I solaced my loneliness by making as much noise as I ever could on my violin. My mathematics may have been weak, and my classics uncertain, but it was impossible to ignore my existence. I had not been up a fortnight when the president of the Cambridge University Musical Society called upon me. He believed I played the violin. "How did he know that?" I asked. He laughed out, "Everybody in the place knows it." Then and there he requested me to join the Musical Society, and play a solo at the next concert. I readily agreed, and from that time I became solo violinist at the Cambridge Musical Society, and played a solo at nearly every concert in the Town Hall for the next three years.

I confess to some nervousness on my first public appearance at a University Concert. It was a grand night. Sterndale Bennett, our new professor of music, himself conducted his "May Queen," and I think Mr. Coleridge, an enthusiastic amateur and old musical star at the University, since very well known in London, sang. I had selected as my *cheval de bataille*, Rode's air in G with variations, and to my own surprise, when my turn came to go on, I was quite shaky. The hall was crammed, the Master of Trinity sat in the front row with other heads of colleges and their families. I tuned in the anteroom. Some one offered me a glass of wine. I had never resorted to stimulants before playing, but I rashly drank it; it was in my head at once. Sterndale Bennett conducted me to the platform. I was a total stranger to the company—a freshman in my second month only. My fingers felt limp and unrestrained, my head was half swimming. The crowd looked like a mist. I played with exaggerated expression. I tore the passion to tatters. I trampled on the time. I felt the excess of sentiment was bad, and specially abhorrent to Sterndale Bennett, who followed my vagaries like a lamb, bless him forever!

But the thing took. The style was new; at least it was unconventional and probably daring, for I really hardly knew what I was about. The air was listened to in dead silence, half out of curiosity no doubt; but a burst of applause followed the last die-away notes. I plunged into the variations; I felt my execution slovenly and beneath my usual mark; but I was more than once interrupted by applause, and at the close of the next cantabile movement of extreme beauty, which I played better—a sort of meditation on the original air—the enthusiasm rose to fever pitch; men stood up in the distant gallery and waved their caps, and I remained holding my violin, unable to proceed with the last rapid variation. When silence was restored I played this atrociously; I hardly played it at all; it was quite wild. Sterndale Bennett, seeing that it was all up with me that night, hurried and banged it through anyhow; but the critical faculty of the room was gone—so was my head. I had won by a toss, and although then, and often afterward, owing to neglect of practice, I was frequently not up to my own mark, my position as solo violinist at the University Concerts was never disputed up to the time that I took my degree.

One day as I was sitting in my arm-chair with an open book upon my knee, contemplating vaguely the row of china musicians' heads on little brackets over my mantelpiece, a knock came at the door. My "oak was sported," and I accordingly "did the dead." I was in no mood for interruption. In front of me, in the centre of my china row of busts—Handel, Mozart, Haydn, Chopin—stood Mendelssohn's bust, raised above the rest and draped with black velvet, with F. M. B. in gold on the velvet. The china face at times, as the light caught the shadows about the delicate mouth, seemed to smile down upon me. The high forehead surrounded by wavy hair, the aquiline nose—— What? more knockings! I rose at last, and opening the door brusquely was confronted by a strange figure with a sort of wide plaid waistcoat, well-made frock-coat, heavily-dyed thin whiskers, and dark wig (as I well saw when the broad-brimmed hat was off), yellow gloves, and patent boots. Middle-aged? No—in spite of the wig and showy get-up—old, very old, but oddly vigorous, inclined to *embonpoint*, ruddy, florid, perhaps choleric face, marked features overspread now with a beaming smile and a knowing twinkle in the rather rheumy eyes.

I never saw such an odd man. My anger evaporated. I laughed out almost, and instinctively extended my hand and shook that of the irresistible stranger warmly, although I did not know him from Adam.

"Beg pardon," he said, "may I come in? I tell you, my friend, my name is Venua—never heard of me—no matter—old Venua knows you; heard you play at the Town Hall—got the stuff in you; you can play. Old Venua, dey say to me, he know all about it—he can tell you how to play. Forty year ago you should have heard me play de fiddle. I play de fiddle now; gif me your fiddle—vonderful tone your fiddle—where is your fiddle?"

All this was uttered without a pause, very rapidly.

The strange, rambling, stuttering, energetic, decided old creature had now rolled into my room; he had sat down and pulled out an enormous silk pocket-handkerchief. Then an old gold snuff-box. "This gif me by ze Grand Duke of Hesse Darmstadt. You take a pinch? Oh no! You are young man. You know noding of snuff—bad 'abit—young man, bad 'abit! never you take snuff! Old Venua can't get on widout his snuff. All de bigwigs take snuff with old Venua—but where is your fiddle? bring him out I say. Vonderful tone—let me see him."

What a jargon! Was it Italian, French, or German-English? I could never make out. In an old book, only the other day, I met with a short biography of a certain Venua, violinist, who flourished at the beginning of this century. Old Venua, of Cambridge, was undoubtedly this man. He was very long past his prime and utterly forgotten. I brought him out the fiddle;

he put it to his chin; in a moment I could see he had played—his touch, execution, all but his intonation were gone, but his style was first-rate and his expression admirable in intention.

From that day I and old Venua became close allies. He used to ask me to dine with him, generally on Sunday, and his ceaseless flow of anecdote and dramatic style of conversation amused me greatly.

He had known Paganini, he had seen Beethoven, he had chatted with Spohr, he remembered the first Napoleon. He mimicked Haydn's style of conversation, violin in hand, as though he had been intimate with him too. Yet this was in 1859, and Haydn died in 1809.

"Gif me a sobjech," says Haydn. "Zo!—here—Tra-la-doi-e-dee-dee, etc., etc. Zat will do, mein freund. Haydn—make you on zat sobjech—a beautiful melody, and work it wonderful; gif you him a start off, he do all the rest. No quartet like the Haydn quartet, my young freund—he is the great master of the string instrument—he knows the just combinazione—he gif all their due. Spohr he all first fiddle—he make all de rest lacqueys to first fiddle. Mendelssohn he make an orchestra of his quartet. Beethoven vonderful always. Mozart he learn all of Haydn—he come after him and die before him. He never write quartet better zan de Papa Haydn—he find new ideas and he write new things—he great master of vat you call de form—of his composition—but in de string quartet Haydn ze great creator—a Brince—a real Brince and founder of ze quartet art!"

Venua loved the violin, and his impromptu lectures upon it taught me much—always characteristic, humorous, genial, and to the point.

"If you want to make a man irritable, discontented, restless, miserable, give him a violin."

"Why?" said I.

"Because," he replied—and I will now resume to some extent the use of my own language—"the violin is the most exacting and inexorable of non-human things. A loose joint somewhere and he goes 'tubby' (a term used to express a dull vibration), a worn finger-board and he squeaks, a bridge too high and his note grows hard and bitter, or too low and he whizzes, or too forward and one string goes loud, or too backward and two strings go soft and weak; and the sound-post (*i.e.* the little peg which bears the strain on the belly and back), mein Gott! dat is de Teffel." But, correcting himself, he added, "No, the French are right, they call it the soul of the violin, *l'âme du violon;* and it is the soul—if that is not right, all the fiddle goes wrong. A man may sit the whole morning worrying the sound-post a shade this way or that, and at last, in despair, he will give it up; then he will go to the bridge and waste his whole afternoon fidgeting it about, and then he will give that up. A hair's-breadth this way with the bridge—oh! the fourth string is lovely; but, bah! the second and third are killed; a little back then, and now the fourth is dead, and the *chanterelle* (*i.e.* first string) sings like a lark—misery! it is the only string vat sing at all. Give him a fiddle!" cried the old gentleman, gesticulating; "yes, give him a fiddle, it will make him mad!"

Interspersed with such droll exaggerations were excellent hints, such as, "Leave your bridge and your sound-post alone if ever you get the fiddle to sound near right; don't change your bridge unless you are absolutely obliged—sound-board, neck, head, nut, everything, but not the bridge; a fiddle and a bridge that have lived for years together love each other as man and wife; let them alone, my young freund, vy make mischief?" and old Venua's eye twinkled as he chuckled at his own joke, and never ceased talking and flourishing his arms.

It was Venua who first taught me about the fabric of the violin what my old master, Oury—who was a pupil of Mori—first made me feel about violin playing—a tender love and sympathy for the instrument as well as the art.

What was Venua's connection with Cambridge I never could make out. He seemed independent. He had long ceased to teach or play, yet he was frequently away, and appeared only at intervals, always retaining the same lodgings at Cambridge, and generally giving me a call when he was in town. When I came up, about a year after leaving the University, for my voluntary theological examination, I inquired for my old friend Venua; but he was gone, and no one could give me any news of him. I never saw him again. He remained to me simply a detached episode in my musical life.*

From the time that I entered the Church I have never played to any real purpose. I resolved to make that sacrifice, and no subsequent reflection has led me to repent of my decision. I could never have played the violin by halves, and had I come up to London and entered the Church in the character of a fiddling parson, I should in all probability never have got credit for, or applied myself seriously to win, any other position. At all events, I should have been heavily weighted and laid

* As this is passing through the press there comes to me news that he died and was buried at Cambridge.

myself open to many temptations. I should always have been coming West in search of musical society and distraction, and people would have said, as indeed my old friends have said, and as my caricaturists continue to say, "He should have stuck to the one thing which he could do well, and not meddled with theology." These good people sometimes gave me credit for having made an heroic sacrifice. They knew nothing about it. The sacrifice I made was a very small one. From the age of eight to the age of twenty-three I had played the fiddle in season and out of season. Applause had lost its charm for me. I was hardened to flattery. My own critical taste disenchanted me with my own performances. Nothing but the best suited me, and I knew I never could attain to that as an executant myself, because I never could take up the violin professionally. Then, fiddling was not my only taste. I had a passion for oratory, for literature, for the study of human nature, and for church work. For a time my new parochial sphere with its special enthusiasms expelled everything else.

CHAPTER II.

HEARING MUSIC.

Would you rather be blind or deaf? Most people will illogically reply, "Neither.!" but when pressed, nine out of ten will be found to answer, "Leave me the sight of my eyes—let me be deaf." Yet all experience shows that they are wrong. Deafness tries the temper more, isolates more, unfits for social converse, cuts off from the world of breathing, emotional activity, tenfold more than blindness. There is something as yet unanalyzed about sound, which doubles and intensifies at all points the sense of living: when we hear we are somehow more alive than when we see. Apart from sound, the outward world has a dreamlike and unreal look—we only half believe in it; we miss at each moment what it contains. It presents, indeed, innumerable pictures of still-life; but these refuse to yield up half their secrets. If any one is inclined to doubt this, let him stop his ears with cotton wool for five minutes, and sit in the room with some intelligent friend who enjoys the full use of his ears, and at the end of five or ten minutes let the two compare notes. Of course, we must suppose that both are doing nothing, except the one taking stock of his loss, and the other taking stock of his gain.

I sit, then, in my chair stone deaf. I look up at the pictures on the wall—a man driving a goat, a haystack, and some pigs — an engraving of Millais's " Black

Brunswicker." I am tired of the sight of it. I notice the bird on his perch; his mouth is wide open, he looks to me as if he were in a fit. I point at him in an alarmed manner; my friend shakes his head with a smile —the bird's only singing. I can't say I am glad to hear it, for I cannot hear anything. Presently my friend rises and goes to the door, opens it—what on earth for? Why, in jumps the cat. I suppose he heard it outside; it might have mewed till doomsday, as far as my ears were concerned. My strange companion has no sooner sat down on his chair, than he jumps up as if stung. He points out, in answer to my bewildered look, that the legs are loose; he must have heard them creak, I suppose. Then he goes up to the clock, and begins winding it up; he must have noticed that it had left off ticking. I might not have found that out for hours. Another start! he rushes from the room, I follow— the maid has spilt the coal-scuttle all down the stairs; he probably heard the smash. My wife might have fallen down-stairs and broken her neck, and I should have known nothing about it. No sooner are we alone again, than he once more rises, I know not why; but I perceive he is met at the door by some one who has called him; it is of no use for any one to call me.

There happens to be a kettle on the fire, and at a particular moment my prudent friend rises. I should never have thought of it—the kettle is going to boil over; he *hears*. All this is insupportable. I am being left out of life—it is worse than being shut up in the dark. I tear the wool out of my ears long before the expiration of the ten minutes, and my friend addresses me as follows:

"I pass over the canary, the cat, the chair, the coal-scuttle, and the kettle. You happened to find out about them a day after the fair by using your eyes; but besides all this, of how much vivid life were you deprived—how many details of consciousness, how many avenues of thought were lost to you in less than ten minutes! As I sat, I could hear your favorite nocturne of Chopin being played in the next room. Perhaps you did not know it was raining; nor should I have noticed it, only I heard it on the skylight. I therefore rang the bell, ordered a trap-door open in the roof to be shut, and sent the carriage for a lady who would have otherwise had to walk home. You did not notice a loud crack behind you; but, in fact, a hot coal flew out of the fire, and I seized it in time to prevent mischief. The postman's knock reminded me of some letters I ought to write, and I made a note of them. The band playing outside put me in mind of some concert-tickets I had promised to send. A neighboring church-bell reminded me of the fact that it was Wednesday, and about a quarter to eleven o'clock. Punch and Judy heard in the distance reminded me of the children, and some toys I had promised. I could hear the distant whistle of a train. The pleasant crackling of the fire behind me was most genial. I let a poor bee out who was buzzing madly upon the window-pane. I heard a ring at the street-bell; presently I heard a well-known voice in the hall. I knew who had arrived; I knew who met him; I could shrewdly conjecture where they went together, and I guessed not unnaturally that the children's lessons would be neglected that morning, since a far more agreeable companion had stepped in to monopolize the eldest daughter. Of all which things, my poor friend, you knew nothing, because your ears were stuffed with cotton wool."

Alas! too many of us go through life with our ears stuffed with cotton wool. Some persons can hear, but not well; others can hear common sounds and musical sounds, and no one would suspect in them any defect, until it some day turns out that they do not know the difference between "God save the Queen" and "Auld lang syne." Thus we reach the distinction between the common ear and the musical ear. Then, in connection with the musical ear, there are mysteries. Some cannot hear sounds lower than a certain note; others cannot hear them higher than a certain note, *as musical sounds.*

The mystery of the musical ear has not been solved. Yet some things are known about it. There is probably no ear so radically defective—except a deaf ear—as to be incapable of a certain musical training. The curate who arrives in a High Church parish without a notion of the right note to intone upon, and with the vaguest powers of singing it when it is given him, in a few months learns to take fairly the various pitches in the service.

But still the question remains—a physiological one—why is one ear musical and another not? Professor Helmholtz, whose discoveries in the sound-world are only comparable to the discoveries of Newton in the world of light, has put forth an ingenious theory somewhat to this effect: He discovered within the ear, and soaked in a sensitive fluid, rows and rows of microscopic nerves—several hundred in number—each one of which, like the string of a pianoforte, he believed vibrated to some note; therefore, we were to infer that just as a note sung outside a piano will set up in the corresponding wire a sympathetic vibration, so any sound or sounds in the outer world represented by a nerve wire, or nerves in the ear, could be heard by the ear; and, as a consequence, I suppose any absence of or defect in these internal nerve wires would prevent us from hearing the sound as others better constituted would hear it.

WHAT IS THE MUSICAL EAR?

The next direct question of musical ear now becomes one of inherited tendency and special training. The musical ear is the ear that has learned—by constantly using the same intervals—to recognize the tones and semi-tones of the usual scale, and to regard all variations of quarter-tones as exceptions and subtleties not to be taken account of in the general construction of melody and harmony. Now, our octave, and our division of the octave into tones and semi-tones, is not artificial, but natural, founded as much upon certain laws of sound-vibration as our notation (if I may say so) of color is founded upon the laws of light-vibration. But although the selection of eight notes with their semi-tones is the natural and scientific scale, seeing that the ear is capable of hearing impartially vast numbers of other vibrations of sound which produce vast numbers of other intervals, quarter-notes, etc., what we have to do in training the musical ear is just to harp on the intervals which compose the musical scale in various keys, and on these only. In this way the ear is gradually weaned from sympathy with what is out of tune—ceases to be dog-like or savage-like, and becomes the cultured organ for recognizing the natural order and progression of those measured and related vibrations which we call musical sound. Of course, a tendency like this can be inherited just as much as any other, and in almost all cases it can be improved and cultivated.

I have mentioned Professor Helmholtz's theory, but have reason to think that he is not, on reconsideration, prepared to indorse it fully. The little rows of minute nerve-wires, each vibrating to a definite sound, are indeed a fascinating idea; but whether true or false, it enables us, by a kind of physical parable, to understand the sort of way in which the ear, being capable of perceiving a large variety of sounds, may be trained to give the preference to certain ones by constantly allowing itself to be exercised by their vibrations, and accustoming itself to select certain notes, and establish between them definite and fixed relations. The exact physical mechanism which enables the ear to do this may have yet to be discovered, but that it exists there can be no doubt, and the use and cultivation of it is in fact the use and cultivation of what we call "an ear for music."

And now I feel I owe the reader an apology. When I have some subject which I am desirous to discuss, something over which I may have been brooding for years, my first instinct is to plunge into the middle of it; my second is to begin at the beginning; my third (and this is the one I generally succumb to) is to begin before the beginning. Thus the important remarks which I am about to make on hearing music have been fairly pushed aside, first, by one preface on the sense of hearing generally, and second, by another preface on the musical ear in particular; but *In medias res* shall be my motto now; no more dallying with the subject; no more strutting in front of the curtain; no more prologue—the actors wait, the bell rings, the curtain rises; let us hope there is a good audience.

This is an afternoon "AT HOME." These words, you will observe, are printed in very large type. In a corner of the card we gather from the small word "music," the quite mixed and genial nature of the whole entertainment. Signor Boreo Guffaw, the well-known bass singer, is expected to look in, a few amateurs have promised to help if necessary, and every one who knows Mrs. de Perkins is aware that this is one of those two annual assemblies in which that well-meaning lady endeavors to pay off the various dinners and "At Homes" which she may herself have been exposed to during the last year. De Perkins, who is elderly, engaged in the city, and not wealthy, won't give dinners; he does not like these "At Homes;" but he is told that they are necessary—and then Guffaw, who taught Mrs. de Perkins before she was married, is very good-natured, and so is every one; and the rooms, not very large, are soon full, the staircase early ceases to be navigable, and Mrs. de Perkins, who really is rather nice, stands at the door, and does her best to catch every one's eye, although, by a certain wild and anxious look in her face, we know that she is wondering why Guffaw does not begin.

Jammed into a niche which just fits me if I hold my arms quite stiff, and stand up stark and straight, I presently hear the eminent foreigner begin "In questa Tomba 'scura." Do I enjoy this song? In the first place I am ill at ease. I crane my neck to look round the corner. I can just see the portly basso with his thumbs in his waistcoat pockets; but just opposite me stands my hostess receiving more guests, and the consequence is that Guffaw's "Tomba" is mixed up with all kinds of *sotto voce's*—".So glad you've come," "How's —— ?" "You mustn't talk," "Tea in the next room"—while in front of me conversation, momentarily suspended, recommences, all about some garden party and some one being lost, and where they were found, and who they were with, and so on.

Do I enjoy the music? Whether I do or not, I intend to get out of this miserable niche—away to the other room, where there is tea. The song is over, and there is naturally a pause in the conversation: at last I find some one that I wish to talk to. I am just explaining with unequalled lucidity the new scheme for boring the Channel Tunnel—attracting, in short, more than one attentive listener—when up trips my anxious but smiling hostess : " You must really listen to this gentleman who is playing—a clergyman, you know, most gifted ; he plays nothing but the oldest masters, Bach, and that sort, you know. Hush ! hush !" and she glides off tapping and silencing people right and left, just as they have got into a nice chat and are beginning to make way—as I was, in fact.

I look round me. Disappointed, cross, irritable-looking faces, which a moment before were smiling and animated, and from the distance the hard tinkle of the perfectly self-satisfied musician grating upon every one's nerves—why ? Not because it is so bad ; simply because it is not wanted then and there. Gradually, as the everlasting fugue goes on and on, or runs into another fugue, people begin to talk feebly. I begin about the Channel again, but by this time my audience has dispersed ; my most devoted hearer—a lady who suffers frightfully from sea-sickness—does not seem to remember where I left off. I can't quite remember myself—we drop the subject. I have to begin all over again, but with something different, to some one else ; then at last the fugue leaves off. Did any one enjoy the music ? Then Guffaw is put on to sing a duet just as I was telling that capital story about the sparrow in church. Well, of course it was no good, all the point was taken out of it because I had to hurry over it and end in a guilty kind of underbreath. I did not stay to hear the new amateur tenor, Mr. Flutuloo, who, I am told, sang with an eyeglass fixed rigidly in one eye, while he positively wept with the other. I can believe that the sensation he created may have been considerable ; I was a great deal too sore about the Channel Tunnel and the sparrow, etc., to care; in short, I left Mrs. de Perkins's At Home in a very bad humor after, I regret to say, hearing some music, but certainly not enjoying it. The moral of this is—

1. Let it be either music or conversation, but not both.
2. If music, let all the audience be musical, and all the musicians good.
3. Don't cram the room and suffocate the singers, but ask a moderate company, let them all be seated, and let the conversation in between be limited to the merest interchange of courtesies.
4. Avoid the current musical "At Home." The De Perkins method never answers; it offends the real musicians, encourages musical impostors, and bores the company.

Some people enjoy themselves at concerts. But "some people" and "concerts" are vague terms. You must go with the right people, and you must go to the right concerts. These right conditions will, of course, vary according to taste and cultivation. The right people for *you* are in all cases the people with whom you are musically in sympathy. The right concerts for *you* are the concerts you can at least in some measure enjoy and understand. The classical pedant sneers at people who delight in ballad concerts and hate Wagner; but the greatest composers have not been above ballads, and although there are bad ballads, yet the characteristics of a ballad—namely, that it should be lyrical, simple, and easily understood—are not bad characteristics. Some of the greatest men have been infinite losers because they happened to be generally unintelligible, while inferior people have exercised an influence out of proportion to their merits, simply because they made themselves generally understood. And be it observed, that this element of intelligibility is one common to the ballad and all the *greatest* works of art. The greatest men all "strike home." The transfiguration is simple—so is the Moses of Michael Angelo. So is Handel's *Messiah* taken as a whole. So is the *Elijah* of Mendelssohn. They are a great deal more than simple, but they are *that*.

There are other kinds of mixed concerts which have their excuse, but they are private; there are no contradictions, no aggravations, no jolts in them. We are not shocked out of one phase of emotion into another; we are not compelled to swallow an Italian *buffo* song after a duet from Mozart's requiem, or a ballad of Claribel, followed by a bit of Spohr's *Last Judgment*. And yet the programme is mixed, varied—as the conversation of friends is varied, flitting birdlike through many lands, pausing above giddy precipices, gliding over summer seas, lingering in bright meadows, poised above populous cities, lingering about the habitations of man. But no more prosy efforts to describe what is indescribable; let the curtain rise once more and let the actors themselves appear before me.

She is fair, with brown-red hair; she is serene, with one of those quiet, equable temperaments, whose privilege it is to blend others into harmony by yielding to each new wave of thought and feeling as it rises, with that sort of simple, unaffected pleasure, the very sight of which makes others happy. Alas! she has been dead these many summers; yet it is the privilege of memory to unlock the doors of old rooms, and find there suddenly, as in a dream, the scenes that have faded out of the real world forever. For a moment I close my eyes. It is an autumn evening by the sea. How pleasantly the waves came plashing in as we paced the shore in the deepening night! We spoke of those weird songs of Schubert which seem like sad eyes looking out into the sunset over some waste of measureless waters; we spoke of those Nocturnes of Chopin, like dream scenes, painted on tinted backgrounds.

"His life," said Ferdinand, "was what Novalis would have called a dream within a dream."

"Yes," I answered, "but a dream always starting from reality and breaking into it again."

"And is not that reflected in his music?" rejoined Estelle. "It makes it sometimes quite terrible to me, the harsh contrast between the reality and the dream, a chord, a transition bar, and then fainter and fainter grows the shadow-land, so intensely real and passionate the moment before—it darkens and melts into a thin, cold mist—just as those gorgeous shadows of purple and orange on the sea, which seemed a minute ago almost substantial, melt and leave the cold sea dark, and the air keen and sharp."

"Yes, that was the history of Chopin's life; the love of Madame Sand was his dream, and the awakening was the cold sea and the sharp, keen air that killed him."

"But before the end what dreams haunted him, fragments of the never-forgotten days, embalmed in fugitive melody, and mystically woven harmonies! I think he must have lived over again perfectly in such moments. They were the realities; and the outer-life, latterly at least, became the dream. Listen!

* * * * * *

"What sweetness is here, this grassy bank, these drooping citron flowers, these glowing azaleas, fringing the summer islet, set like a jewel in the bosom of the Mediterranean! The name of Lucrezia Floriani rises to my lips, the name of the Prince Karol, who is Chopin. Time is not. These skies are eternally blue. This welling up of crystal water, just kissing the fringe of drooping blossom against the shore; this hum of insect life, breaking the silence, only to make the summer air more slumbrous; the little rain-cloud on the horizon, which, toward evening, will creep up, until the distance is blotted out, and the black sky is rent with forked lightning—such things entered into Chopin's soul, and live forever in his profound and strange musical reveries.

"But apart from this deeply personal element, the deepest thing of all, as it is in the nature of every true Pole, was the undertone of sad patriotism; this pierces when least expected; this is never long absent. Listen!

* * * * * *

"It is a dazzling crowd, glittering with diamond lights—a profusion of rare jewels; the halls are filled with perfume, the strains of a mazurka are in the air. They seem to call forth as by magic, and support with the breath of some mystic life, these floating, swaying forms of beautiful women, and these countrymen of Chopin, without a country; and as the dance goes weaving on, with a certain dreamy and pensive grace, we perceive that in the heart of the music there is a deep wound, a minor chord of inextinguishable pain, hidden by lovely arabesques of subtle sweetness, winning, beguiling, subduing, but never for long hiding the forlorn sorrow of a hopeless but undying patriotism. Now it is a Polonaise. Listen!

* * * * * *

"What enterprise, what indomitable effort to achieve the impossible, what frantic exploits, as of one resolved to die on the battle-field, but before dying to overwhelm with deeds of intrepid valor his terrible and relentless foe ! The pauses are the pauses of sheer exhaustion ; in them we catch through the sulphurous clouds a sight of remote battle-scenes and distant combinations, until the warrior rises again in his strength, and once more for a time his enemies fly scattered."

"I shall think of all this when I play your favorite Polonaise." She drew her shawl close to her—the mist crept round the bay—it was no longer summer ; we went in, we three, how happy, how harmonious, blended by the grace—the free, the tender grace—of one lovely and beloved presence !

* * * * * *

Unlock the door—let no footfall from the present disturb this shadow-scene. It is the old room — the familiar room. I see her there. There is no sense of strangeness or unreality about her ; she smiles, as she was wont to smile, she moves softly—her fingers turn the music leaves—the candles are lighted—her face is half in shade—I can hear her low melodious laugh. I seem to be once more holding my Stradivarius violin lovingly. What ! there is no sign of dust, or age, or neglect about this long-closed room. As we go back to past chapters of a beloved story, so have I gone back to read again a fragment of life, and as I look, and look, and look, the intervening years roll away, the shadows become real, " till only the dead seem living, and only the living seem dead."

Let it be Mendelssohn's D minor trio. The playing of that night remains with me. We seemed alive—sensitively alive to every vibration ; her fingers caressed the cool ivory keys lovingly, the Stradivarius spoke rapturously to the lightest touch of the bow, the full-toned violoncello gave out the deep but tender notes, like the voices of the sea in enchanted caves. How clean and "seizing," as the French say, was her rendering of the opening movement! How wonderfully woven-in were the parts! We all three made but one, yet retaining our perfect individualities. A mystic presence invisible seemed to be with us; we felt as if playing in the presence of the great, the gentle Mendelssohn; and though we played, so absorbed were we, that we seemed at the same moment to be following our own music like listeners, in ourselves and out of ourselves. Between the movements we spoke not. I marked the flush upon her cheek—the bright light in her eyes. He was grave, intensely preoccupied—the dream-power was upon us all. The peace and full contentment of the slow movement with its rich and measured flow of melody melting at last into that heavenly trance at the close, which leaves us at the open gates of Paradise; then the sudden break at the scherzo, as though a joyous troop of lower earth-spirits had burst in to tear us away from the divine contemplation, and toss us back into a world of wild uproar and merriment; then a slight pause before the tempestuous, but intensely earnest, conclusion. Here is the battle of life, with its suspense, its failure, its endeavor—striving for the victory, its wild and passionate overthrow, its indomitable recovery and untamed valor; that is the bracing and sublime atmosphere of the last movement more true to life than ecstasy, more wholesome than peace, more dignified than pleasure; and that is where the D minor trio leaves us.

Then we drifted into talk of Mendelssohn. As she sat she occasionally played some fragment from a concerto—some striking chord from the *St. Paul*, some passage from *Ruy Blas*, or an echo from the incomparably delicate overture to the beautiful "Melusine," till one said "Sing," and she sang from Schumann, the ballads from Heine—those tragedies and melodramas in three verses, or in two lines, and Brahm's "Guten Abend, Gute Nacht." Then followed songs without words, and sitting in the shadow I saw her face in the light, and felt her spirit rise and fall upon the pulses of invisible sound, in unison with ours. Then came some of Ernst's reveries on the violin, and so the evening wore away, and we took no account of the hours.

Were there any other listeners? Yes, at times one and another of them would recall a passage—a likeness between Mendelssohn and Bach, a phrase of Scarlatti, or a combination of Wagner in a Brahms movement.

This, if you like, was a mixed programme, but its parts were mixed with subtle sympathies, and united by the finest threads of thought and emotion. Thus we moved on from one delight to another with no sense of unpleasant or disjointed break—as those who pass out of a lovely grotto into the sunlight, and after winding through hedgerows of May bloom to the quiet shore, pass back into a garden of tall trees and smooth lawns, and thence to some lovely conservatory filled with tropical bloom, thence to a marble vestibule, thence to halls of tapestry, and luxurious couches and repose. And there has been no break—nothing has jarred upon us in the midst of variety. Hand in hand we have been with friends; we have seen smiles upon dear faces. We have poured forth words, and soul has been revealed to soul; and without, the world of fair things has imaged the life of vivid and inexhaustible thought and feeling within. Compare, I pray you, these parables of "Hearing Music" aright, with the strange and disjointed legend of "Mrs. de Perkins and her musical At Home."

* * * * * *

I will take a wider sweep. I have received the keenest national impressions from music.

At midnight I heard the players pass by. The warm Italian air, scarce chilled by the night, came in from the orange gardens. I leaned my head forward to breathe its full fragrance. The musicians had come from yonder lighted palace; now they pass on up through the groves of citron and myrtle, from the distant deep shadows; the regular pulse of the music brings back the feeling of the dance; it is a mere echo, a shadow dance—fainter and fainter now; I can hear it no more. I look up, the stars burn like gold.

All Italy in a moment is resumed for me in that slight picture. A few bars of music, heard at random, may conjure it up again—first the emotion, then the picture.

* * * * * *

The feast of the Kermess was over in Amsterdam. The town filled with country-people had been emptying all through the night. The booths in the market-places were struck. I stood high up, looking over the network of canals toward the Scheldt. Above my head I heard the cry of the wild swan, winging its way southward from Sweden, and below a rough chorus of men and women came over the bridge. It was loud, boisterous singing, but in parts well defined, rhythmic, and full of a strong charm; they passed into a side street; the drinking chorus seemed to split into fragments and then to cease. How often has it since rung in my ears, and so often has it brought back with it the hearty, coarse, eager life of Holland, and the keen, brackish odor of the wind blowing in from the North Sea.

But in each case observe the peculiar, direct power which music has of dealing with the nerve centres. It is not the image which is recalled and which brings back the feeling; but the sound awakes directly a peculiar rhythm of nervous wave-motion, which is the physical vehicle for a peculiar feeling. Thus a breath of the past in a desert at first unpeopled, and the very atmosphere of a past moment is restored, in which mystic air the forms of dead scenes and persons begin to live and grow again, and at last become intensely vivid. In this, note that music differs from every other art. The painter and poet alike depend directly upon scenes and concrete images for their emotion; but the musician depends directly upon emotion for his scenes and images, and even when these are absent, he is not less potent—sometimes more so; for he can handle and mould the temperature of the mind itself at will, wind up feeling unconnected with thought through every semitone, modulate and change it, fit and unfit us for exertion, make us forget the hard, persistent images of pain and trouble, and the coarse realism that damps joy—by creating an atmosphere within, in which these cannot breathe, and so are expelled as to any power they may have to move us—actually expelled for a season from the mind.

There is a phrase, "I was carried away by the music." That expression is true to feeling; it means, "When I heard this or that, I ceased to be affected by the outward things or thoughts which a moment before moved me; I entered a world of other feeling, or—what I before possessed was so heightened and changed that I seemed to have been 'carried away' from the old thing in a moment." But it would be still truer to say, not "music carried me away," but "music carried away, or changed, the mood, and with it the significance of the things which occupied me in that mood."

The easy command over the emotions possessed by sound, and elaborated by the art of music, is due to the direct impact of the air-waves upon the drum of the ear, which collects them and sends them to the seat of consciousness in the brain by means of the auditory nerve. The same, of course, is true of the waves of color upon the eye, scent upon the nose, and vibrations of touch taken by the brain even from the most distant nerve in the body. But the auditory nerve has in some things a strange advantage and prerogative of power over the others. First, the distance from the ear to the brain is shorter than that of any other of the sensitive surfaces, so the time taken to convey the impressions of sound is less, and therefore the impact more direct. This measured by time is infinitesimal, but measured by emotional effect it counts for much. Secondly, the vibrations of sound as distinguished from the vibrations of light, and even the vibrations of touch, which are, after all, differently local—the vibrations of sound induce a sympathetic vibration on every nerve in the body; they set it going, in short, as the strings of a piano are set going by the stroke of a hammer on the floor, and when the sound is excessive or peculiar, all the great ganglionic centres are disturbed, the diaphragm and many other nerves and muscles are influenced, the stomach is affected, the spine "creeps," as we say, the heart quickens and throbs with strong beatings in the throat. Thus a curiously sympathetic action is set up through this physical peculiarity which sound has of shaking, moving, and at times causing to tremble the human body.

But the cause of the sympathetic action of the great ganglionic centres under the pulsations of sound lies deeper still. It is to be found in the fact that the auditory nerve is closely connected, at its origin in the *medulla oblongata* of the brain, with that of the important *nervus vagus* or *pneumogastric* supplying the heart, lungs, and the most important abdominal viscera. It is also in intimate communication with the branches of the *great sympathetic nerve* from the *ganglia* which supply the muscles regulating the tension of the ear's drum, and which modify the effect of the waves of sound upon it. And these branches, again, are in direct communication with the *vagus* and the great ganglionic centres, controlling the action of the heart and stomach. Thus excitation of the auditory nerve readily agitates these close neighbors, and they proceed to spread the influence far and wide through all the delicate network of sympathetic nerve telegraphy which pervades the entire system. Thus the effect of sound is speedily propagated through myriad side-channels, until the whole body is thrilling with its confluent waves.

Now we can explain, perhaps, why it is that our musical sensations are different in small rooms and large ones, or, to speak more closely, why the relations between the volume of sound and the space to be filled must be suitable in order to produce the right effect. I can sit close to a piano and listen to a "Lied ohne Worte." I can take in every inflection of touch with ease, not a refinement is lost; but if I go to the end of a long room, the impact is less direct, the pleasure is less intense; the player must then exaggerate all his effects, hence a loss of refinement and ease. Public players and singers constantly make shipwreck thus in private rooms. Accustomed to vast spaces, they roar and bang until the audience is deaf, and the only reason why the unknowing applaud on such occasions, and the only difference, as far as they are concerned, between the professional and the amateur, is simply that the first is so much louder than the second. This makes them clap their hands and cry "Bravo!" but in reality they are applauding a defect.

The only musical sounds which really master vast spaces like the Albert Hall are those of a mighty organ or an immense chorus. The Handel Festival choruses are fairly proportioned to the Crystal Palace, but on one occasion, when a terrific thunderstorm burst over Sydenham in the middle of *Israel in Egypt,* every one beneath that crystal dome felt that, acoustically, the peal of thunder was very superior to the whole power of the chorus, because the relation between the space to be filled and the volume of sound required to fill it was in better proportion. But there is still something which has not yet been said for small sounds in large places. Transport yourself in imagination to the Albert Hall on some night when, as is usually the case, there is but a scanty orchestra, and presently a new mystery of sound will present itself to you. At first you will be disappointed. Any one can hear that the hall is not properly *occupied* by the sound; the violins should be trebled at least, several of the wind instruments doubled, etc. You think you will not listen to this charming E flat symphony of Mozart; you cannot help feeling that you lose a delicate inflection here, a staccato there, a flute-tone, a pianissimo on the drum, or a whole piece of counter melody —owing to the scattered conditions of isolated vibrations lost in space.

But you have still something to learn, something like a new musical truth, which few people seem yet to have noticed. Listen! The sounds from the band reach you too late, perhaps; they are not simultaneous. The impact on the ear is somewhat feeble, you must even strain attentively to catch what is passing ; but the more you do so the easier it becomes, just as the eye, in looking through a lens, may see all dim, but gaze on until the objects grow sharp and clear. The nerves of the eye have adapted themselves to the new conditions ; the longer you look the better you see. So in these vast, uncomfortable spaces, the longer you listen the better you hear. A certain special training is required, and then gradually a new quality is perceived—we must give the process a new name—"sound filtering." From this point of view, which it requires some delicate and attentive ear-culture to appreciate, new delights are born from the defective space conditions usually complained of. I have heard the voice of Madame Lemmens-Sherrington in the extreme distance at the Crystal Palace, when she was exerting herself to the utmost, and it sounded like a voice from heaven, full of unearthly, far-away sweetness ; the same intensity and volume in a small room would have been intolerable. I have heard Bottesini on the double-bass in the open air with similar effect.

Listen to an orchestra or quartet, however fine, in a moderate-sized room ; there is the catgut, the rosin, the scrape, the bite of horse-hair on strings ; the earthly cannot be completely got rid of. But space will filter all that, and leave nothing but a kind of spiritual disembodied sound, like the tones of those plugged pipes in the organ that seem to steal out of some remote cloudland with a certain veiled sweetness that makes us hold our breath.

Since I have learned to listen to these peculiar effects in all their strange gradations, a new class of musical impressions has been revealed to me, and I have become much reconciled to hearing music in vast spaces. I do not go there for the kind of normal impressions, for the direct study, for the strong, immediate impact gained from music in a moderately sized room—I lose much of all that; but I gain a number of new abnormal effects, which also have a power over certain hidden depths and distant fastnesses of the emotional region.

Music has a vast future before it. We are only now beginning to find out some of its uses. With the one exception of its obvious and admitted helpfulness, as an adjunct of religious worship, as a vehicle for and incentive of religious feeling, I had almost said that we had as yet discovered none of its uses. It has been the toy of the rich; it has often been a source of mere degradation to both rich and poor; it has been treated as mere jingle and noise—supplying a rhythm for the dance, a kind of Terpsichorean *tomtom*—or serving to start a Bacchanalian chorus, the chief feature of which has certainly not been the music. And yet those who have their eyes and ears open, may read in these primitive uses, while they run, the hints of music's future destiny as a vast civilizer, recreator, health-giver, work-inspirer, and purifier of man's life. The horse knows what he owes to his bells. The factory girls have been instinctively forced into singing, finding in it a solace and assistance in work. And for music, the health-giver, what an untrodden field is there! Have we never known an invalid to forget pain and weariness under the stimulus of music? Have you never seen a pale cheek flush up, a dull eye sparkle, an alertness and vigor take possession of the whole frame, and animation succeed to apathy? What does all this mean? It means a truth that we have not fully grasped, a truth pregnant with vast results to body and mind. It means that music attacks the nervous system directly, reaches and rouses where physic and change of air can neither reach nor rouse.

Music will some day become a powerful and acknowledged therapeutic. And it is one especially appropriate to this excited age. Half our diseases, some physicians say all our diseases, come from disorder of the nerves. How many ills of the mind precede the ills of the body! Boredom makes more patients than fever. Want of interest and excitement, stagnation of the emotional life, or the fatigue of overwrought emotion, lies at the root of half the ill-health of our young men and women. Can we doubt the power of music to break up that stagnation? Or, again, can we doubt its power to soothe? to recreate an overstrained emotional life, by bending the bow the other way? There are moods of exhausted feeling in which certain kinds of music would act like poison, just as whip and spur which encourage the racer at first, tire him to death at last. There are other kinds of music which soothe, and, if I may use the word, lubricate the worn ways of the nervous centres. You will ask what music is good for that? We reply, judgment and common-sense, and, above all, sympathy, affectional and musical sympathy, will partly be your guide, but experience must decide. Let some friend well versed in the divine art sit at the piano, and let the tired one lie on a couch and prescribe for herself or for himself. This will happen: "Do not play that *Tannhäuser* overture just now, it wears me out, I cannot bear it;" or, "Yes—sing that 'Du bist die Ruh,' and after that I must hear Mendelssohn's 'Notturno,' out of the *Midsummer Night's Dream;*" and then—and then—what must come next must be left to the tact and quick sympathy of the musician. I have known cases where an hour of this treatment did more good than bottlefuls of bark or pailfuls of globules; but I do not wish to overstate the case. I merely plead for an unrecognized truth, and I point to a New Vocation—the vocation of the Musical Healer.

How many a girl might turn her at present uncared-for and generally useless musical abilities to this gentle and tender human use. Let her try. At the end of the *séance*, let her and her patient note the abatement of the headache brought about directly by the counter excitement of a nerve-current set up by music. Let her friend admit that she has suffered less during that hour—the mind having been completely called off from the contemplation of a special pain, and the pain meanwhile having passed or abated. There are cases chiefly connected with disorders of the spine, cases of apathy, where music is almost the only thing which seems to stir the torpid nerves and set up a commotion, quickening the heart and flushing the cheek. Then, I say, let music open the shut gate, and let health come in that way, *cœlestis janitor aulæ*. But I want, before I pass, to fix my musical healer upon the reader's mind. She is gentle; she is glowing with health, but not boisterous; she has a quick sympathy for pain; she has a cool, soft hand that does the hot brow good; she rather moves than walks; the sound of her footfall is seldom heard. Oh, Alma! the fostering one, the healing presence, you are in many households, but you hardly know your powers; the sick bless you; they love to hear your voice; but days and weeks pass, and you never exercise your gifts for them. You are a beautiful musician, but your music would not make you the healer without your tact in applying it, your sympathy, your quick judgment, your watchfulness of effect, your faculty of giving yourself when you sing and when you play. It is the union of musical talent with personal qualities like yours that will give you grace to apply the medicine of music to disease.

Have you ever thought of that? You have played casually to the weary, the idle, or even the sick; but you have not with reflection played to refresh, to stimulate, or to soothe; and you cannot do this all at once.

1. You must have the idea of doing it: that is, you must conceive of music as a therapeutic art.

2. You must gain a certain easy command of a wide range of compositions that you may select your remedies wisely.

3. You must take care to establish between yourself and your patients that kindly rapport which will predispose them to listen to you; it must be the hand of something like a friend upon the white keys or upon the strings of a zither, an instrument of heavenly soothing qualities, as of harps in the wind at sunset. It must be the voice of something like a friend; the voice that has said with no feigned earnestness, but with the wide, warm love of a Christlike nature, "I wish I could do you good." Such a voice will sing well and pleasantly, and bring peace.

4. Self-training, judgment, and experience generally. The music-healer must indeed have gifts of mind, but hers will be almost as much a vocation to be learned as that of nursing itself. She must study different kinds of temperament and disease, watch and write down and remember the effect which certain pieces or kinds of music have on certain temperaments. But the fascination of the new calling would lie in the delight of its exercise, the variety and endless excitement and surprises of its results, the incessant study of character, the

constant self-training and cultivation of sympathy for a definite and immediate end, and in the intense happiness of feeling that upon the waves of heavenly melody and harmony which lifted up your own soul, another's pain and distress were floating away, and that you had been the active agent in procuring this pleasure, this relief, this recovery.

Let some pen more competent than mine expand this new doctrine of "music considered as a therapeutic." If it found support from any well-accredited medical authority, with what faith and favor would it be received by thousands of sufferers! with what alacrity would spring up right and left our musical healers, coveting and exercising earnestly the best gifts of character and training! It would not be long before we had a handbook on the subject, with suggestions for a course of treatment based on actual experience.

Music is not only a body healer; it is a mind regulator. The great educational function of music remains almost to be discovered. The future mission of music for the million is the Discipline of Emotion.

What is the ruin of art? Ill-regulated emotion.

What is the ruin of life? Again, ill-regulated emotion.

What mars happiness? What destroys manliness? What sullies womanhood? What checks enterprise? What spoils success? Constantly the same—ill-regulated emotion. The tongue is a fire; an uncontrolled and passionate outburst swallows up many virtues and blots out weeks of kindness.

There is one thing more important than knowing self; it is governing self. There is one thing better than crushing impulse; it is using impulse. The life of the ascetic is half true, the life of the voluptuary is the other half of the truth. The stoic may be said to be blind at least of one eye. The cynic is very nearly blind of both, since the power and the passion and the splendid uses of existence are hidden from him, and all these go wrong in various ways, from abusing, misusing, or neglecting the emotional life.

The Greek was not far wrong when he laid such stress on gymnastics and music. Of music, indeed, in its modern, exhaustive, and subtle developments, as the language of the emotions, he knew nothing; but his faint guess was with a certain fine and unerring instinct in the right direction; shame upon us that, in the blaze of modern music, we have almost missed its deepest meaning! The Greek at least understood how sound regulated motion, which is, after all, only the physical expression of emotion. Not a procession, not a social gathering, not a gymnasium, nay, not even an important oration, was thought complete without the introduction of musical sound; and that not as a mere jingle or pastime, but to regulate the order, the variety, the intensity of bodily motions, actions, and words, so that throughout there might be an elaborate discipline carried on through musical sound—a discipline which, thus learned at the schools, met the Greek again at every turn in his social and political life, and ended by making his earth-life that rounded model of physical and intellectual harmony and perfection which have made at once the despair and wonder of sculptors, poets, and philosophers of all ages.

And we, living in the full development of this divine art of music, put it to less practical uses than the Greek, who never went beyond music as a rhythmic and melodic regulator of dancing, feasting, and oratory!

It remains for us to take up the pregnant hint, and

claim modern music as the great organ of emotional culture and emotional discipline. This practical view of the unique and perfect functions of the musical art is, I think, sufficiently new to require a little further explanation.

"How," it will be asked, "apart from mere pleasure—pleasure, if you will, of a harmless and elevating kind—am I a bit better for the hearing of music?"

In answering this question, I leave out the effect produced on bodily health through the agitation of the nervous centres by musical sound, as dwelt upon above.

I will come to close quarters again with Music and Morals, and I will show how hearing music in the right way gets up, as it were, the steam power of emotion, collects it, concentrates it, and then puts it through such innumerable stages of discipline that the very force of emotion which, allowed to run wild, brings ruin into life, grows, through the right hearing of great and skilful music, docile, controlled, indefinitely plastic, or at the call of the will, resistless in might.

Music, in short, is bound, when properly used and understood, to train us in the exercise of our emotions, as the gymnasium trains us in the exercise of our limbs. The Greek understood both these uses; we probably understand neither.

First, then, music rouses the emotions. Inward activities, long dormant or never before awakened, are called up, and become new powers within the breast; for, remember, emotion nerves for action. The stupidest horse that goes up hill to the sound of bells, the timidest soldier that marches to battle with fife and drum, the most delicate girl who spins round tireless in the dance, the poorest laborer who sings at his work—any of them is good enough to prove that music rouses and sustains emotion.

But, secondly, music disciplines and controls emotion. That is the explanation of the art of music, as distinguished from the mere power of the musical sound. You can rouse with a stroke; but to guide, to moderate, to control, to raise and depress, to combine, to work out a definite scheme involving appropriate relations and proportions of force, and various mobility—for this you require the subtle machinery of an art; and the direct machinery for stirring up and regulating emotion is the wonderful vibratory mechanism created by the art of music.

I wish to give here a short example of the way in which a train of abstract emotion, capable of being fitted to different ideas, or capable of underlying more than one series of mental events (so long as the relations of them be similar and parallel), can be roused and developed in a fixed artistic form by music. My present limits will not allow me to take one of the great symphonies of Beethoven or Mendelssohn for this. I will select a "Lied ohne Wörte;" let us take, for instance, No. 10, the fourth Lied of the Second Book. I will mention the bars by their numbers, instead of using technical terms, such as a key of D or F, subdominant, tonic, etc. It is difficult to describe mental states apart from particular thoughts; but as far as possible we will try to do so, and so express the consciousness of a state of mind which might be equally appropriate to several separate and distinct, though similar and parallel, trains of thought.

Understand what I mean by similar and parallel trains of thought. Let me even appeal to the eye, and put my similar thoughts in parallel columns, thus:

I. Man losing his temper.   I. Sea ruffled with wind.
II. Man lost his temper.   II. Sea convulsed.
III. Smashes the furniture. III. Thunder and lightning.
IV. Is appeased by wife.   IV. Blue sky, wind drops.
V. All is forgiven and forgotten.   V. Sun breaks out, sea calms.

One and the same train of emotion or general cast of feeling may fitly underlie such two progressive scenes; but the events must in every case be similar in tone and run parallel; only in this sense does music, as it is sometimes loosely said, mean all sorts of things to different people.

I now return to an emotional analysis of Lied IV., of Book II., Mendelssohn. With the first bars of rapid semi-quavers, increasing from p to sf, we are thrown into a state of restless emotion, dashed (bars 4, 5, 6) with suspense, as when one heaves and holds his breath at a passing thought of some agitating possibility; (7, 8, 9, 10), the flash of suspense passes off, lowering back the tone of mind to its first state; that state, instead of subsiding as before, passes into a reflex sort of reasoning upon itself, as though one said (15, 16, 17, $\frac{1}{2}$18), "But why should I disquiet myself in vain?" ($\frac{1}{2}$18, 19, 20). "I will resist, I will shake it off (21); I will be free (22); the cloud has passed (23); I see my joy (24, 25, 26, 27, 28, 29, 30). O ecstatic vision! I lose myself in this splendid revelation, I float out upon the tide of triumph. Now I rest, bathed in tranquil peace and perfect satisfaction (31, 32, $\frac{1}{2}$33); I prolong the dream." But already the ecstatic glow has cooled ($\frac{1}{2}$33, 34, 35, 36), a faint touch of earth bitterness, a misgiving (D sharp) has crept in (37, 38, 39, 40, 41, 42), and is confirmed until the vision of bliss is almost obliterated, and the emotion is in danger of sinking back at once to its first condition of morbid restlessness; but that would be monotonous (45). At this point it is, therefore, caught by new reflex action of the feelings, and a struggle takes place (46, 47, 48, 49, 50, 51), represented by the opening subject struggling up in the bass, checked, then struggling up in the treble, checked at *sf*, and then *cresc.*, struggling up (51) once more. Then there is a pause, emotion is at a standstill, and at last grows almost tepid and indifferent; dropping at 57, *p* and *dim.*, almost listless, when at 60 the struggle recommences with fresh violence, the great effort of the mind to cast out the restless, passionate broodings of the first page (60 to 71) produces a storm of conflicting emotions, in which now one side, now another seems uppermost, till at last the mind, trembling on the morbid verge, passes over the line with a kind of wilful and helpless self-surrender; but this time the experiences through which it has passed make it impossible quite to repeat the morbid and restless series, and (72) only half the first subject is given, the emotion is hampered, it does not run easily, it cannot get on; then (76) the same phrase over again, *piu f*, with growing impatience. A change of some sort is evidently at hand (81); the old subject is tossed away as worthless and unfit for the purpose, as the spirit feels itself breathed upon once more, and held by some new force, through a series of bars (81 to 87), until expectancy is crowned, and with a crescendo of ascending octaves, which makes us fairly hold our breath, while the action of the pulse is rapidly quickened, suddenly— but this time on a higher pitch, and with quite bewildering power of effect—the glory breaks again upon the soul, and we seem "rapt from the fickle and the frail," and caught up into that splendid air of joy and bounding triumph. The poor shaken and earth-worn spirit is thus held for a little space in Paradise. It is its last gleam of perfect peace. Already at 103, the vision has well-nigh faded out; at 111 the light of common day has been fairly reached, and the perilous struggle between morbid brooding and noble endurance is in danger of recommencing. Four times, at 119, 123, 125, and 126, the morbid passage reminding us of the opening phrase, knocks ($f\!f$) passionately for admittance, and is sternly negatived by the bass. At 129, 130, 131, there is a very natural pause of brief exhaustion at p. At 132 the emotion is stirred, but this time less strongly; we feel that a new and more normal life is now going to open out, into which indeed we are not permitted to enter, for the Lied draws to its close. The vision of triumph has had its own chastening and purifying effect, although the triumph of joy is evidently not near; still the restless and passionate mood of anxious brooding, which so unfits for the life that has still to be lived out, has also passed. The last unemphatic memory of it occurs at 138; not even *half* the first subject, as before, is repeated—only *one bar* of it, and the emotion is then left unimpassioned and suspended on a long D, the same chord for six bars, without change in treble or bass, serving to close the piece, and leaving the mind in a self-contained and reconciled, if not a happy mood, ready now to enter without harrowing preoccupation upon the more ordinary phases and pursuits of life.

Now if music does really rouse and then take in hand and rule at its will, and thereby teach us to rule, the emotions, it is obvious that we are, when we hear music intelligently and sympathetically, *actually cultivating abstract habits of mind which may afterward be transferred as trained forces to the affairs of daily life.* As the study of Euclid trains the mind in the abstract, so the study of music trains the emotions in the abstract.

If you want to touch and train this emotional life, music is your all-powerful ally.

The time is not distant when this great truth will be understood and practised in connection with our toiling masses—our artisans, our poor, our laborers, our degraded denizens of back streets, cellars, and foul alleys. There are millions whose only use of the emotional life is base, undisciplined, and degraded. Pleasure with many means* crime; restraint, the real handmaid of pleasure, is unknown; system, order, harmony in their feelings, habits of self-control, checking the impulses, moderating and economizing the feelings, guiding them to powerful purposes and wise ends and wholesome joys—of all this our masses are chiefly ignorant; yet if what I have maintained be true, all this music would mightily *help* to teach and to give.

I have known the oratorio of the *Messiah* draw the lowest dregs of Whitechapel into a church to hear it, and during the performance sobs have broken forth from the silent and attentive throng. Will any one say that for these people to have their feelings for once put through such a noble and long-sustained exercise as that, could be otherwise than beneficial? If such performances of both sacred and secular music were more frequent, we should have less drunkenness, less wife-beating, less spending of summer gains, less pauperism in winter. People get drunk because they have nothing else to do; they beat their wives because their minds are narrow, their tastes brutal, their emotions, in a word, ill-regulated; they spend their wages because they have no self-control, and dawdle in public-houses, where money must be spent, simply in the absence of all other resources; and they starve in winter because they have not acquired the habit of steady work, which is impossible without study and wholesome recreation—or that steady thrift and self-control which is impossible apart from disciplined emotion.

The question of music for the people will some day become a great government question. A few thousands spent on promoting bands, cheap and good, accessible and respectable, would save the country millions in poor-rates. I do not say that music will ever shut up all our prisons and workhouses; but I venture to believe that as a chief and sovereign means of rousing, satisfying, and recreating the emotions, it would go far to diminish the number of paupers and criminals. It would help them to save, it would keep them from drink, it would recreate them wholesomely, and teach them to govern their feelings—to use, and not invariably abuse, their emotions.

One Saturday afternoon I stood outside a public-house, and saw the groups of men standing round the door. Those that came to the door did not enter; those who came forth with lighted pipes, paused; a slatternly girl or two, with a ragged child in her arms; a wife who had followed her husband to look after the Saturday wages, which were going straight to the gin-shop; a costermonger with his cart drew up; the idle cabmen came across the road; even a few dirty, stone-throwing, dog-worrying boys ceased their sport; and two or three milliners' "Hands" stood still. And what was it all about? I blush for my country! A wretched cornet with a harp, no two strings of which were in tune, the harpist trying wildly to follow "The Last Rose of Summer" with but two chords, and always in with the wrong one. The weather was bitterly cold, the men's hands were in their pockets, the girls shivered; but they were all taking their solace. This was the best music they could get: it seemed to soothe and refresh them. Oh, that I could have led those people to some near winter pavilion, or even a cold garden, where they could have walked about and heard a popular selection of tunes, an overture, anything, by a common but excellent German band! What good that would have done them! How they would have enjoyed it! And supposing that every Saturday they could look forward to it, admission twopence apiece, the men would be there with their wives and children; they would spend less on the whole family than they would have squandered on themselves in one drunken afternoon. They could meet their friends, have their chat and glass of ale, or cup of coffee, in the winter garden; they would go home sober; and being satisfied, recreated, having had their exercise and company, would be more likely to go to bed early than to get drunk late. Surely all this is better than boozing in public-houses.

Oh, what a vast, what a beneficent future has music in the time to come! Let its true power and use be once understood; let some one man who loves the people, and is willing to consult their tastes without pandering to them, open a promenade for the lower stratum of the population, at a low price, on Saturday afternoon, and let us see the result. Let the musical part be under some fit and intelligent musical dictator, and let some able and sympathetic administrator, intimately and wisely in sympathy with the masses—a Miss Octavia Hill—organize the refreshments, the admissions by payment, the general distribution of tickets, passes, advertisements, accommodation, etc. Let this be tried fairly —at first, of course, with an outlay of charitable funds —and then I prophesy four things:

1. It will soon be self-supporting.

2. It will have a definite and marked influence upon the crime and intemperance of the district.

3. It will promote thrift, and increase the sum, now lamentably small, of the people's wholesome pleasures.

4. It will become a national institution, and spread in a short time throughout the length and breadth of the land.

Then shall music, ceasing to be the luxury of the rich and the degradation of the poor, open the golden gates of a wider and a happier realm of recreation for the masses. In its wake might follow, under similar management, a regenerated and popular drama, pictorial exhibitions, short and systematic lectures to groups in separate alcoves, electrical experiments, the microscope, the telescope, and a thousand other elevating and instructive *séances*—to each *séance* one halfpenny apiece extra, or one penny to frank for the whole.

Once get the people together by the power of music, you can mould them; one closed chamber of their minds after another might be unlocked; and were the scheme conducted with ability, and carefully watched, we should soon hail the dawn of a new era of popular enlightenment and genial instruction combined with an almost boundless variety of accessible, innocent, and elevating enjoyment.

CHAPTER III.

OLD VIOLINS.

THE construction, the history, the sound of the violin would make a romantic work in three volumes as sensational as, and far more instructive than, most novels. The very pine-wood smells good, to begin with. The forests of the Southern Tyrol, which now teem with saplings, when the old violins were made, from 1520 to 1750, still abounded in those ancient trees, so eagerly and often vainly sought out by modern builders, and which the old viol-makers found to possess the finest acoustic properties.

The mighty timbers were felled in late summer. They came in loose floating rafts from the banks of the Garda; they floated down the Mincio to Mantua. Brescia was in the midst of them. From Como they found their way to Milan, and from Lake Maggiore direct, *via* the Ticino and the Po, to Cremona.

What market days were those! What a timber feast to select from; and what cunning lovers and testers of wood were the old viol-makers, the fathers of the violin! The rough heaps of pine, pear, lemon, and ash, beloved of the Brescians—of maple and sycamore, preferred by the Cremonese—lay steaming dry and hard in a few hours beneath the sun of the southern Alps.

Before a beam was bought, the master passed his hand over the surface. He could tell by touch the density of its fibre. Then he would take two equal slips of deal and weigh them, and judge of their porousness. The very appearance of the wood would guide him to its probable vibrational powers. Then he would, perchance, before leaving the market, cut strips of equal length, and elicit their relative intensities by striking their tongues. He would often select for a definite purpose, looking for a soft, porous piece, or a specially hard and close-fibred grain—a certain appearance he would instinctively associate with rare acoustic properties. The seller would be eager to find the pieces, useless to other customers, invaluable to an Andreas Amati, for he was sure that the viol-maker would buy what suited him at a long price. After the lapse of nearly two centuries, we can trace such favorite beams by peculiar stains, freckles, and grainings. When, after cutting up a dozen trees, once in two or three years a piece of fine acoustic wood was found, it was kept for the master's best work. The same pine-beam will crop up in the bellies of Stradivarius at an interval of years. Another can be traced in the violins of Joseph Guarnerius, and after his death Carlo Bergonzi got hold of the remnants of it, and we detect it by a certain stain in the fibre.

The anxiety to retain every particle of a precious piece of wood is seen in the subtle and delicate patching and repatching of backs and bellies. The seams are only discoverable by a microscope, so perfect is the cabinet work. How different from the modern maker at Madrid, whom Tarisio relates as having to repair a damaged Stradivarius, and, finding the belly cracked, sent it home with a brand-new one of his own manufacture!

The properties of fine violin wood are very mysterious. Only to be surrounded by a selection of fine violins is an experience which cannot be forgotten. Sit in the room with them with your eyes shut, and, although you may not touch one of them, you will soon be aware of ghostly presences. Even the old seasoned backs and bellies of unstrung violins are full of the strangest echoes, and Mr. Hill, the violin-maker, tolls me that as he sits in his workroom, where old violin carcasses are piled in hundreds on shelves and cupboards pell-mell, ribs, bellies, and backs, he constantly hears them muttering and humming to themselves, in answer to his tools, the stroke of his hammer, the sound of his voice.

Let us now look at the violin anatomically. It is a miracle of construction, and as it can be taken to pieces, put together, patched, and indefinitely repaired, it is almost indestructible. It is, as one may say, as light as a feather and as strong as a horse. It is composed of fifty-eight or seventy pieces of wood. Wood about as thick as a half-crown, by exquisite adjustments of parts and distribution of strain, resists for several centuries an enormous pressure. The belly of soft deal, the back of hard sycamore, are united by six sycamore ribs, supported by twelve blocks with linings.

It appears that the quick vibrations of the hard wood, married to the slower sound-waves of the soft, produce the mellow but reedy *timbre* of the good violin. If all the wood were hard, you would get the tone light and metallic; if all soft, it would be muffled and tubby.

There is every conceivable variety of fibre both in hard and soft wood. The thickness of back and belly is not uniform; each should be thicker toward the middle. But how thick? and shaved thin in what proportions toward the sides? The cunning workman alone knows. As a rule, if the wood be hard he will cut it thin; if soft, thick; but *how* thin and *how* thick, and exactly *where*, is nowhere writ down, nor can be, because nowhere for handy reference are recorded the densities of all pine and pear and sycamore and maple planks that have or shall come into the maker's hands.

The sound-bar is a strip of pine wood running obliquely under the left foot of the bridge. It not only strengthens the belly for the prodigious pressure of the four strings, whose direction it is made to follow, for vibrational reasons, but it is the nervous system of the violin. It has to be cut and adjusted to the whole framework; a slight mistake in position, a looseness, an inequality or roughness of finish, will produce that hollow teeth-on-edge growl called the "wolf."

It takes the greatest cunning and a life of practical study to know how long, how thick, and exactly where the sound-bar should be in each instrument. The health and *morale* of many an old violin has been impaired by its nervous system being ignorantly tampered with. Every old violin, with the exception of the "Pucelle," has had its sound-bar replaced, or it would never have endured the increased tightness of strings brought in with our modern pitch. Many good forgeries have thus been exposed, for in taking the reputed Stradivarius to pieces, the rough clumsy work inside, contrasting with the exquisite finish of the old masters, betrays at once the coarseness of a body that never really held the soul of a Cremona.

The sound-post, a little pine prop like a short bit of cedar pencil, is the *soul* of the violin. It is placed upright inside, about one eighth of an inch to the back of the right foot of the bridge, and through it pass all the heart-throbs or vibrations generated between the back and the belly. There the short waves and the long waves meet and mingle. It is the material throbbing centre of that pulsating air column, defined by the walls of the violin, but propagating those mystic sound-waves that ripple forth in sweetness upon ten thousand ears.

Days and weeks may be spent on the adjustment of this tiny sound-post. Its position exhausts the patience of the repairer, and makes the joy or the misery of the player. As a rough general rule, the high-built violin will take it nearer the bridge than the low-built, and a few experiments will at once show the relation of the "soul" to tightness, mellowness, or intensity of sound. For the amateur there is but one motto: "Leave well alone."

The prodigious strain of the strings is resisted first by the arch of the belly; then by the ribs, strengthened with the upright blocks, the pressure among which is evenly distributed by the linings which unite them; and, lastly, by the supporting sound-bar, sound-post, and back. Many people, on observing the obvious join between the neck and the head of old violins, fancy that the *head* is not the original. It is the *neck* that is new. All the necks of old violins have thus been lengthened, and the old heads refixed, for the simple reason that Corelli's finger-board will not do for Paganini, and mightier execution requires an ampler field for its eccentric excursions.

The scroll, or head, fitted with its four simple screws of ebony, box, or rosewood, is the physiognomy of the violin. At first all fiddle-heads look alike—as do all pug-dogs, or all negroes, and, indeed, England, Wales, Italy, Holland, and most other countries have their general faces; so have violins—but a practised eye sees the difference at a glance. Look for half an hour every day at a late Joseph Guarnerius, an early Nicholas Amati, and a grand pattern Strad., and you will be surprised that you could ever have confounded their forms. What is called the "throwing" of the scroll betrays the master's style like handwriting, and he lays down his type in every curve, groove, and outline. A keen eye can almost see the favorite tool he worked with, and how his hand went. These subtleties are like the painter's "touch," they can hardly be imitated so as to deceive one who has mastered the individual work of the great makers.

The ebony finger-board must be nicely fitted, as also the neck, to the hand of the player; on its even smoothness and true curve depends the correct stopping of the notes. You cannot, for instance, stop fifths in tune on a rough or uneven finger-board. The button to which the tail-piece is fastened is full of style, and not, like the pegs, a thing to be dropped and changed at will; it is a critical part of the violin, takes a good third of the leverage of the whole strain, is fixed like a vice, rooted in the very adamant of the wood, carefully finished, and cut round, pointed, or flat, according to the taste of the maker.

The purfling, more or less deeply embedded, emphasizes the outline of the violin. It is composed of three thin strips of wood, ebony, sometimes whalebone, the centre of two white strips; it is often more or less embedded, and betrays the workman's taste and skill. The double purfling and purfling in eccentric patterns of some of the old violins is very quaint, but a doubtful adjunct to the tone. But, strange to say, prior to 1600, appearances were more thought of than tone. The old guitars and viols are often so profusely carved or inlaid with tortoiseshell, ivory, and silver, that they have but little sound, and that bad. I do not think that this has ever been noticed before, but it is undoubtedly a fact that attention to tone only dates from the rise of the violin proper in the sixteenth century, and is, in fact, coincident with the rise of the art of modern music.

I come now to the Cremona varnish. What is it? About 1760 it disappeared, and never reappeared. All the Cremonas have it. Was it a gum or an oil, or a distillation from some plant, or some chemical once largely in use and superseded, as the old oil lamps have gone out before gas and paraffine? How was it mixed? Is the recipe lost? No one seems to be able to answer these questions definitely. There it lies, like sunlit water, mellow, soft, rich, varying in color — golden, orange, or pale red tint on the Guarnerius! rich gold, deep orange, or light red on the Stradivarius back; and when it rubs softly away rather than chips off hardly, like the German and French imitations, it leaves the wood seasoned, impregnated, and fit to resist heat, cold, and the all-destroying worm for ages. Mr. Charles Reade gives one account of the matter. He thinks the wood, cut in winter, varnished in the hot summer months, was first bathed several times in oil; thus, he says, were the "pores of the wood filled, and the grain shown up." The oil held in solution some clear gum. "Then upon this oil varnish, when dry, was laid some heterogeneous varnish, namely a solution in spirit of some sovereign, high-colored, pellucid, and, above all, tender gum." These gums were reddish yellow and yellowish red, and are accredited with coloring the varnish. On the other hand, it must be stated that, although the difficulties in the amber theory are great, Mr. Perkins, the eminent chemist, has discovered amber in the varnish of Joseph Guarnerius, and he believes the coloring to be derived from an herb common throughout Piedmont, and, following out his conviction, Mr. Perkins has made a varnish which certainly does resemble very closely the Cremonese hue and gloss. Dod, who died in 1830, professed to have got the Cremona recipe, and while employing John Lott and Bernard Fendt to make his violins, always varnished them himself; and, indeed, his varnish is very superior, and his violins are highly prized. But perhaps in a general description like this to discuss further the varnish theory would be superfluous.

The bridge of the violin is to many a true Asses' Bridge; you may try and try again, and its true position will still be represented by an unknown x. It is but a small piece of hard boxwood, 2 inches by $1\frac{1}{2}$ in size; it is quaintly perforated; it clings closely to the violin's belly with its two little thin feet; is about as thick, where thickest, as a five-shilling piece, thinning steadily toward the top, which obeys the curve of the finger-board and lifts the strain of the four strings. The bridge is movable; but it is so important and all-essential to the propagation of any sound at all, that it may be called the wife of the violin. All old violins have had many bridges in their time; but there is no reason why the union, if happy, should not last for forty or fifty years. A perfectly harmonious marriage is as rare between violins and their bridges as it is between men and women, though in either case there is a considerable margin for the gradual adjustment of temperaments. Although the old violin is very capricious in his choice, and often remains a widower for years, he does not object to elderly bridges, and when he finds one he can get on with, will obstinately resent any rash interference with the harmony of his domestic arrangements.

This is a point not nearly enough considered even by wise violin doctors and repairers. The heartless substitution of raw young bridges for old and tried companions is common and much to be deplored, and a sensitive

THE SENTIMENT OF THE BRIDGE.

old Strad. will never cease to spar with the fresh, conceited, wayward young things, utterly incapable of entering into his fine qualities, and caring naught for his two hundred years of tonal experience; and the jarring and bickering go on until he gets rid of one after another and settles down, if not with his old favorite, at least with some elderly and fairly desiccated companion. I do not believe in bridges being worn out. After a year or two the hard box-fibre yields very little under the cutting of the strings; there is a considerable margin for the shifting of the strings, and no string but the first will materially grind. Rather than change so precious a thing as a congenial partner, glue, mend, patch, repair her, just as you would her priceless old husband; if he is in the prime of life at about one hundred and fifty, she may well be a little made up at sixty or seventy. Thirty years ago my Stradivarius, 1712, grand pattern, came by gift into my possession. I soon found it did not get on with its bridge—a new, sappy, crude, thick thing, which seemed to choke and turn sour its mellow vibrations. About that time I received the present of a very old bridge from the violin of F. Cramer. It was delicate, exquisitely finished, evidently very old. I thought its build too slight, but clapped it on at once, and the old violin waked as out of a long sleep, like a giant refreshed with wine. It was then some time before I found exactly the right place, and for several years, on and off, I fidgeted about with the bridge. One day, in shifting it, I snapped it; but after trying other bridges, I glued the old one together, and once more the violin found its old sweetness and solace. Years passed, I left off playing, the Strad. lay neglected, got damp, and its joints loosened. I lent it to a cunning doctor; he "fixed it up" again, but sent it back with a new bridge, and sounding

—well, like files and vinegar! I recovered the old bridge that he declared now worn out. I restored it to its beloved husband, now only in his one hundred and seventy-first year; he received his lost wife with effusion, and I think the harmony made by the two was never more perfect than it is now. Truly *amantium* not *iræ*, but *separacio amoris integratio est.*

A word about violin strings. The positive thickness of the strings depends upon the temperament and build of the violin, providing that the player's fingers are equal to thick or thin strings. Thick strings will mellow the screaminess of a Stainer, elicit the full tone of a Joseph Guarnerius or grand Strad., while the older violins of Brescia, and even the sweet Nicolas Amati, will work better with thinner strings; but in such matters the player must come to the best compromise he can with his fingers and his fiddle, for the finger will often desire a thin string when the fiddle cries out for a thick one. New violins as a rule will take thicker strings than the fine old sensitives of the sixteenth or seventeenth centuries. Of the English, French, German, and Italian strings, the Italian are the best; and of the Italian, the Roman hard and brilliant, a little rough, and Neapolitan smooth, soft, and pale are preferred. Paduans are strong, but frequently false. Veronese are softer and deeper in color. The Germans now rank next, and the white smooth Saxon strings are good substitutes for, but no rivals of, the Italians. The French firsts are brittle, the Italian strings sound well, and the French patent fourth silver string, perfectly smooth and shining, is preferred by some soloists to the old covered fourth. The English strings, of a dirty green and yellow color, are very strong, and good enough for hack work in the orchestra. The best and strongest strings are made from the intestines of spring lambs killed in September, and the superiority of the Italian over others is explained by the climate, for in Italy the sun does what has to be done artificially in more northern latitudes.

The demand for the interior of the September lamb being out of all proportion to the supply, there is a vast sale of inferior strings always going on at high prices. In string selection the objects are three :

1. To suit the constitution of your instrument, and choose that thickness and quality of string which will develop tone with the greatest ease, roundness, and freedom.

2. To choose strings which will give good fifths—a matter sometimes a little dependent on the shape of your own fingers and the cut of your finger-board, but also controlled by the relative thickness of your strings.

3. To avoid false strings—an epidemic which rages incontinently among E violin strings. Spohr's recipe for detection was to hold the string between the fingers and thumbs, and if, when he set it vibrating from one end to the other, only two lines appeared, he decided that it was true ; if a third, it was deemed false. Once on, however, there can never be any doubt.

It is only necessary to glance at the enormous variety of shapes that the viol tribe has assumed, both before and after the creation of the violin, to judge of the inexhaustible dominion which the conception seems to have exercised over the human mind. The collector who cannot play, and the player who cannot collect, are alike victims of this mania for violins. Of what interest can they be to the collector, who keeps dozens of them, unstrung and unmended, in cupboards and cabinets, and shows them about to his bewildered guests like old pots or enamels ?

Look at a fine specimen or two, on and off, when you have the chance, and the mystery may possibly dawn upon you too.

There, in a small compass, lies before you such a wonder of simplicity, subtlety, variety, and strength as perhaps no other object of equal dimensions can possess. The eye is arrested by the amber gloss and glow of the varnish, the infinite grace of the multitudinous curves, the surface, which is nowhere flat, but ever in flowing lines—sunlit hollows of miniature hills and vales, irregular, like the fine surface of a perfectly healthy human body. Its gentle mounds and depressions would almost make us believe that there is a whole underlying system of muscle—a very living organism, to account for such subtle yet harmonious irregularity of surface. It is positively alive with swelling and undulating grace.

Then the eye follows with unabating ardor the outline, dipping in here or bulging there, in segments of what look like an oval or a circle, but which are never any part of an oval or a circle, but something drawn unmechanically, like a Greek frieze, after the vision of an inward grace.

Its voice may be as fair as its form and finish; yet unstrung and silent, more truly can it be said of a violin than of any human creature, that "it is a thing of beauty and a joy forever," for its beauty grows with the mellowness of age, its voice is sweeter as the centuries roll on, and its physical frame appears to be almost indestructible.

And the player, who is not always a judge of a genuine violin, but goes by the sound qualities which suit him—he naturally adores what is, within its limits, scientifically the most perfect of all instruments.

The four strings, of course, limit and define its harmonic resources. In combination, and viewed collectively in the quartet alone, is it able to compass the extended developments of harmony in bass, tenor, and treble clef; but as a tone-producing instrument it has no rival. It possesses *accent* combined with *sustained and modified tone*. The piano has accent, but little sustained and no modified tone; the organ has accent, and sustained, but in a very imperfect sense, modified tone; the violin possesses in perfection all three. With the stroke of the bow comes every degree of *accent;* with the drawing and skilful *sostenuto* of up and down bowings the notes are indefinitely *sustained* to a degree far exceeding the capacity of the human lungs; while every pulse of emotion is through the pressure of the finger communicated to the vibrating string, and the tone trembles, shivers, thrills, or assumes a hard, rigid quality, passing at will from the variety of a whisper to a very roar or scream of agony or delight.

Can the soul of the musician fail to yield loving or utter allegiance to the sovereign power of the violin, which is so willing and ideal a minister of his subtlest inspirations—equal to the human voice in sensibility and expression, and far superior to it in compass, execution, variety, and durability?

The hotter suns and splendid river supplying the fine wood-market, and the commercial prosperity enjoyed by Cremona, seem to have attracted and fixed the manufacture of the violin; and there became a growing demand, not only from all the churches, but also throughout the palaces of Italy. We must ever view that central square of Cremona, where stood the Church of St. Dominic, with feelings of the deepest interest. Standing opposite the façade on our right hand lies the house of the Amati; there worked Andrew, the founder of the school, making, in 1550, close copies of the Brescians, Gaspar and Maggini.

There were the boys, Anthony and Jerome, who afterward made jointly those violins so much sought after; but oddly enough reverted to the tubbier model, and over-grooved the sides of their bellies and backs, thinning their tone, until the genius of Jerome discerned the error and reverted to the Brescian type.

Here was born the great Nicolas Amati, 1596–1684, who struck out his own model, flattened, and in his best time scarcely retaining a trace of the vicious side-groove of the earlier Amatis.

On the same work-bench, as students in the school of the immortal Nicolas, sat Andrew Guarnerius and the incomparable Stradivarius, finishing their master's violins and copying for years his various models with supreme skill and docility.

Almost next door, probably on the death of Nicolas Amati, Stradivarius set up his shop, opposite the west front of the big church; there for fifty years more he worked with uninterrupted assiduity; and next door to him the family of the Guarnerii had their work-rooms, and in that little square were all the finest violins made in the short space of about one hundred and fifty years. The body of Stradivarius lies in the Church of the Rosary, not a stone's-throw from his own house; and so these great men died, and were buried, working in friendly rivalry, and leaving their echoes to roll from pole to pole.

The great Nicolas (1596–1684) began to change his model, reverting to the later Brescian in all but his sound holes and two curves, about 1625. His violins increased in size, and would have increased in power, had it not been for a remnant of the early Amati side-grooving, which is said to thin the tone. The dip from the foot of the bridge is thought to be too great, but the upper part of the grand pattern is truly noble. Some of his scrolls have been criticised as too small and contracted, but there is nothing of this in a 1676 specimen before me; and although the corners are pointed and highly elegant, there is nothing weak; yet the whole is full of feminine grace.

The varnish, when not as is usual rubbed off, inclines to light orange with clear golden tints. The tone is so sweet and sensitive that it seems to leap forth before the bow has touched the strings, and goes on like a bell long after the bow has left them. To a fine Joseph Guarnerius you have sometimes to lay siege, and then you are rewarded; but the Nicolas Amati is won almost before it is wooed.

The incomparable Antonius Stradivarius, or Stradivari, lived between 1644-1737. His latest known violin bears date 1736, and mentions his age, ninety-two. He worked without haste and without rest. His life was interrupted only by the siege of Cremona in 1702. But his art knew no politics, and the foreign courts of Spain and France were quite as eager to get his violins as the Governor of Cremona, or the Duke of Modena.

Up to about 1668 he was simply the apprentice of Nicolas; we find scrolls and sound-holes cut by the pupil on the master's violins. He even made and labelled for Nicolas.

In 1668 he leaves his master's shop and sets up for himself. But for thirty years this consummate student, while making every conceivable experiment with flutes, guitars, and violins, practically copied closely the best models of Nicolas Amati.

Still we notice that from 1686-1694 his sound holes begin to recline, his form grows flatter, his curves extended, his corners tossed up and pointed, the scroll bolder, varnish inclining away from the browns and light orange to the rich yellows and light reds. Notice the way in which his purfling at the corners, like a little curved wasp's sting, follows no outline of the violin, and is not in the middle of the angle, but points freely toward the *corner* of the angle. What *chic!* as the French say.

In 1687 the master makes his long pattern—not really longer, but *looking* longer because of the contracted sides. The Spanish Quatuor, inlaid with ivory, illustrates the fancy and skill of the workman.

It was not until Stradivarius had entered upon his fifty-sixth year that he attained his zenith and fixed his model, known as the grand pattern. Between 1700 and 1725 those extraordinary creations passed from his chisel, even as the master-pieces on canvas passed from the brush of Raphael. The finest of these specimens—like that possessed by Mr. Adams, the Dolphin, and by Mr. Hart, the Betts Strad.—fetch from £300 to £1000.

To try to describe these instruments is like trying to describe the pastes, glazes, and blues of Nankin China. Beneath the tangible points of outline, scroll, character, and variety of thickness and modification of form, dependent on qualities of wood known to the master, there lie still the intangible things which will hardly bear describing, even when the violin is under the eye—one might almost say under the microscope. A rough attempt by contrast may be made in detail. Take but one detail for the benefit of the general reader, the inner *side curves* and angles of the middle boughts.

In Gaspar and Maggini those curves are drooping at the corners, longish and undecided in character; in

Duiffoprugcar they amount almost to wriggles. Nicolas Amati balances the top and bottom of his hollow curve with a certain mastery, but it still has a long oval sweep, with a definite relation of balance between the top and the bottom angle. Having mastered this sweep, Stradivarius begins to play with his curves and angles. He feels strong enough to trifle, like a skilled acrobat, with the balance. He lessens the oval, and tosses up his lower corner with a curious little crook at the bottom ; the top angle towers proudly and smoothly above it, yet it is always graceful—delicious from its sense of freedom, almost insolent in its strength and self-confidence. There is a touch about Stradivarius here as elsewhere ; it is that which separates the great masters everywhere from their pupils—Raphael from Giulio Romano, Paganini from Sivori, Stradivarius from Carlo Bergonzi. The freedom of Stradivarius becomes license in Carlo Bergonzi and over-boldness in Joseph Guarnerius ; for, although the connection between Joseph and Stradivarius has been questioned, to my mind it is sufficiently clear.

Although Stradivarius worked down to the last year of his life, still, after 1730, feeling his hand and sight beginning to fail, he seldom signed his work. We catch one, and only one, glimpse of him as he lived and moved and had his being at Cremona in 1730, Piazza Domenico. Old Polledro, late chapel-master at Turin, describes "Antonius, the lute-maker," as an intimate friend of his master. He was high and thin, and looked like one worn with much thought and incessant industry. In summer he wore a white cotton night-cap, and in winter one of some woollen material. He was never seen without his apron of white leather, and every day was to him exactly like every other day. His mind was always riveted upon his one pursuit, and he seemed neither to know nor to desire the least change of occupation. His violins sold for four golden livres apiece, and were considered the best in Italy; and as he never spent anything except upon the necessaries of life and his own trade, he saved a good deal of money, and the simple-minded Cremonese used to make jokes about his thriftiness, and the proverb passed, "As rich as Stradivarius."

A traveller who lately visited his house, still standing in the square of Cremona, remarked that it was heated through with the sun like an oven. He said you might sit and sweat there as in a Turkish bath. That was how the Cremona makers dried their wood, and so it was their oils distilled slowly and remained always at a high temperature, their varnish soaked into the pine bellies and sycamore backs beneath the tropical heat of those seventeenth century summers!

Joseph Anthony Guarnerius del Gesu IHS (1687–1745) towers a head and shoulders above the other illustrious Guarnerii, viz., Andrew and Joseph, his sons, Peter, brother of Joseph (*son*), Peter of Mantua, son of "Joseph *Filius* Andreæ." The loud and rich tone of the later Joseph del Gesu violins makes him the formidable rival of Stradivarius. Paganini preferred his Joseph, now in the Municipal Palace of Genoa, to all others.

Who was Joseph's master? The idea that Joseph, or any one who lived either in Amati's or Guarnerius's house—Amati on the right, Guarnerius on the left of Stradivarius, in the same square at Cremona—was entirely unaffected by the great man's influence, has always seemed to me absurd. That influence has been denied as vehemently in late years as it used to be formerly taken for granted. Still, the great Joseph is claimed as the pupil of Joseph, son of Andrew—that Andrew who sat by the side of Stradivarius in Nicolas Amati's workshop. With this I find no fault; but if the influence of Stradivarius cannot be seen in earlier Josephs, the later Josephs show undoubted signs of the master, who between 1700 and 1730 had eclipsed all his predecessors. In some details Joseph's undoubted reversion to Brescian influence, and that early, is interesting—the flat model, the long sound-holes, and, it must be added, often the rough work. Still, in Joseph's middle period there occurs that very high finish which reminds one of Stradivarius. The elegance of the Strad. scroll is never attained, perhaps not even aimed at. The Josephs of about 1740 are most in request. They are large and massively made, the wood of finest acoustic property, the Brescian sound-hole toned down and rounded more like Stradivarius. A fine genuine violin of this period will not go for less than two hundrd guineas, and four hundred would not be an out-and-out price. The Guarnerius head or scroll is often quaint and full of self-assertion. The violin has the strongest make, temper, and stamp; the fourth string is often as rich as a trumpet. His last period is troubled by certain inferior violins called prison fiddles. The tale runs that Joseph was imprisoned for some political offence, and was supplied with refuse wood by the jailer's daughter. The prison fiddle is a boon to forgers; their bad fiddles pass freely for interesting " prison Josephs."

With Carlo Bergonzi (1718–1755) and Guadagnini (1710–1750) the great Cremona school comes to an end. The very varnish disappears, the cunning in wood-selection seems to fail the pale reflectors of a dying art, and the passion for vigor and finish has also departed. The violin, although it culminated, was not exhausted at

Cremona ; but it would lead me into a new branch of my subject to deal with the other schools. These, after all, are but reflections, more or less pale or perfect, of the incomparable Cremonese masters.

CHAPTER IV.

PAGANINI.

WHO is this man who rises up suddenly in the world of music, and whose fame passes with the brightness and rapidity of a meteor through the civilized world; who, at the moment when Baillot, Spohr, Rode, and Lafont seemed to have explored the heights and depths of the violin, opened up new vistas full of strange, unparalleled mysteries, and gave us glimpses into a hell, purgatory, and paradise beyond the dreams even of Dante; whose gaunt and supernatural figure startled and fascinated the crowds that thronged about him, a solitary man among men, but so unlike them that he seemed to belong to another race, and to discourse in the weird music of another world; who bowed to none, yet was idolized by all; whose engagements were negotiated by kings and ministers; who could spurn the prayers of princes and grand duchesses, and yet received honor at their hands, and was alternately decorated by the pope, and anathematized by the clergy? Who was this exceptional being reigning supreme for forty years without a rival over the conflicting schools of Italy, Germany, and France; at whose approach the greatest masters confessed themselves vanquished; who, although he set the fashions, fired whole populations, invented a new school, yet, in his own peculiar greatness, had no masters, no equals, and has left no followers? This man, who has stamped so indelible an impression of himself upon the musical world, while his name will survive as the synonym of wonder and mystery to the remote ages—this Hercules of the violin was Nicolo Paganini.

That a man's grandmother, or even his father and mother, are of some consequence when he derives lustre or gain from them of any kind, no one will deny; but when he sheds back upon them the only kind of reflex glory which they are capable of receiving, the glory of an imperishable name, no one will blame the biographer for skipping a few dull and stupid antecedents.

Paganini *père* may have been a street porter, as some pretend; or small tradesman, as others, probably in the right,'affirm. He was a sharp man; he was a cruel man; he did overmuch to develop his son's talents, and overmuch to ruin his health, and, probably, is chargeable with having destroyed his mental and moral equilibrium for life. Nicolo's mother was a sweet, amiable woman. She loved her boy, she believed in him, she often stood between him and the rod, she prayed for him, and saw one night in a vision a celestial being, who told her that the boy would become the greatest violinist that ever lived. How far this dream, which she lost no time in communicating to father and son, increased the father's severity, and fired the boy's ambition, we cannot tell; but the dream seems to have been a well-established fact, and years afterward, when the mother was old, and the son at his zenith, she reminded him of it, as of an incident which had been familiar to both of them throughout their lives.

In these early days of boyhood were probably laid the seeds of that idiosyncrasy of temperament which became at once the glory and curse of his life. Little as we know about the human brain, it is tolerably certain that its particles move in physical grooves and acquire methodical arrangements, which correspond to what we call mental qualities and states of mind. Illness may perpetuate some and modify others. Great severity may have a similar effect; recurrent outward action, for instance, may create intense propensity in certain directions, and thus impart the perseverance of mania to inward dispositions; the nervous system at the same time, if it does not break down, becomes over-developed, and is then endowed with an almost supernatural sensibility. Something of this kind appears to have been the case with Paganini. He was by nature very delicate. At four years old he was nearly buried alive; he lay for a whole day in a state of catalepsy, and was already placed in his shroud, when he revived, but with a nervous system which from that time forward showed signs of a strange and unnatural susceptibility. By his own temperament, as soon as he could hold the violin, he was urged to an intense and dangerous application. For the least fault he was severely beaten by his father, which seemed only to increase an ardor which should, for his own sake, have been rather moderated. Precocity was still further forced on by starvation. Had it not been for his mother, he might never have survived this brutal treatment. We shall see by and by how lovingly he remembered her in the midst of his triumphs.

Paganini was born at Genoa on the 10th of February, 1784. After exhausting his father's instruction, he was taken in hand by Signor Servetto, of the Genoese theatre; then Giacomo Costa, chapel-master, taught him, and the child was often seen playing in the Genoese churches on a violin almost as large as himself; but, like Mozart before him, and Mendelssohn after him, Nicolo was the despair of his masters, who were in turn angry with his innovations, and astonished at his precocious facility. In his ninth year he appeared at a concert, and electrified every one with variations on the French air, *La Carmagnole*. This triumph impelled his avaricious father to discover some one who could further teach him; the young talent was to be pressed and squeezed to its utmost limit, in order to produce the golden harvest.

At Parma lived the celebrated musician Rolla. To Rolla was the boy taken; but Rolla was ill. While waiting in the ante-room little Nicolo took up a violin, and played off at sight some difficult music which he found lying on the table. The invalid composer raised himself on his bed to listen, and eagerly inquired who the great master was who had arrived and was playing in his ante-room. "A mere lad!—impossible!" but on Paganini's making his appearance as an humble pupil, Rolla at once told him that he could teach him nothing. Thence to Paër, who was glad to make his difficult charge over to Ghiretti, and this master gave him three lessons a week in harmony and counterpoint. It is not clear that this extraordinary genius owed much more to any one but himself—his indomitable perseverance and his incessant study. His method is to be noted. For ten or twelve hours he would try passages over and over again in different ways with such absorption and intensity that at nightfall he would sink into utter prostration through excessive exhaustion and fatigue. Though delicate, like Mendelssohn, he ate at times ravenously, and slept soundly. When about ten he wrote twenty-four fugues, and soon afterward composed some violin music, of such difficulty that he was unable at first to play it, until incessant practice gave him the mastery.

In 1797 Paganini, being then thirteen years old, made

his first professional tour ; but not as a free agent. His father took him through the chief towns of Lombardy, and, not unnaturally, prescribed the task and pocketed the proceeds. But the young neck was already beginning to chafe against the yoke. In 1798 he escaped, with his father's tardy consent, to Lucca, where a musical festival in honor of St. Martin was going on. He there gave frequent concerts, and was everywhere met with applause, and, what was more to the purpose, with money. Surrounded by men of inferior talents, a mere inexperienced boy, without education, without knowledge of the world, with nothing but ambition and his supreme musical genius, he now broke wildly away from all wise restraints, and avenged himself upon his father's severity by many youthful excesses. He gambled—he lost—he was duped by his companions ; but he made money so fast, that he soon owned about £1000. It is pleasant to think that he at once thought of giving some of this to his father and mother ; it is unpleasant to record that his father claimed, and eventually got, almost the whole sum from him. But it did not much matter now, for everything seemed literally to turn into gold beneath those marvellous fingers, and bad luck proved nearly as profitable to him as good.

By the time he had reached seventeen, Paganini was a confirmed gambler. He had little left but his Stradivarius violin, and this he was on the point of selling to a certain prince, who had offered him £80, a large sum at the beginning of this century even for a Stradivarius. Times have changed, and in these latter days we think nothing of giving £300 for a genuine instrument of the first class. But the reckless youth determined to make a last stand for his violin. "Jewels, watch, rings, brooches," to use his own words, "I had disposed of all; my thirty francs were reduced to three. With this small remains of my capital I played, and won 160 francs! This amount saved my violin, and restored my affairs. From that time," he adds, "I abjured gaming, to which I had sacrificed a part of my youth, convinced that a gamester is an object of contempt to all well-regulated minds." The violin he narrowly missed losing was given him by Parsini the painter, who on one occasion brought him a concerto of extraordinary difficulty to read at sight, and, placing a fine Stradivarius in his hands, said, "This instrument shall be yours if you can play that concerto at first sight in a masterly manner." "If that is the case," replied Paganini, "you may bid adieu to it;" and, playing it off at once, he retained the violin. Easy come—easy go. Some years later at Leghorn, being again in great straits, he was obliged to part, for a time at least, with this same Stradivarius; but this disaster was only the means of procuring him the favorite Guarnerius, upon which he ever afterward played. In his need, Monsieur Livron, a distinguished amateur, lent him this splendid instrument, and was so enraptured by his playing that he exclaimed, "Never will I profane the strings that your fingers have touched. It is to you that my violin belongs." This violin is still shown at Genoa under a glass case.

At the age of seventeen Paganini appears to have been entirely his own master—weak in health, nervous, irritable, and excitable; his wild and irregular habits and pursuits were, at this critical age, threatening to hurry him to an early grave, when an event occurred which, although but too characteristic of the looseness of Italian manners, probably saved his life.

Suddenly, in the midst of new discoveries and unexampled successes, Paganini ceased to play the violin. He retired into the depths of the country, and devoted himself for three years to agricultural pursuits, and to the society of a lady of rank who had carried him off to her Tuscan estate, and to the guitar. With the sole exception of the late Regondi, no such genius had ever been concentrated upon this limited and effeminate instrument. But the lady's taste ran that way, and the great violinist lavished for a time the whole force of his originality and skill upon the light guitar. He wrote music for it, and imitated it on the violin, but seldom touched it in after life until quite the close, although, as we shall presently see, he was able to produce a prodigious effect upon it when he chose. These years of country life and leisure, during which he was delivered from the pressure of crowds, the excitement of public performances, and, most of all, the grinding anxieties of life, had the effect of bracing him up in health, and prepared him for that reaction toward intense study and exhausting toil which left him without a rival—the first violinist in the world.

In 1804 he returned to Genoa, where he seems, among other things, to have given lessons to a young girl of fifteen, named Catherine Calcagno, who appears to have caught something of his style, and to have astonished Italy for a few years; but after 1816 we hear no more of her. And now the neglected violin was taken up once again, but this time with maturer powers and settled intentions. There is a strange thoroughness about Paganini—nothing which any previous musician knew or had done must be unknown or left undone by him; there was to be no hitting him between the joints of his armor; no loop-hole of imperfection anywhere. He now occupied himself solely with the study of his instrument, and with composition—wrote four grand quartets for violin, viol, guitar, and violoncello; and bravura variations with guitar accompaniment. At the age of twenty-one (1805) he made a second professional tour, passing through Lucca and Piombino, and in one convent church, where he played a concerto, the excitement was so great that the monks had to leave their seats to silence the uproar in the congregation. It was at the end of this tour that Napoleon's sister, the Princess Eliza, offered the new violinist the direction of the court music, and gave him the grade of captain in the Royal Guard, with the privilege of wearing that officer's brilliant uniform on state occasions.

Between 1805 and 1812, while in the service of the Princess Eliza, afterward Grand Duchess of Tuscany, Paganini probably reached his acme of power, if not of fame. He had for years been at work upon new effects and combinations, but, at the very time when each new exploit was being greeted with frantic applause, he betook himself to an exhaustive study of the old masters. Something he seemed to be groping after —some clue he wished to find. How often had he thrown over Viotti, Pugnani, Kreutzer; how often had he returned to their works! All were found utterly inadequate to suggest to him a single fresh thought, and it was nothing short of a new world that he was bound to discover.

In studying the ninth work of Locatelli, entitled "L'Arte de Nuova Modulazione," his brain was set suddenly to going in the peculiar direction of his new aspirations. Every original genius seeks some such clue or point of departure. Something in Locatelli's method inflamed Paganini with those conceptions of simultaneous notes struck in different parts of the instrument;

the hitherto unknown management of the screws, in which the violin was tuned all sorts of ways to reach effects never heard before or since ; the harmonic flying out at all points ; the arpeggios and pizzicatos, of which more anon—these, which were in after years brought to such perfection, were born out of infinite study and practice, under the stimulating influence of the Grand Duchess and her court.

It is at this season of his life that Paganini appears most like other people, the idol of the court, untouched as yet by any definite malady, occupying an official post, and systematically laboring to perfect a talent which already seemed too prodigious to belong to any one man. All conditions seemed most favorable to his peace and pleasure, could they have only lasted ; but this was not possible. They continued until he had achieved the last step in the ladder of consummate skill, and no longer. Probably all his executive peculiarities were developed at this time. It was at Florence, for instance (and not in a prison), that Paganini first played upon only two—the first and fourth—strings, and then upon one—the fourth—string. Being in love with a lady of the court, who reciprocated his attachment, he gave out that he would depict upon his violin a *Scène Amoureuse ;* the treble string, we presume, was the lady, and the fourth string the gentleman. The emotional dialogue was carried on between the two in a manner which fairly overcame the audience with delight, and led to the Grand Duchess requesting him to try one string alone next time. How he succeeded in that exploit is known to all the world, for he ever afterward retained an extreme partiality for the fourth string.

In 1808 he obtained from the Grand Duchess leave to travel. His fame had preceded him. Leghorn, where seven years before he had forfeited his famous Stradivarius and won a Guarnerius, received him with open arms, although his appearance was marked by an amusing *contretemps*. He came on to the stage limping, having run a nail into his heel. At all times odd-looking, he, no doubt, looked all the more peculiar under these circumstances, and there was some tittering among the audience. Just as he began, the candles fell out of his desk—more laughter. He went on playing; the first string broke—more laughter. He played the rest of the concerto through on three strings, but the laughter now changed to vociferous applause at this feat. The beggarly elements seemed of little consequence to this magician. One or more strings, it was all the same to him; indeed, it is recorded that he seldom paused to mend his strings when they broke, which they not unfrequently did. Whether from abstraction or carelessness he would allow them at times to grow quite ragged on the finger-board, and his constant practice of plucking them, guitar-like, with the left hand, as well as harp-like with the forefinger of the right hand, helped, no doubt, to wear them out rapidly.

At Ferrara both he and his violin met with a different reception. A singer had failed him, and he had induced a *danseuse* who had a pretty voice to come to the rescue. Some graceless fellow in the audience hissed her singing, which caused Paganini to take a revenge little suited to the occasion. In his last solo he imitated the cries of various animals, and suddenly advancing to the foot-lights, caused his violin to bray like an ass, with the exclamation, "This is for him who hissed!" Instead of laughter, the pit rose in fury, and would have soon made short work of him and his violin, had he not escaped by a back door. It appears that the country folk round Ferrara called the town's people, whom they hated, "asses," and were in the habit of singing out "hee-haw!" whenever they had to allude to them; hence the angry reception of Paganini's musical repartee.

We get but fugitive glances of the great artist during this professional tour, but it is too true that at Turin he was attacked with that bowel complaint which ever afterward haunted him like an evil demon, causing him the most frightful and protracted suffering, and interrupting his career sometimes for months together. His distrust of doctors and love of quack medicines no doubt made matters worse, and from this time his strange appearance grew stranger, his pallor more livid, his gauntness and thinness more spectral and grotesque, while greatly, no doubt, in consequence of suffering, his face assumed that look of eagle sharpness, sometimes varied by a sardonic grin, or a look of almost demoniacal fury, which artists have caricatured and sculptors have tried to tone down. Indeed, he must have been altogether an exceptional being to behold in the flesh. People who knew him say that the figure which used still to be exhibited at Madame Tussaud's, some twenty-five years ago, was a remarkable likeness. He looked an indifferently dressed skeleton, with a long parchment face, deep dark eyes, full of flame, long lank hair, straggling down over his shoulders. His walk was shambling and awkward, the bones seem to have been badly strung together, he appeared as if he had been fixed up hastily on wires and the wires had got loose. As he stood, he settled himself on one hip, at a gaunt angle, and before he began, the whole business looked so unpromising, that men wondered how he could hold his violin at all, much less play it!

It must have been at his first visit to Florence, before

his appearance was familiar, as it afterward became, to the inhabitants of that city, that we get one of those side-views of the man which are more precious than many dates and drier details.

Slowly recovering from illness, Paganini repaired to Florence, probably in May of the year 1809. He must have then lived in almost complete solitude, as he does not appear to have been recognized there before the month of October, when he was officially recalled to his duties by the late Princess, now Grand Duchess, at the Court of Florence.

Those who have wandered in spring-time about the environs of Florence, know the indefinite charm there is in the still and fertile country, without the walls of the city. Outside the gate of the Pitti, on the summit of a steep hill, stands Fiesole, bathed in clear air and warm sunshine. How many an invalid has walked up that winding and rugged path, gathering, here and there, a sweet wild-flower, resting from time to time to drink in the delicious air, until pure health seemed borne back to the feeble frame upon the soft and fragrant breeze.

Alone, on a bright morning, a tall, ungainly figure goes slowly up the hill toward Fiesole. He pauses at times, he looks round abstractedly. He is talking to himself out loud, unconscious of any one near him—he gesticulates wildly—then breaks out into a loud laugh; but stops suddenly, as he sees coming down the hill a young girl, carrying one of those large baskets full of flowers so commonly seen in the streets of Florence. She is beautiful with the beauty of the Florentine girls; the brown flesh-tints mellowed with reflected light from the white road strewn thick with marble-dust; under the wide straw hat the free curls flow dark and thick, clustering about her temples, and lowering the forehead.

Suddenly the large black eyes, so common among the Italian peasants, seem transfixed with something between wonder and fear, as they fall upon the uncouth figure approaching her. In another moment, conscious of the stranger's intense gaze, she stands motionless, like a bird charmed by a serpent; then she trembles involuntarily from head to foot. A strange smile steals over the pale and haggard face of Paganini—was he, then, conscious of exercising any mesmeric power? At times he seemed so full of some such influence that individuals, as well as crowds, were irresistibly drawn and fascinated by his look.

But the strange smile seemed to unloose the spell, the startled girl passed on, and the solitary artist resumed his walk toward Fiesole.

Heavy clouds riven with spaces of light were driving before the wind. Over the bridge Delle Grazie, up the hill once more without the gates of Florence, we pass toward a ruined castle. A storm seems imminent, the wind whistles and howls round the deserted promontory, the bare ruin that has braved the storms of centuries stands up dark against the sky, and seems to exult in the fury of the elements, so much in harmony with its own wild and desolate look. But what are those low wailings? Is it the wind, or some human being in anguish? The traveller rushes forward—in a cavity of the deep ruin, among the tumbled stones, overgrown with moss and turf, lies a strange figure—a lonely, haggard man. He listens to the wind, and moans in answer, as though in pain. Is he the magician who has conjured up the tempest, and is the scene before us all unreal? or has the tempest entered into his soul, and filled him with its own sad voice? Indeed, as he lies there, his pale, almost livid face distorted, his wet hair streaming wildly about his shoulders, his uncouth form writhing with each new burst of the hurricane—he looks the very impersonation of the storm itself. But, on being observed, his look becomes fixed—the stranger insensibly recoils, and feels awkwardly the sense of intrusion. If the strange man is in pain he wants no help; thus rashly exposed to the weather, hardly recovered from his grievous malady, he may well be actually suffering; but most likely he is merely possessed for the time by certain emotions impressed upon his sensitive and electric organization by the tempest from without. He is drinking in the elemental forces which, by and by, he will give out with a power itself almost as elemental.

Some of us may have walked in the soft moonlight under the long avenue (Cascine) that runs by the brink of the rushing Arno straight out of Florence. We can remember how the birds love those trees, and the broken underwood beneath them. When the city sleeps, the heart of those woods is alive; even the daylight birds are sometimes aroused by the nightingales, as they answer each other in notes of sweetness long drawn out, and tender raptures that seem to swoon and faint into the still more tender silences of the summer night. But suddenly the birds' song is checked—other strains of incomparable sweetness arise in the wood. The birds are silent, they pause and listen; the notes are like theirs, but more exquisite—they are woven by a higher art into phrases of inspiration beyond even the nightingale's gift. The strange whistler ceases, and the birds resume, timidly, their song; again the unearthly music breaks forth, and mingles with theirs. As we push apart the bushes, we discover the same weird figure that but lately lay moaning in the storm among the ruins upon yonder hill.

The person to whom we owe, substantially, the above glimpses, met this extraordinary man again in the streets of Florence a few days later. A merry party of young people, laughing and shouting, pass by toward the Uffizi. We listen to their ringing voices, occupied with themselves, and, youth-like, caring for nothing at the time but their own gayety, when suddenly the voices fall, the twanging of the guitar ceases; a curious murmur runs through the merry throng, and not a pleasant murmur; a tall, pale man, with eyes on fire, and strange, imperious look, has pushed brusquely in among them.

He seizes the guitar, and, sweeping its strings with passion, causes it to wail like a zither, then peal out like the strains of a military band, and finally settle into the rich chords and settled cadences of a strong harp. All resistance and murmuring cease as the astonished party follow him, spell-bound. His cravat flies loose, his coat-tails wave madly to and fro, he gesticulates like a maniac, and the irresistible music streams forth louder, wilder, more magical than ever, he strides, leaps, dances forward with the guitar, which is no longer a guitar, but the very soul of Nicolo Paganini. A few days later still the mystery was cleared up. Paganini had been officially called to Florence by the Grand Duchess to superintend the court concerts, and the whole of the town was soon ringing with his name.

About the age of thirty, at which time, as we shall presently narrate, Paganini became free never again to be bound by any official appointment, the great violinist had exhausted all the possible resources of his instrument. From this time Paganini, incredible as it may appear, seldom, if ever, played, except at concerts and rehearsals, and not always even at rehearsals. If he ever practised, he always used a mute. Mr. Harris, who for twelve months acted as his secretary, and seldom left him, *never* saw him take his violin from its case. At the hotels where he stopped the sound of his instrument was never heard. He used to say that he had worked enough, and had earned his right to repose; yet, without an effort, he continued to overcome the superhuman difficulties which he himself had created with the same unerring facility, and ever watched by the eager and envious eyes of critics and rivals. In vain! No false intonation, no note out of tune, no failure was ever perceptible. The *Times* critic, reviewing him in London some years before his death, says his octaves were so true that they sounded like one note, and the most enormous intervals with triple notes, harmonics and guitar effects, seem to have been invariably taken with the same precision. In the words of a critical judge, M. Fétis, "his hand was a geometrical compass, which divided the finger-board with mathematical precision." There is an amusing story told of an Englishman, who followed him from place to place, to hear him play in private, in the hope of discovering his "secret." At last, after many vain attempts, he managed to be lodged in the next room to the great artist. Looking through the key-hole, he beheld him seated on a sofa, about to take his violin from its case—at last! He raises it to his chin—but the bow?—is left in the case. The left hand merely measures with its enormous wiry fingers a few mechanical intervals, and the instrument is replaced in silence; not even then was a note to be heard!

Yet every detail of rehearsal was an anxiety to him. Although he gave a prodigious number of concerts, he was always unusually restless and abstracted on the morning of the day on which he had to perform. He would be idle for hours on his sofa—or, at least, he seemed to be idle—perhaps the works were then being wound up before going to rehearsal. He would then, before starting, take up his violin, examine it carefully, especially the screws, and, having satisfied himself, replace it in its shabby-worn case without striking a note. Lastly, he would sort and arrange the orchestral parts of his solos, and go off to rehearsal. He was very unpunctual, and on one occasion kept the whole band waiting for an hour, and was at last found sheltering from the rain under a colonnade, rather than take a cab. This was in London. At the rehearsal there was always the most intense eagerness on the part of the band to hear him play, and when he came to one of his prodigious cadenzas, the musicians would rise in their seats, and lean forward to watch every movement, and follow every sound. Paganini would then just play a few commonplace notes, stop suddenly, and, turning round to the band, wave his bow, with a malicious smile, and say, "Et cætera, Messieurs!" If anything went wrong he got into a paroxysm of fury; but when things went well he freely showed his satisfaction, and often exclaimed, "Bravissimo sieti tuti virtuosi!"

He could be very courteous in manner, and was not personally unpopular with his fellow-musicians, who stood greatly in awe of him. No one ever saw the principal parts of his solos, as he played by heart, for fear of the music being copied. The rehearsal over, he carried even the orchestral parts away with him. He would then go straight home, take a light meal, throw himself on his bed, and sleep profoundly until his carriage arrived to take him to the concert. His toilet was very simple, and took hardly any time; his coat was buttoned tightly over his chest, and marked the more conspicuously the impossible angles of his figure; his trousers hung loose for trousers of the period; his cravat was tight about his neck. He sweated so profusely over his solos that he always carried a clean shirt in his violin trunk, and changed his linen once at least during the concert. At concert time he usually seemed in excellent spirits. His first question on arriving was always, "Is there a large audience?" If the room was full he would say, "Excellent people! good, good!" If by any chance the boxes were empty he would say, "Some of the effects will be lost." He kept his audience waiting a long time, and he would sometimes say, "I have played better," or "I have played worse," and occasionally his first solo would be more effective than his last. After once or twice trying the music of Kreutzer and Rode in public, he decided never to play any but his own, and said to his secretary, Mr. Harris, "I have my own peculiar style; in accordance with this I regulate my compositions. I had much rather write a piece in which I can trust myself entirely to my own musical impressions." "His art," observes M. Fétis, "was an art born with him, the secret of which he has carried to the grave."

Some have pretended that, as Paganini never cared to play except in public, his art was nothing to him but a means of making money. It would be, perhaps, nearer the truth to say that his art was so entirely himself, that he did not require, except at seasons, and chiefly for others, to give it outward expression. He needed no more to play than Beethoven needed to hear. Happier than Beethoven, he was not deprived of the power of realizing outwardly the art in which he inwardly lived; but probably the creations of his spirit infinitely outstripped the utmost limits even of *his* executive powers, until in his eyes they seemed, after all, the faint and inadequate symbols of his wild and inspired dreams.

There are times when the deepest feeling is the most silent—music may come to the aid of words; but there is a point at which music itself is a mere beggarly element. What made Paganini so exceptionally great was the portentous development, the strength and independence, of the emotional fountain within. The whole of life was to him nothing but so many successions of psychological heat and cold. Incidents immediately became clothed with a psychic atmosphere—perhaps the life of emotion was never so completely realized in itself, and for itself, as in the soul-isolation of Paganini. That life, as far as it could be individually expressed, was uttered forth by his violin. On his concert bills he used to put,

Paganini fara sentire il suo violino.

What the tempest had told him his violin would proclaim; what the summer night had whispered was stereotyped in his soul, and the midnight song of birds came forth from the Cremona depths at his bidding. Nor was there any phase of passion unknown to him, save, alas! the phase of a pure and lasting love. His wild soul had early consumed itself with unbridled excesses, and although in his maturer years he grew more sober in such matters, it was not before he had fathomed the perilous depths of more than one *grande passion*, and made himself master of all its subtle expressions.

When, then, we are told that he seldom played, we must remember that his inmost life was itself one vast cosmos of imaginary concord and discord—he *was* music, although only at times "the tides of music's golden sea" would burst forth with incomparable splendor, and gather a kind of concrete existence in sound; yet to him his own inspirations were as real—perhaps more real—without it. For music exists apart from physical vibrations, nor can such vibrations, however subtle and varied, express it wholly as it lives in the creative heart. The ear of the soul hears what no ear of sense can hear, and a music fairer than anything on earth is often sounding in the spirit of the true musical seer. Nay, does he not feel, like Beethoven, the bitter descent when he formulates his thoughts upon paper, strikes the keys, or sets in vibration the strings which after all are but feeble apologies for the ideal beauty, the intense, the subtle, or exalted harmonies of the inner life?

Shall we now assist at one of Paganini's performances? How many descriptions have been written, and how inadequate! It is hardly possible to do more than describe a few salient peculiarities. But even our pale sketch would be incomplete without such an attempt.

Enter Paganini—a shudder of curiosity and excitement runs through the crowded theatre, the men applaud, the women concentrate a double-barrel fire of opera-glasses upon the tall, ungainly figure that shuffles forward from the side scenes to the foot-lights, with such an air of haughtiness, and yet so many mechanical bows. As the applause rises again and again, the apparition stands still, looks round, takes in at a glance the vast assembly. Then, seizing his violin, he hugs it tightly between his chin and chest, and stands for a few seconds gazing at it in motionless abstraction. The audience is now completely hushed, and all eyes are riveted upon one silent and almost grotesque form. Suddenly Paganini raises his bow and dashes it down like a sledge-hammer upon the strings. The opening of the concerto abounds in solo passages, in which he has to be left almost without accompaniment; the orchestra is reserved for the *tuttis* and slight interludes. Paganini now revels in his distinctive and astonishing passages, which hold the audience breathless. At one time torrents of chords peal forth, as from some mimic orchestra ; harmonic passages are thrown off with the sharpness and sonority of the flute accompanied by the guitar, independent phrases being managed by the left hand plucking the strings, while the right is playing legato passages with the bow. The most difficult intervals are spanned with ease—the immense, compass-like fingers glide up and down every part of the key-board, and seem to be in ever so many places at once. Heavy chords are struck indifferently with the point or heel of the bow, as if each inch of the magic wand were equally under control ; but just when these prodigious feats of skill are causing the senses to reel with something like a painful strain, a low, measured melody steals forth and penetrates the souls of all present, until some of the audience break out into uncontrollable applause, while others are melted to tears, overpowered by the thrilling accents. Then, attenuated as it were to a thread—but still distinctly audible and resonant—the divine sound would die away ; and suddenly a grotesque flash of humor would dart up from a lower sphere and shift the emotional atmosphere, as the great maestro too soon dashes, with the impetuosity of a whirlwind, into the final " rondo " or " moto perpetuo."

Paganini was not inexorable about encores—he was always gratified by applause. After the concert the people often waited outside to accompany him to his hotel. He seemed delighted with this kind of homage, and would go out at such seasons and mix freely with them ; but he was often quite inaccessible, and bent upon absolute seclusion.

Let us now resume the chronological narrative. Toward the end of 1812, Paganini quarrelled with his royal patroness, the Grand Duchess of Tuscany. She had given him leave, as above mentioned, to wear at court the uniform of captain of the body-guard, and one night he appeared in the orchestra attired in this splendid costume. The Duchess seems to have thought this inappropriate, and sent word desiring him to change his uniform for an ordinary dress. The offended artist declined point-blank, and that evening threw up his appointment and left the Florentine Court and all its works forever. It is not at all improbable that Paganini, who could now command any sum of money, had grown tired of official duties, which could no longer shed any new lustre upon him, and that, longing to be free, he gladly availed himself of the first ready pretext for flight. In vain his royal mistress sent after him, imploring him to return. Paganini was inexorable, and it was even whispered that the Duchess's entreaties were prompted by a feeling still more tender than the love of music—a feeling which Paganini had ceased to reciprocate.

Paganini was very fond of Milan, and he stayed there during the greater part of 1813. He visited that city three times in five years, staying often for several months, and giving in all thirty-seven concerts, most of them at the Scala.

It was in 1814 that he first made the acquaintance of Rossini at Bologna. The great composer, like every other connoisseur, regarded him with admiration and astonishment, and a friendship was then begun which was strengthened when the two celebrities met in 1817 at Rome, and in 1831 at Paris.

Paganini treated his fellow-musicians and rivals with simple and unaffected courtesy. He expressed his great admiration of Spohr's violin-playing, and he went all the way from Genoa to Milan to hear Lafont. When they met, Lafont proposed that they should give a concert, in which each should play a solo. "I excused myself," says Paganini, "by saying that such experiments are always impolitic, as the public invariably looked upon them as duels. Lafont, not seeing it in this light, I was compelled to accept the challenge." Commenting upon the results, he added with singular candor and modesty: "Lafont probably surpassed me in tone, but the applause which followed my efforts convinced me that I did not suffer by comparison." Although usually anxious, more for the sake of others than for himself, to avoid such contests, he never declined them; and a similar trial of skill took place between him and the Polish violinist, Laprinski, in 1818, at Plaisance, the two artists remaining excellent friends.

At this time Paganini's health seems to have been in an unusually critical condition. We have noticed that he seldom consulted doctors, and when he did so he was not in the habit of following their advice; but his credulity was worse than his scepticism. He dosed himself immoderately with some stuff called "Leroy;" he believed that this could cure anything. It usually produced a powerful agitation in his nervous system, and generally ended in upsetting the intestinal functions. Sometimes it seems to have deprived him of the power of speech.

In 1816 he went to Venice, where he seems fairly to have collapsed after giving a few concerts. However, in the following year (1817) he was much better, and went to Genoa to see his mother, taking Milan *en route*. He has been called avaricious, suspicious of his kind, and devoid of all natural affection. He, no doubt, loved money, and had a general distrust of his friends, but it is certain that he was attached to his mother, and took care to supply her with every comfort. She writes to him some years later:

> I am delighted to find that after your travels to Paris and London, you purpose visiting Genoa expressly to embrace me. My dream has been fulfilled, and that which God promised me has been accomplished—your name is great, and Art, with the help of God, has placed you in a position of independence. We are all well. In the name of all your relations I thank you for the sums of money you have sent. Omit nothing that will render your name immortal. Eschew the vices of great cities, remembering that you have a mother who loves you affectionately. She will never cease her supplications to the All-powerful for your preservation. Embrace your amiable companion for me, and kiss little Achille. Love me as I love you. Your ever affectionate mother,
> THERESA PAGANINI.

The "amiable companion" seems to have been a cantatrice, Antonia Blanchi di Como, with whom he appears to have lived at one time, and who bore him his only son, "the little Achille."

In the same year, 1817, he arrived in Rome in time for the Carnival, where he excited the greatest enthusiasm. He was frequently to be found at the palace of Count de Kaunitz, the Austrian Ambassador, where he met all the great people in Rome, and among them M. de Metternich, who did his utmost to persuade him to visit Vienna. From this time Paganini determined, sooner or later, to visit the principal cities in Germany and France, but the state of his health was still very precarious. In 1818–19 he gave concerts at Verona, Plaisance, Turin, and Florence, after which he visited Naples for the first time. His advent had been long looked for with feelings of jealous expectation and distrust. The chief professors and musicians of the place, who had never heard him, were not very favorably disposed. They, however, gave him a reception, on which occasion a piece of music was casually placed before him, full of the most ingenious difficulties that could be devised. Paganini was not unaccustomed to this kind of trap, and upon being requested to play it at sight, he merely glanced at it and played it off with the greatest ease.

But he had even worse foes than the professors. He seems to have got into damp apartments close under St. Elmo, and his lungs, at no time very strong, now showed unmistakable signs of consumption. The landlord, fearing that he would die in his house, actually turned him and all he possessed out into the street, where his friend, Ciandelli, happening to come by at the very nick of time, administered a sound thrashing to the brutal host with a stick, and took the invalid artist to a more comfortable lodging. In 1820 he returned to his favorite city, Milan, where he founded a musical society, conducted several concerts, and received various crowns, medals, and decorations. In December of the same year he returned to Rome, and in the following year, 1821, paid a second visit to Naples, giving concerts at the Fondo and the Theatre Nuovo. At the end of the year he crossed over to Sicily, but the people of Palermo hardly appreciated him; and in 1822 he was again at Venice and Plaisance. From thence he would have gone straight to Germany, in accordance with the proposals of Metternich; but on his way to Pavia, in 1823, he was attacked by his old complaint, and for some time it did not seem likely that he would recover. He was advised to go to Genoa for rest, and while there he recovered sufficiently to give concerts at the Theatre St. Augustine, when the prophet in his own country for once attracted enthusiastic crowds. The Milanese, who had never expected to see him alive again, gave him an enthusiastic reception at the Scala, on the 12th of June,

1824. He seems to have been still unable to tear himself away from Italy, for in the same month he returned to Genoa, then passed to Venice, and in 1825 he was at Trieste. Then he proceeded, for the third time, to Naples, and going over to Palermo, for the second time, he now met with a most astonishing success. He remained in Sicily for a whole year, and seems in this delicious climate to have recovered his health sufficiently to undertake a long professional tour. He was then detained in Italy for nearly two years more, for in 1826 he visited again Trieste, Venice, and gave five concerts at Rome. In 1827 he was decorated by Pope Leo XII. with the Order of the Golden Spur. He then repaired to Florence, where a disease in one of his legs stopped his progress for several months. It was only in the spring of 1828 that he went on to Milan, where he at length gave his farewell concert, before starting on his long-projected visit to Vienna.

To dwell upon the reports of his first appearance at Vienna would be only to repeat what has already been said. "The first note that he played on his Guarnerius," writes M. Schilling in the *Lexique Universel de Musique*, "indeed, from his first step into the room, his reputation was decided in Germany. Acted upon, as by an electric spark, a brilliant halo of glory appeared to invest his whole person; he stood before us like a miraculous apparition in the domain of Art!" He gave concerts in the capital of Austria on the 13th, 16th, and 18th of April, 1828. The greatest players and musicians from all parts flocked to hear him. Mayseder, Jansa, Slawich, Strebinger, Böhm, united in extolling the new prodigy. In a very few days Vienna seemed to be turned upside down—no class of people was unmoved by the presence of this extraordinary man. The newspapers were full of verses and articles on Paganini. Cravats, coats, gloves, hats, shoes, and even cigar-cases and snuff-boxes—everything was now *à la Paganini*. The fashionable cooks called new dishes by his name; any great stroke at billiards was a *coup à la Paganini*.

He stayed several months at Vienna, but time did not injure his popularity; his talent bore the most critical inspection all round—he was at once colossal in the breadth and majesty of his effects, and microscopic in the perfection and subtlety of his details. At the acme of his fame he left Vienna, and commenced a tour through Austria, Bohemia, Saxony, Poland, Bavaria, Prussia, and the Rhenish Provinces. Prague was the only city which failed to appreciate him. There was a stupid rivalry, of which we find traces in the days of Mozart, between Vienna and Prague, and it was generally understood that whoever was applauded at Vienna was to be hissed at Prague, and *vice versâ*. But on reaching Berlin the great artist was received with such an ovation, that he is said to have exclaimed, on his first appearance, "Here is my Vienna public!"

From this time to the end of his life, the wildest stories began to be circulated about him, chiefly in the Italian and French newspapers; but the *Leipzig Gazette du Monde Elégant* cannot be held quite blameless, for it inserted one of the most extravagant of these tales. One man gravely affirmed that Paganini's miracles of skill were no longer to be wondered at, because he had seen the devil standing close behind him moving his arms for him. Another eye-witness wrote that he had for some time observed a beautiful woman at Paganini's concerts; he went to the theatre in the hope of again seeing her on the occasion of Paganini's last performance. The master appeared, played divinely; the house was crammed, but where was the lady? Presently—in one of the soft pauses—a deep sigh was heard; it proceeded from the beautiful lady; tears were streaming down her cheeks. A mysterious person was seated by her side, with whom Paganini exchanged a ghastly smile; the lady and her cavalier soon rose; the strange cavalier grasped her hand—she grew deadly pale. They proceeded out of the theatre. In a narrow by-path stood a carriage with coal-black steeds—the horses' eyes seemed on fire; the two entered, the carriage vanished—where, apparently, there was no road at all. The inference of all which is that Paganini was in league with the devil! It is strange but true that these absurd legends gained some credence among the ignorant populace of Italy and France, though they were probably laughed at in Germany.

But other stories of a different kind annoyed him far more. He was a ruffian who had murdered one mistress, and decamped with another man's wife; he was an escaped convict; he was a political busybody. He was a spy, a thief, an immoral swindler; he had been in prison, it was said, for years, and had thus learned his skill upon one string, all the others having been broken. It is necessary, even at this time of day, to give a distinct denial to this last legend. Paganini's morals were not above, but they were not below, the average of the somewhat dissolute state of society in which it was his misfortune to have been born and bred. He never committed a murder, or fought a duel, or betrayed a friend, or left without provision those whom he had given just claims upon him. As to politics, he knew nothing and cared nothing for them; and he never read the newspapers except when they contained something about himself. In Paris they pasted up a coarse wood-cut of

Paganini chained in a dungeon about the walls and hoardings of the city. Paganini describes himself as having stood before it in mute astonishment, until a crowd gathered round him, and, recognizing the likeness, mobbed and hustled him in the most inconvenient manner. It was these reports that he afterward bitterly complained of, and M. Fétis, at his request, drew up a letter, which was afterward published throughout Europe, in which the aggrieved violinist vindicates his character from the current calumnies. His protestations, however, were far from stilling the rumors, and, when he arrived in London, some years later, there was no absurd and extravagant tale about him that was not eagerly caught up and circulated throughout the length and breadth of the land. A lesser man might have courted this sort of notoriety, but Paganini, who could do without it, was intensely annoyed and wounded. We cannot follow the great violinist in detail through his German campaign, in the years 1828-29-30, but some notion of his way of life may draw his personality a little closer to the reader ere we prepare to greet him on our own shores.

Ill health, at times acute suffering, which turned his pale bony face to a green, livid hue, an intensely susceptible nervous system, an outward life alternating between scenes of highly-wrought excitement, amazing exertion, and fitful repose—these causes combined to produce a character singular for its mingled abstraction and plasticity. At times he seemed in the body, at other times out of the body; sometimes he appeared to be only semi-conscious of life, at other times more intensely conscious than any dozen people put together. Physical causes acted at times oddly and instantly upon his brain; at others they found him like stone. He was not always open to impressions, which at certain moments would find him so receptive that he became the utter incarnation of them. He was full of contradictions, which he cared little to explain either to himself or to others. He travelled with the utmost speed from place to place; in the hottest weather he would have all the carriage windows closed. Although latterly his lungs affected his voice, which became thin and feeble, he delighted to talk loudly when rattling over the roads; the noise of the wheels seemed to excite him, and set his brain going. He never entered an inn on the road, but would sit in his carriage until the horses were ready, or walk up and down wrapped in his great cloak, and resent being spoken to. Arrived at his hotel, he would throw all his doors and windows open, and take what he called an air bath; but he never ceased to abuse the climate of Germany, and said that Italy was the only place fit to live in. His luggage was extremely simple—a small napkin might have contained the whole of his wardrobe; a coat, a little linen and a hat-box, a small carpet-bag, a shabby trunk, containing his Guarnerius violin, his jewels, a clean shirt, and his money—that was all. He carried papers of immense value in a red pocket-book, along with concert tickets, letters, and accounts. These last no one but himself could read, as he knew hardly any arithmetic, and calculated, but with great accuracy, on some method of his own. He cared little where he slept, and seldom noticed what he ate or drank. He never complained of the inns—every place seemed much alike to him—out of Italy; he detested them all equally. He seldom noticed scenery, or paid attention to the sights of foreign towns. To himself he was the only important fact everywhere. He often started without food in the early morning, and remained fasting all day. At night he would take a light supper, and some chamomile tea, and sleep soundly until morning. At times he ate ravenously. He remained taciturn for days, and then he would have all his meals sent up to his room; but at some hotels he would dine at the table d'hôte, and join freely in conversation. He lay on his sofa doing nothing the greater part of every day; but when making plans for the publication of his works or the founding of a musical institution, which at one time occupied much of his thoughts, he would stride up and down his room, and talk in a rapid and animated manner. After dinner he habitually sat in his room in total darkness until half-past ten, when he went to bed. Sometimes from sixty to eighty people, eager to see him, would wait upon him at his hotel in the course of the day. When compelled to see visitors, he was polite; but the intrusion of strangers fatigued and annoyed him, and he often refused himself to every one. He would bolt his door, and not take the least notice of any knocks.

He would sit for hours almost motionless in a kind of trance, and apparently absorbed in deep thought; but he was not always averse to society. He was fond of conversing with a few friends, and entered into whatever games and recreations were going on with much zest; but if any one mentioned music, he would relapse into a sullen silence, or go off to some other part of the room. He disliked dining out; but when he accepted he usually ate largely of everything on the table, after which he was generally attacked by his old bowel complaint. At the time, however, he would eat and drink largely without any inconvenience. Although he mixed freely with the world, like Chopin, he was a solitary man, and reserved to the last degree. No one seemed to be in his confidence. He had an excellent memory—yet certain faces seemed to pass from him absolutely. His fidelity to both his parents was not the least remarkable point in his strange character, and although ardently attached to money, he could be generous at the call of what he considered duty, and even lavish when charity was concerned—indeed, he frequently gave concerts for the benefit of the poor, remembering the time when he had been a poor man himself.

Paris, always eager for novelty, the self-elected critic of the civilized world in all matters appertaining to art, was by this time imperative in her demand to see and hear Paganini; so, early in the spring of 1831, he set out for that fashionable capital. Fame had preceded him with every kind of strange rumor—he could not only play on one string, it was said, but his fiddle still gave forth strange music when all the strings were removed. The old calumnies revived. The town was placarded with villainous wood-cuts of him in prison. Others represented him in caricature, playing on one string. In short, expectation was wound up to its highest pitch, when he suddenly arrived, in bad health, and immediately gave a performance at the Opera-House, on March 9th, 1831. The calm and judicious veteran of the Royal Conservatory of Music in Belgium, M. Fétis, who knew him well, and heard him often, and to whose work I am so much indebted for the present sketch, can find no other words to express the sensation which he created on his first appearance at Paris than "universal frenzy." The whole city flocked to hear him, the professors and virtuosi crowded round him on the platform, as near as they dared approach, in order to watch him play, after which they were no wiser than before. At the end of each piece the whole audience, it is said, rose *en masse* to recall him; the tongue of envy forgot to wag, and rivalry was put out of court. It was hoped that he might have thrown some light upon certain prodigious violin studies which he had published, and which had long been known at Paris. No one could play them, or even conjecture how some of them were to be played; nor did Paganini reveal the secret, which lay, no doubt, partly in a peculiar way of tuning the instrument, as well as in a length and agility of finger which he alone possessed.

About the middle of May he left Paris for London, and the *Times* newspaper, which, at that time, hardly ever noticed concerts, devoted half a column in a vain attempt to give some idea of his first performance at the King's Theatre. Paganini, to save himself trouble, had agreed, for an enormous sum of money, to let himself to a speculator during his stay in England, who made all arrangements for him and took the proceeds. This plan has since been adopted by several illustrious artists, M. Joachim among them; and, although it has been stigmatized as wanting in dignity, it is probably, on the whole, the most satisfactory to the artist, though not always to the public. An attempt was made to double the prices at the Opera-House, which raised great indignation; the prices ultimately charged were the usual Opera charges—no more and no less—and this was doubtless thought exorbitant for a concert, although the solo performer was supported by an orchestra and some of the best Opera singers, the famous Lablache among them. The crowd at the doors on the first night was excessive, and the pit was full to overflowing, but the boxes were thin. Paganini was suffering at that time from the inroads of his old complaint, aggravated by the rapid encroachments of his last fatal malady, consumption. He appeared contrary to the advice of his physicians, and was received with the usual tumult of applause. From a heap of contemporary criticism struggling vainly with the difficulty of the subject, we extract a few passages from the pen of an eye-witness, which strikes us as unusually graphic.

Mr. Gardner, of Leicester, writes : " At the hazard of my ribs, I placed myself at the Opera two hours and a half before the concert began. . . . . . The concert opened with Beethoven's second symphony, admirably played by the Philharmonic band, after which Lablache sang 'Largo al Factotum,' with much applause, and was encored. A breathless silence, and every eye was watching the action of this extraordinary violinist ; and as he glided from the side scenes to the front of the stage, an involuntary cheering burst from every part of the house, many rising from their seats to view the Spectre during the thunder of this unprecedented cheering—his gaunt and extraordinary appearance being more like that of a devotee about to suffer martyrdom than one to delight you with his art. With the tip of his bow he sent off the orchestra in a grand military movement with a force and vivacity as surprising as it was new. At the termination of this introduction he commenced with a soft streaming note of celestial quality, and with three or four whips of his bow elicited points of sound that mounted to the third heaven and as bright as the stars. . . . . . He has long legs and arms, and his hands in his playing often assume the attitude of prayer, with the fingers pointed upward. It was curious to watch the faces of Lindley, Dragonetti, and the other great players, who took up places on the platform to command a good view of him during his performance ; they all seem to have agreed that the like had never been heard before, and that in addition to his marvellous eccentricities and novel effects, he had transcended the highest level of legitimate art that had ever been reached."

It has often been asked in what respects Paganini's playing differed from that of other great violinists—in what has he enriched the art—what has he discovered or invented? These questions have been to some extent answered by the painstaking Professor of Music, Guhr, who had many opportunities of watching him closely.

He was peculiar, first, in his manner of tuning. Sometimes the first three strings were tuned half a note higher, the G string being a third lower. Sometimes he tuned his G to B; with a single turn of his peg he would change the pitch of his G string, and never fail in his intonation. These artifices explain, no doubt, many of his extraordinary intervals.

Secondly, in his management of the bow he has had many imitators, though none have approached him in the romantic variety and "fiend-like power with which he ruled over the strings." His ordinary *staccato*, played with a very tight bow, was prodigiously loud and firm, like the strokes of a hammer, while his method of dashing the bow on the strings, and letting it leap through an infinity of tiny staccato notes with unerring precision was wholly his own invention.

Thirdly, his *tremolo* use of the left hand exceeded anything which had been attempted up to that time. This effect has been, like every other one of his inimitable effects, driven to death by subsequent violinists.

Fourth, his use of harmonics, now universally known to violinists, was then absolutely new. Formerly only the open harmonics had been used, and that very charily; but Paganini astonished the world by stopping the string with the first finger, and extracting the harmonic simultaneously with the fourth. By sliding up the first finger together with the fourth, he played entire melodies in harmonics, and got, on an average, about three octaves out of each string; his use of double harmonics in rapid passages, and such trifles as four simultaneous A flats, are still problems which few if any hands but his have been able to solve.

Lastly, his habit of plucking the strings, sometimes with the right, sometimes with the left hand, and producing those rapid *pizzicato* runs, on an accompaniment of a harp or guitar, was absolutely new; beyond these things it was found impossible much farther to analyze his playing. His secret, if he had any, died with him; his music does not reveal it. Although he wrote quartets, solos, duets, and sonatas, fragments of about twenty-four of which are in existence, only nine were found complete; of these the Rondo known as "Clochette," and often played by M. Sivori, and "Le Streghe," are perhaps the best known. The celebrated variations on the "Carnival de Venise" do not appear to have been published as he played them, though both Ernst and Sivori claim to play the Paganini Carnival. M. Fétis considers his finest compositions have not been preserved—among those he reckons a magnificent concerto played at Paris in 1813, and a grand military sonata for the fourth string only.

The rest of Paganini's story is soon told. Broken in health, after an absence of six years, he returned to Italy, where he was now nearly worshipped by his countrymen. He had grown immensely rich, and bought various properties in Tuscany. He played at concerts from time to time, and was always most generous in giving his talents for the benefit of the poor.

Mr. Dubourg, in his valuable work on the violin, asserts that he went to America; but of this I can find no trace in the biography of M. Fétis, nor in any other documents which I have as yet come across. In 1835 Paganini lived much between Milan and Genoa. The Duchess of Parma had conferred the Order of St. George on him in 1834.

In 1836 he got into bad hands. He lent his great name to the establishment of a Casino in Paris, which failed. He was obliged to go to Paris, and the journey, no doubt, hastened his end. His consumption grew worse; he could not bear the cold; he was annoyed by the unscrupulous speculators, who tried to involve him in their own ruin, and then refused to bear the burden with him. They even succeeded in mulcting him in the sum of 50,000 francs, and he was actually detained by legal proceedings until he had paid the whole sum.

But his days of speculation and glory were alike numbered. In 1839 he was a dying man. He struggled with indomitable energy against his deadly foe. He now often took up the guitar, which, in the spring-time of his life, had been so intimately associated with his first romantic attachment. He was a great admirer of Beethoven, and not long before his death he played one of that master's quartets, his favorite one, with astonishing energy. In extreme weakness, he labored out to hear a requiem of Cherubini for male voices, and soon afterward, with all his last energies, he insisted upon being conveyed to one of the churches in Marseilles, where he took part in a solemn mass of Beethoven. His voice was now nearly extinct, and his sleep, the greatest of consolations, was broken up by dreadful fits of coughing; his features began to sink, and he appeared to be little more than a living skeleton, so excessive and fearful was his emaciation. Still he did not believe in the approach of death. Day by day he grew more restless, and talked of passing the winter at Nice; and he did live on till the spring.

On the night of May 27th, 1840, after a protracted paroxysm, he suddenly became strangely tranquil. He sank into a quiet sleep, and woke refreshed and calm. The air was soft and warm. He desired them to open the windows wide, draw the curtains of his bed, and allow the moon, just rising in the unclouded glory of an Italian sky, to flood his apartment. He sat gazing intently upon it for some minutes, and then again sank drowsily into a fitful sleep. Rousing himself once more, his fine ear caught the sound of the rustling leaves as they were gently stirred by some breath of air outside. In his dying moments this sound of the night wind in the trees seemed to affect him strangely, and the summer nights on the banks of the Arno long ago may have flashed back upon his mind, and called up fading memories. But now the Arno was exchanged for the wide Mediterranean Sea, all ablaze with light. Mozart in his last moments pointed to the score of the Requiem, which lay before him on his bed, and his lips were moving, to indicate the effect of kettledrums in a particular place, as he sank back in a swoon; and it is recorded of Paganini that on that fair moonlight night in May, as the last dimness came over his eyes, he stretched out his hand to grasp his faithful friend and companion, his Guarnerius violin, and as he struck its chords once more, and found that it ceased to speak with its old magic power, he himself sank back and expired, like one broken-hearted to find that a little feeble, confused noise was all that was now left of those strains that he had created and the world had worshipped.

He left £80,000 to his son, Baron Achille Paganini, and about £45 a year to Antonia Bianchi, with whom he had long since quarrelled. He had previously provided for his mother. His violin he left to his native city, Genoa, with directions that no other artist should ever play upon it.

We have no heart to dwell upon the wretched strife over his dead body. Paganini, who had no great opinion of the Catholic religion or the Catholic priests, died without confession and the last sacraments. He was, accordingly, refused burial in consecrated ground by the Bishop of Parma. For a long time his corpse remained at a room in the hospital at Nice. The body then lay for four years at Villa Franca, when, owing, it was affirmed, to the ghostly violin sounds that were heard about the coffin, his son, by paying large sums of money, got permission to bury his father with funeral rites in the village church near what had been his favorite residence, the Villa Gajona. This last tribute was tardily paid to the ashes of the immortal musician in May of 1845.

CHAPTER V.

WAGNER.

WAGNER is the most powerful personality that has appeared in the world of music since Beethoven. But indeed he seems to me, in his wide range as poet, dramatist, musician, and philosopher, almost alone in the history of Art.

Beethoven was a musician only. His glory is to have carried the art of music to its extreme limits of development; no one has yet gone beyond him.

Wagner said, "I have invented nothing." You cannot invent metre after the Greeks, or the modern drama after Shakespeare, or coloring and perspective after the Italians: there is a point at which an art ceases to grow and stands full-blown like a flower.

Most people admit that in music, as in other arts, that point has been reached. What then remained? *This,* according to Richard Wagner: to concentrate into one dazzling focus all the arts, and, having sounded and developed the expressional depth, and determined the peculiar function of each, to combine them at length into one perfect and indivisible whole.

Words seem childishly inadequate to render all at once such a conception as this. Slowly we may master some of its details and allow them to orb into a perfect whole. If you stand at the foot of one of the Alps, you can see but a little portion of it—a hamlet, a sloping patch of vineyard, and a pine copse beyond; but as you ascend the winding path the prospect opens to right and left ; cascades leap by to lose themselves in the torrent below ; you plunge into the gloom of a forest and emerge on to the higher meadows and pleasant scenes of pastoral life ; yonder the soil grows rocky, and tumbled boulders lie around you ; the cloud lifts, and a vista of mountains and valleys is suddenly opened up, and pressing forward you leave far below the murmurs of one world, and. raise your enraptured eyes to the black eagle, as he wheels aloft in the golden air beyond the stainless and eternal snows.

So when we are brought face to face with such a varied, complex, and immense intelligence as that of Richard Wagner we are apt to dwell on a part—a peculiarity of the music—a turn of the drama—a melody, a situation, an eccentricity. But the secret lies, after all, in the unity of effect. Close your eyes after a day in the Alps, and, as the visions pass before you, all will grow clear to your inner consciousness, and the varied scenes you have realized only in succession will at last arrange themselves into one great and majestic whole.

"Perhaps he has some talent for music," said the sick man, as he heard little Richard, then only seven years old, strumming a tune from *Der Freyschutz* on the piano. It was Louis Geyer, his step-father— painter, author, and actor—then on his death-bed, thinking of the future, planning as dying men plan, and hitting the mark as they often hit it, quite at random. The child's vivid temperament and eager, sensitive mind had always made him a favorite with the actor and the poet, and he thought of making a painter of Richard, but the boy seemed to have no turn for it. His mother, a woman full of life and imagination, was less anxious and more wise. She let him grow, and happily he was left to her, "with no education," as he says, "but life, art, and myself."

Indeed any attempt to hasten Wagner's development, or to fix his career, would doubtless have failed. From the first, the consciousness of his own force has been one of his strangest and strongest peculiarities. At times it seems to have almost intoxicated him—at others it sustained and cheered him in utter loneliness; it has dominated all who have come in personal contact with him, and bent the minds and wills of the rebellious like reeds before the wind.

And the reason is evident. Wagner was always prodigious in his ability. Like those very fast trotters that flash along the highways of England and America, he has been in the habit of passing every one on the road, and passing them easily. But the consciousness of power bred in him a singular wilfulness. At school he could learn anything, but he would learn only as he chose and what he chose. When *his* time came he mastered, with incredible rapidity and accuracy, Greek, Latin, mythology, and ancient history. As for his music-master, he soon sent him to the right-about, telling him he would learn music in his own way. Indeed the variety of influences, and the rapidity with which he absorbed them, one after the other, quite unfitted him for going into harness early in any one direction.

At the age of seventeen he had dipped into most literatures, ancient and modern, glanced at science, learned English in order to read Shakespeare, weighed several schools of philosophy, studied and dismissed the contending theologies, absorbed Schiller and worshipped Goethe (then eighty-four years old), turned away from the conventional stage of Kotzebue and Iffland, tasted politics, and been deeply stirred by the music of Beethoven.

There was doubtless a great indistinctness about his aims at this time. To live, to grow, to feel, to be filled with new emotions, and to sound his enormous capacities for receiving impressions and acquiring facts—this had hitherto been enough; but the vexed question was inevitable: to what end?

The artistic temperament could give but one answer to that—"Expression!" Creation itself—man, the world, the universe, is nothing but that. There is ever this imperious divine necessity for outward expression. This is the lesson of the ages and of the universe, of which we see but a little speck realized upon our tiny and overcrowded planet. But this burning thought turns the mind of man itself into a divine microcosm—he, too, begins to obey in his higher activities what he perceives to be the supreme law of the divine life. He, too, must flash into self-consciousness, and breathe in form, until all that slept in the silence of his heart comes forth swift and radiant with the wind and fire of emotion, and stands at last like an angel, full of wreathed melodies and crowned with stars.

Such to the artist soul is the beloved parable of earth. The life within must become outward; all that we are is dying to be born—is craving to realize itself, to know, to possess, to adore!

It is quite obvious that life is here seized, not from the intellectual, but from the emotional side. The intellect is used to fathom, to formulate, to economize, and represent, in their most impressive forms, the feelings which would otherwise be wasted and misspent; but the intellect, which has played so important a part in Wagner's system, is always the second, never the first factor, and its function has been to analyze the various expressional media of the past and present, and to create some form or combination more exhaustive and powerful than all the rest.

Wagner was willing to be led; but he could not help feeling that an artist now is the heir of all the ages, that now for the first time he can stand and gauge the creations of the past in poetry, painting, drama, and music, and ask himself, how far, through these, has the inner world of the mind found utterance. Wagner had the unconscious but inflexible hardihood to take up each art in turn, weigh it, and find it wanting. Each fell short of the whole reality in some respect. Painting leaves out motion and solidarity, sculpture possesses solidarity without motion, and usually without color. Poetry without drama appeals to the senses chiefly through the imagination; in itself it has neither sound, color, nor solidarity. The spoken drama lacks the intensity which it is the unique function of musical sound to give; while mere pantomime, whether of dance or drama, lacks the indefinite power of sound as well as the definite suggestion of words; and, lastly, musical sound alone provokes the eternal "why?" which can only be answered by associating the emotion raised with thought, for music is without solidarity, color, or thought, while possessing motion and sound in the highest perfection.

It will be said, "Yes, but each art is complete in itself." True, but not complete as a means of expressing thought and feeling. You urge, "But the power of art lies often in its suggestiveness. I read a poem and shut my eyes, and the vision is more splendid than anything that could be presented outwardly." Yes, indirectly, because you have imagination; the vision was beautiful, but its quality depended on *you*, not on the *art*. Art is for expression, and that art is best which expresses most. Do not confuse the effects of imagination and association with the effects of art. A barrel-organ or a daub may serve to set a-going imagination and memory, but art has to do with expression, and is defective *quâ* art just where it begins to make these demands upon imagination and memory.

Those who have traced Wagner's career from boyhood know how patiently he has questioned every art, how passionately he has surrendered himself to it, for a time; how willing he would have been to rest; how inexorably experience and feeling have urged him on until, like the hardy navigators of old, he broke at last into a new and undiscovered ocean. At the age of eleven he had read Shakespeare. Surely dramatic expression of thought and feeling could go no farther. But he would test it as a form of art by experiment, and see how it worked. He immediately constructed a drama, horrible and thorough—a cross between *Hamlet* and *King Lear*. Forty-two characters suffered death in the first four acts, so that in the fifth, in order to people his stage at all, most of them had to reappear as ghosts. The Shakespearian method was closely adhered to, and for several years he continued to brood over it lovingly.

Here was a form intensely individual, self-conscious —in which man explored the depths of his own nature. On that rough wooden stage of the Globe Theatre so vivid were the characters, so rapid and complex the feelings, so perfect and expressive the pantomime, that the want of stage trappings and accessories was hardly felt. Still, it was a restrained expression; it was too mosaic; the individuals lacked an universal element in which to live and move and have their being; we sit fascinated and bewildered with the subtle analysis and changing episodes; but the characters do not run up into universal types, they are too entirely absorbed by their own thoughts and feelings. The contest here is not with Fate and Time, as on the Greek stage, but with Self and Society.

Excited, but oppressed, by the complex inner life of the Shakespearian drama, Wagner still felt the need of wedding the personal life to some larger ideal types, and intensifying the emotional element by the introduction of musical sound. Then the cramped wooden stage of the Globe Theatre vanished, and in its place rose the marble amphitheatre, open to the sky, embedded in the southern slope of the Athenian Acropolis. In the classical drama nothing was individual—the whole life of Greece was there, but all was summed up in large and simple types. The actors speak through fixed masks. All fine inflection is lost—all change of facial expression sacrificed to massive groupings and stately poses, regulated by the shrill pipe and the meagre harp. But still there is in the dramas of Æschylus, Euripides, and Sophocles a breadth of expression which enables the soul to shake itself free from its accidental surroundings and enter into general sympathy with the wider life of humanity. It is this escape into the ideal which the modern self-conscious spirit most needs; this merging of discordant self in the universal harmony which drew Wagner toward the theatre of the Greeks. There we start from the gods, the ideal representatives of human thought and emotion. Zeus is in Agamemnon, Ares in Achilles, Artemis in Iphigenia, Aphrodite in Phædra; and there is something prophetic and sublime in the spontaneous growth of these types beneath the human touch, until they transcend the gods and conquer Olympus itself. Cassandra is greater than the gods in her consciousness of injustice; Prometheus is sublime in his god-like defiance of fate; Antigone triumphs through voluntary sacrifice. It is the inexorable progress of the human conscience toward a higher Olympus, a purer deity ; men come from gods, but excel the gods. Then follows the inevitable decline, "the dusk of the gods," and, lastly, the assertion of man's divinity and the rehabilitation through man of the divine idea.

This thought Christianity should eternally present ; but as its votaries unhappily trampled upon one half of human life, and caricatured the other all through the Middle Ages, the Renaissance insisted upon reviving the types of Greek beauty and force, in order to restore the balance and reassert the place and dignity of the downtrodden senses. That protest, in the teeth of our modern religious narrowness, will continue to be popular until the reconciliation between the old and the new world-spirit is reached in a higher, freer life, recognizing and making room for the development in due balance of every part of human nature. The Greek view of life may not be adequate, but it had elements which we want ; and to study Art we must still go to Athens. Within his limits the Greek remains our supreme standard.

For what the Greek was, and for what he saw, his theatre found an almost perfect art-form. The dance or science of pantomimic motion was part of his daily education. His body was trained in the Palæstra, or gymnasium, and his life was one of constant drill to enable him to take part in the games and national festivals. The elastic tongue of Homer had been enriched and fired by a hundred poets before the full development of the Greek drama, and hymns and songs, set to rhythmic and choral melodies of every character and variety, supplied him with ready emotional utterance upon all occasions. Add to this the profound enthusiasm which still accompanied the ancient rites, the Delphic oracles and the Eleusinian mysteries, and we have all the materials which were woven into one harmonious whole by Æschylus—poet, warrior, stage manager, and religious devotee.

The soul of the Greek drama, freed from accidental associations, must now be melted down in the new crucible.

Wagner found there an intense earnestness of purpose —the devout portrayal of a few fundamental types—the large clear outline like the frieze of the Parthenon—a simple plot and well-developed phases of feeling as pronounced and trenchant as the rhythmic motions of the *dramatis personæ;* and lastly he found—what he found not in Shakespeare—the Greek chorus. This gave its binding intensity to the whole drama—this provided the universal element in which the actors lived and moved and had their being. The chorus ever in motion—a band of youth or maidens, priests or supernatural beings, fluid and expressive, like the emotions of the vast and earnest assembly—the chorus bore aloft a wail over the agonies of Philoctetes, a plaint for Iphigenia, a questioning of the gods for Cassandra; it enveloped the stage with floods of passionate declamation; it rushed, it pointed, it swayed, it sighed and whispered in broken pathetic accents; it was like the sobbing of the sea on a rocky strand—the sound of the waves in Ionian caves —the wild sweep of the tempest answering back man's passionate plaint, and fitting the simple feelings of the great types on the stage with an almost elemental intensity of expression. The mysterious variety of Greek metres, the varied spasmodic rhythms, can only be understood when the vision of the Greek chorus rises before us in its eager bursts of appropriate but fitful activity. That changing chant, that harsh ringing progression of notes on the Greek scales of which Gregorians are still the Christian relics—we should not call it music, it was not melody, much less harmony; but it was sound inflexions marvellously used to drill declamation, posture, and pantomime. The soul of it has transmigrated in these latter days—it has become the Wagnerian orchestra.

Turn back now, for a moment, to the Shakespearian drama. Chorus, musical sound, band, song, all the voices of universal nature environing man—appalling, consoling, inspiring him—have vanished. A new inner-world, unknown to the Greeks, has taken their place, and man is absorbed with himself. Yet without that universal voice which he can make his own, how he shrinks, dwarfed by his narrow individuality; no longer a part of the great whole and soul of things; nature no longer his mother, the winds no more his friends, the sea no more his comforter! The ideal atmosphere of the Greek chorus is missed; the power of music, however rudimentary, is absent; Shakespeare seems to have felt it; it passes over his sublime creations as an invocation to Music in *Twelfth Night*, or in Ophelia's plaintive song. And this is the point of contact between the old drama of Æschylus and the new drama of Shakespeare; the two stand forever for the opposite poles of dramatic art—the universal type, the individual life—and both are necessary. The individual is naturally evolved from the universal, but once evolved and developed it must be restored to the universal and be glorified by it.

At this crisis, in his quest after a perfect art-form, Wagner found himself confronted with Beethoven's music. He did not believe that drama could be carried farther than Æschylus, Sophocles, and Shakespeare, or music any farther than Beethoven; but he did conceive the project of leading the whole stream of the

Beethovenian music into the channels of Shakespearian drama. The Greek chorus might have been adequate to the simple types of Greek tragedy; but modern life, with its self-conscious spirituality, its questions, its doubts, its hopes, and its immense aspirations — this seemed to require quite a new element of expression. The voice of this inner life had been preparing for four hundred years; when it was ready it turned out to be no inflexible mask, through which a human voice might speak, nor even a mobile chorus, but a splendid and complex organ of expression, fitted so closely about the soul of man as to become the very Æolian harp upon which the breath of his life could freely play.

In the great world-laboratory of Art, Wagner found already all that he required. There was, as he remarked, nothing left for him to invent; the arts of poetry, music, painting, and pantomime had been explored separately and perfected; nay, one step more had been made — the arts had actually been *combined* at different times in different ways. Music with pantomime and poem by the Greeks; music with pantomime, drama, painting, and every conceivable effect of stage scenery and costume, as in modern opera; music and words, as in oratorio or the cantata. But in Greece music was wholly undeveloped as an art; acting had never sounded the depths of individual life and expression. The Shakespearian drama left out music. The cantata and oratorio omitted pantomime and painting; while modern opera presented a meretricious and maimed combination of the arts resulting from a radically defective form.

With a surprising vigor of intellect, Wagner has analyzed the situation, and explained exactly why he felt dissatisfied with the best operatic efforts of the past, and why he seeks to supersede opera with the "musical drama."

I think his critical results may be briefly summed up thus: In the musical drama, poetry, music, scenery, and acting are to be so blended as that each shall have its own appropriate share, and no more, as a medium of expression. The acting must not be cramped by the music, as in common opera, where a man has to stand on one toe till he has done his *roulade*, or pauses in the dead of night to shout out a song about "Hush! we shall be discovered!" when there is not a moment to spare. The music must not be spoiled for the acting, as in ballet and pantomime, where acting is overstrained to express what the sister arts of poetry and music are better fitted to convey. And poetry—which after all supplies the definite basis and answers the inevitable "why?"—must not be sacrificed, as in our opera *libretti*, to the demands of singers for *aria* and *scena;* while the scenery must only attempt effects and situations which can be made to look real. The object of the grand musical drama is, in fact, to present a true picture of human feeling with the utmost fulness and intensity, freed from every conventional expression by the happy union of all the arts, giving to each only what it is able to deal with—but thus dealing with everything, leaving nothing to the imagination. The Wagnerian drama completely exhausts the situation.

Filled with this magnificent conception, Wagner looked out upon the world of modern opera—and what did he see? First, he noticed that the opera had made a false start. It sprang, not from the earnest feeling of the miracle plays, but from the indolent desire of the luxurious Italian nobles to listen to the delicious popular melodies in a refined form. The spontaneous street action (which may to this day be admired in Naples or Florence) was exchanged for a sort of drawing-room stage, and poets were hired to reset the Italian melodies, as Moore reset the Irish melodies, for ears polite. This new aristocratic mongrel art had nothing to do with the real drama. Metastasio himself was only an Italian Mr. Chorley—the very humble servant of everybody's tunes ; but these tunes had to be strung together, so the *recitative*, used for centuries in church, was borrowed ; then the product was naturally a little dull, so the whole had to be whipped up with a dance ; hence the *ballet*, and there you have the three fixed points of the opera— *aria, recitative,* and *ballet*—which to this day determine the form of modern opera. Thus opera, while it had no connection with the real drama, did not even spring from the best musical elements. " From the prosperity of opera in Italy," says Wagner, " the art-student will date the decline of music in that country. . . . . No one who has any conception of the grandeur and ineffable depth of the earlier Italian church music—Palestrina's " Stabat Mater," for instance—will ever dream of maintaining that Italian opera can be looked upon as the legitimate daughter of that wondrous mother."*

As ear-tickling, and not truth of expression, was the chief thing, and as there was nothing much to be expressed, the *arias* became wider and wider of the words, and at last the words became mere pegs, and the music totally irrelevant — as who should dance a jig over a grave.

Gluck's reform consisted in making the operatic tunes once more true to the words ; but the improvement touched the sentiment only, without reaching the

---

* *Music of the Future:* Letter to F. Villot, p. 10.

defective form. In France the form was slightly redeemed by the superior *libretti* and more elaborate pantomime; while in Germany opera arrived as a finished foreign production, and Mozart and others had to go to Italy to learn it. "In expressing my highest admiration of the exquisite beauty of our great masters," says Wagner, "I did not detract from their fame in showing that the cause of their weaknesses lay in the faultiness of the *genre*."* And the defect of *genre* lay chiefly in the immolation of the *libretto* to the exigencies of fixed *aria, scena,* and *recitative.* The drama, which has to be stretched upon that Procrustean bed, must necessarily become disjointed and lifeless in the process. Rossini retarded the progress of the musical drama for at least fifty years through the absolute triumph of melody, in the most fascinating abundance, over the resources of the orchestra and the inspirations of the poet.

"His opera," writes Edward Dannreuther, to whose pamphlet on Wagner I am so much indebted, "is like a string of beads, each bead being a glittering and intoxicating tune. Dramatic and poetic truth—all that makes a stage performance interesting—is sacrificed to tunes. Poet and musician alike had felt this. Goethe and Schiller both found the operatic form, and even the existing stage, so uncongenial, that they took to writing narrative and descriptive plays not to be acted at all, and have been followed in this by Byron, Tennyson, Browning, and Swinburne. Beethoven wrote but one opera, *Fidelio*, in which the breadth of the overture, or overtures, seems to accuse the narrowness of the dramatic form, although the *libretto* of *Fidelio* is very good, as times go. Mendelssohn and Schumann could never find a suitable *libretto*.

* *Music of the Future:* Letter to F. Villot, p. 22.

The conclusion of all this is obvious. The perfect medium which was to combine the apparently unmanageable arts was yet to come, and Wagner proposed to himself the task of harnessing these fiery steeds to his triumphal car, and driving them all together. He must choose his own subject, with a simple plot and a few strong passions and great situations. He must write his own drama, which, without being either orthodox verse or fixed metre, would aim in its mobile and alliterative pathos at following the varied inflexions of natural feeling. He must arrange his own scenery, perfect in detail, and within the limits of stage possibility; and finally he must compose his own music and drill his band, chorus, and characters.

To his prophetic vision the old opera form of *aria*, *scena*, and *recitative* had disappeared. The orchestra in a wondrous fashion floods the soul with an emotion appropriate to the situation. The drama itself advances unshackled by any musical exigency; the music flows on continuously, not imposing a form, but taking its form from the emotion of the sentences as they follow each other. Snatches there are here and there of exquisite melody, broken up by part-singing, with a wild burst of chorus when needful to fulfil the dramatic occasion; but never must action be delayed, never must emotion be belied, never truth sacrificed: only at times, when the expressional power of words ceases, the music will fulfil, deepen, combine, and sometimes lift the drama almost out of itself. Then the spectator is raised into a sphere of ecstatic contemplation; the pageantry passes before his eyes as in a dream, while his soul lives and moves only in the ideal sphere of the varied and intense passions which are being played out before him.

While these perceptions and aims were slowly maturing in him, Wagner found himself constantly at war with his age and his surroundings. At sixteen, he had resolved to devote himself to music, finding in it the ineffable expression for emotions otherwise mainly inexpressible. Musical notes and intervals were to him radiant forms and flaming ministers. Mozart taught him that exquisite certainty of touch which selects exactly the right notes to express a given musical idea. Weber taught him the secret of pure melody, how to stamp with an indelible type a given character, as in the return of the Samiel motive in *Der Freyschutz;* he also perceived in that opera the superiority of legend and popular myth, as on the Greek stage, to present the universal and eternal aspects of human life in their most pronounced and ideal forms. Beethoven supplied him with the mighty orchestra, capable of holding in suspension an immense crowd of emotions, and of manipulating the interior and complex feelings with the instantaneous and infallible power of a magician's wand. Schubert taught him the freedom of song ; Chopin the magic elasticity of chords ; Spohr the subtle properties of the chromatic scale ; and even Meyerbeer revealed to him the possibility of stage effect through the Grand Opera. Shakespeare, Goethe, and Schiller suggested the kind of language in which such dramas as *Lohengrin* and *Rheingold* might be written ; while Madame Schröder Devrient revealed to him what a woman might accomplish in the stage presentation of ideal passion with such a part as Elsa in *Lohengrin,* or Brünnhilde in *Walküre.*

But the immediate result of this, as I have said, was not promising. Contrary to the advice of his friends, he had thrown himself, heart and soul, into the study of music as a profession. Under the Cantor Weinlig, at Leipsic, and while at the University, he produced an overture and symphony, which were played, and not unfavorably received, at the Gewandhaus; but his early work, with here and there an exceptional trait in harmony, was nothing but a pale copy of Mozart.

His health now broke down. He was twenty years old (1833), and he went to his brother, a professor of music at Wurzburg, where he stayed a year, at the end of which time he was appointed musical director at the Magdeburg theatre, where, under the combined influence of Weber and Beethoven, he produced two operas —*The Fairies* and *The Novice of Palermo*—neither of which succeeded. He left his place in disgust, and obtained another post at the Königsberg theatre. There he married an actress—a good creature, who, without being much to blame, does not seem to have materially increased his happiness, but who decidedly shared the opinion of his friends that the composition of "pot-boilers" was superior to the pursuit of the Ideal. The Ideal, however, haunted Wagner, and—Poverty.

In 1836 he left with Mina for Riga on the shores of the Baltic, and there, as *chef d'orchestre* at the theatre, he really appears to have enjoyed studying the operas of Mehul, Spontini, Auber; for, while suffering what he describes as a dull, gnawing pain at the frequent irrelevance of the sentiment to the music, the nobler correspondences and beautiful inspirations gave him far-off glimpses of that musical drama to which he even now dimly aspired.

In the midst of his routine duties Bulwer's novel, *Rienzi*, struck his imagination. There, as on a large and classic stage, was portrayed that eternal revolt of the human spirit against tyranny, routine, selfishness, and corruption, of which the Polish insurrection of 1831 and the Revolution of July were the modern echoes.

Rienzi, a tribune of the people, dreaming of the old austere Republic, in the midst of corrupt Papal Rome—a noble heart, a powerful will at war with a brutal and vulgar age, supported, cheered by the enthusiasm of a devoted and patriotic sister, raised by a wave of popularity to the highest summit of human power, then hurled down by the Papal anathema, betrayed by a mean and cowering aristocracy, banished by the mob that had so lately hailed him as a deliverer, and at last falling by a treacherous hand upon the charred and crumbling ashes of his own homestead, the last great tribune of Rome!—here was a subject with immense outlines, full of situations in which the greatest breadth might be joined to the most detailed inflexions of feeling. In it Wagner, while not departing avowedly from the form of the grand opera then in vogue at Paris, has in fact burst the boundaries. *Rienzi* is already the work of an independent master—it is, at least, prophetic of *Lohengrin* and *Tristan*, while comparing favorably in pure melody and sensational effects with any of the current operas. What rush, triumph, aspiration about the large outlines and tramping measures of the overture—what *élan* and rugged dignity in the choruses—what elevation in Rienzi's prayer, "God of Light!"—what fervor and inexhaustible faith in the phrase, "Thou hast placed me as a pilot on a treacherous and rocky strand"—what imagery, as of vast buildings and ranged towers dimly seen athwart the dull red dawn, in the music of "Scatter the night that reigns above this city," and what chastened exaltation, free from all Italian flourish or ornament, of "Rise, thou blessed sun, and bring with thee resplendent liberty!"

But in 1839, which saw the text and the completion of the first two acts, we are far indeed from the production of *Rienzi;* it struck, however, the key-note of a most important and little-understood phase in Wagner's career—the political phase.

Musicians, poets, and artists are not, as a rule, politicians. Their world is the inner world—the world of emotion and thought, which belongs to no special age or clime, but is eternal and universal. Goethe and Beethoven cared little for revolutions, and have even been deemed wanting in patriotism. But Wagner was a hot politician. He was at one time a mob orator, and was seduced by his illustrious friend Röckel, who was afterward put in prison, to throw himself at Dresden into the rise of Saxony and the agitations of 1848. He was proscribed and banished from German soil, and years afterward, when he had, if not recanted, at all events acquiesced in things as they were, he was obliged to fly from Munich, warned by the friendly king that his life was in danger. The title of but one of his numerous semi-political pamphlets, "Art and the Revolution," gives us the real clue to all this. People have accused Wagner of time-serving and change in politics; but the fact was that he favored social revolution *because* he thought it needful to art revolution. Conventionality and stagnation in art seemed to him the natural outcome of conventionality and stagnation in society; the world must be recalled to feeling and reality before art could again become the ideal life of the people, as it was once in Greece. But when, through royal patronage later on, all impediment to the free development of his art-work disappeared, his revolutionary tendencies also disappeared. He too was, first and foremost, Artist, and he came to realize his vocation, which had to do with Art and with "the Revolution" only in so far as it affected "Art."

But, in fact, no ardent soul could escape the romantic and revolutionary contagion that swept over France, Germany, and even England, between 1830 and 1850. Europe seemed to breathe freely once more after the iron hand of Napoleon I. had been lifted from her oppressed bosom—but then, like a wayward child, she burst into all kinds of excesses.

The atheism of the first revolution, the brutality of Napoleon Buonaparte's administration, the dulness of Louis Philippe's, the revived taste for Greek art, combined with the inflexible dogmatism of the Papal creed —all these conspired to fill the ardent youth of the period with a deep revolt against things as they were. With this came a settled longing for a return of some sort to nature and freedom, and a vague but intense aspiration toward the ideal and immaterial world, which in other times might have taken the form of a religious revolution, but in 1830 broke out in what has been called "Romanticism" in Art. It was seen in the writings of Mazzini and the mutterings of Italian freedom ; in the insatiable and varied developments of Madame Sand's genius, in the wild and pathetic cries of Alfred de Musset, in the sentimentalism of Lamartine, in the vast scorn and bitter invective of Hugo, in the heart-broken submission of Lacordaire, and in the despair of De Lammenais. Byron, Shelley, and Tennyson caught both the most earthly and the most heavenly echoes of the romantic movement in England ; while its inner life and genius have found, after all, their most subtle expression in the music of Beethoven, Mendelssohn, Schumann, Berlioz, Chopin, Wagner, Liszt, and Rubinstein.

"It seems, indeed," writes Wagner, in one of those veins of flashing perception in which he so abounds, "that human sentiment, as if intensified by the pressure of conventional civilization, had sought an outlet for asserting itself according to its own laws of expression. The astounding popularity of music in our time proves the correctness of the supposition that the modern development of this art has met an innate desire of the human spirit."*

Wagner had left Magdeburg for Riga, but he soon came to the end of his tether there. A stupid little provincial town was not likely to become then what Wagner has made Bayreuth since—the stage for turning upside down the art-theories of the civilized world. Pushed by what he calls "despair," without money and without friends, but with that settled faith in himself which has made him independent of both until it has won both, the obscure *chef d'orchestre* resolved to go to Paris and storm the Grand Opera, then at the feet of Rossini and that strange, unscrupulous bric-à-brac composer, Meyerbeer! The small vessel in which he sailed was blown about the Baltic for three weeks, put into many desolate coast-nooks, and nearly wrecked. After many hardships, shared with the rough and often starving crew, the lonely musician arrived in London (1840), with his head full of Paris and the *Grand Opéra*, and with *Rienzi* in his carpet-bag.

While here he playfully seized the musical *motive* of the English people. It lay, he said, in the five consecutive ascending notes (after the first three) of "Rule Britannia;" there was expressed the whole breadth and downright bluff "go" of the British nation. He threw "Rule Britannia" into an overture, and sent it by post to Sir George Smart, then omnipotent musical pro-

---
* Letter to Villot, p. 30.

fessor in London; but the postage being insufficient, the MS. was not taken in, and at this moment is probably lying in some dim archive of the Post-Office, "left till called for."

Crossing to Dieppe, he met the crafty and clever Meyerbeer, who instantly saw the man he had to deal with, and probably conceived in a moment that policy of apparent support but probable intrigue which made him throughout life Wagner's pet aversion.

It has been unwarrantably asserted that Wagner hated the Jews because of Meyerbeer and Mendelssohn, and hated Meyerbeer and Mendelssohn because they were successful; but Wagner's dearest friends have been Jews; he only objected to what he considered the low level of their art theories; and if he hated Meyerbeer and Mendelssohn—two men also at loggerheads, by the way—it was not simply because they had the ear of Europe, but because they and their friends kept every one else out of the field, while Meyerbeer debased musical art to the level of the vulgarest sensation, and Mendelssohn never rose in Wagner's opinion above the plane of a drawing-room prophet, while creating an elegant and pseudo-classic standard of excellence to which every one soon learned to bow down.

In this opinion I shall never concur. Mendelssohn has been to me as much a revelator of the beautiful as Wagner has been of the sublime. Nothing is more painful to me than the bitter opposition between the friends of Mendelssohn and Wagner. These two great spirits were probably as antipathetic as Moore and Wordsworth; but although Wagner is *the* inexorable and colossal development in art since Beethoven, Mendelssohn reigns forever in a sweet wayside temple of his own, full of bright dreams and visions, incense and ringing songs. And partly is he so sweet because, unburthened with any sense of a message to utter, a mission to develop, he sings like a child in the valleys of asphodel, weaving bright chaplets of spring flowers for the whole world, looking upon the mystery of grief and pain with wide eyes of sympathy, and at last succumbing to it himself, but not understanding it, with a song of tender surprise upon his lips.

Wagner passed two terrible years, 1840-42, in Paris. Meyerbeer had given him introductions, and introduced him later to Mr. Joly, a stage-director at Paris, whom he must have known to be on the point of bankruptcy, and who suspended the rehearsal of the *Novice of Palermo* at the last moment. But this was but the end of a series of checks. He wrote an overture to *Faust*. His good friend and faithful ally, Schlesinger, editor of the *Gazette Musicale*, got it rehearsed at the Conservatoire. It sounded quite too strange and *bizarre* to those ears polite, and was instantly snuffed out.

He submitted a *libretto*, "Love Forbidden," to a theatrical manager, but it had no chance, and dropped. Schlesinger now employed him to write, and he wrote articles and novels, and so kept body and soul together. No one would listen to his music, but he was not a bad hack, and was hired for a few francs to arrange Halévy's "Queen of Cyprus" for the piano, and the latest tunes of Donizetti and Bellini for piano and *cornet à piston.*

At night he stole into the Grand Opera, and there, as he tells us, felt quite certain that his own works would one day supersede the popular efforts of Rossini and Meyerbeer. He does not seem to have been dejected like a lesser soul; in what the French called his *immense orgueil*, he was sorry for their want of appreciation, but never dreamed of altering *his* ideas to suit them. "Je me flattais," says the unpaid musical hack, " d'imposer les miennes." Meanwhile the splendid band of the Conservatoire, under Habeneck, consoled him, and on the Boulevards he often met and chatted with Auber, for whom he had a sincere respect and admiration. Auber was at least a conscientious musician of genius, who knew his business, and did not debase what was at no time a very exalted but still a legitimate branch of his art, the *opéra comique ;* and, besides, Auber was a *bon comarade*, and liked Wagner, probably without understanding him.

After months of drudgery, and chiefly penny-a-lining for the *Gazette Musicale*, Wagner felt the imperious necessity for a return to his own art. He took a little cottage outside Paris, hired a piano, and shut himself up. He had done for a time, at least, with the mean, frivolous, coarse world of Paris—he did not miss his friends, he did not mind his poverty. He was again on the wild Norwegian coast, beaten about with storms, and listening to the weird tales of mariners, as in broken and abrupt utterances, or with bated breath, they confided to him the legend common in one form or other to seafaring folk in all parts of the world—the legend of the Flying Dutchman. The tale sprang from the lives and adventures of those daring navigators of the fifteenth and sixteenth centuries, and reflects the desperate struggle with the elements, the insatiable thirst for the discovery of new lands athwart unknown seas ; and it seems to embody forever the avenging vision of men who, resolved to win, had so often dared and lost all. A famous captain, mad to double the Cape of Storms, beaten back again and again, at length swears a mighty oath to persevere throughout eternity. The devil takes him at his word. The captain doubles the cape, but is doomed to roam the seas forever from pole to pole—as the Wandering Jew to tread the earth—his phantom vessel the terror of all mariners, and the dreadful herald of shipwreck. Here was a legend which needed but one inspired touch of love to make it a grand epitome of seafaring life, with its hard toils, its forlorn hopes, and its tender and ineffably sweet respites. The accursed doom of the Flying Dutchman can be lifted by human love alone. The captain, driven by an irrepressible longing for rest, may land once in seven years, and if he can find a woman who will promise to be his and remain faithful to him for one term of seven years, his trial will be over—he will be saved.

The legend thus humanized becomes the vehicle for the expression of those intense yet simple feelings and situations which popular myth, according to Wagner, has the property of condensing into universal types. Immense unhappiness, drawn by magnetic attraction to immense love, tried by heartrending doubt and uncertainty, and crowned with fidelity and triumphant love, the whole embodied in a clear, simple story, summed up in a few situations of terrible strength and inexorable truth—such is Wagner's conception of the drama of the *Flying Dutchman* with its "damnation" motive belonging to the captain, and its "salvation" motive given to the bride—its sailor's subject—its pilot's song—its spinning-wheel home-melody—and its stormy "Ho! e ho!" chorus. The whole drama is shadowed forth in the magic and tempestuous overture, and stands out as this composer's first straightforward desertion of history proper, and adoption of myth as the special medium of the new musical drama.

Six weeks of ceaseless labor, which to Wagner were

weeks of spontaneous and joyful production, sufficed to complete the music of the *Flying Dutchman*. The immediate result in Paris was ludicrous. The music was instantly judged to be absurd, and Wagner was forced to sell the *libretto*, which was handed over to a Frenchman, one M. P. Fouché, who *could* write music. It appeared, with that gentleman's approved setting, under the title of *Le Vaisseau Fantôme*.

This was enough! No lower depth could well be reached, and Wagner was preparing to leave Paris to the tender mercies of Rossini, Meyerbeer, and M. P. Fouché, when news reached him from Germany that *Rienzi*, flouted in the capital of taste, had been accepted in Berlin and Dresden!

It was the spring of 1842, and it was also the rapid and wondrous turn of the tide for Wagner. He hurried to Dresden, to find the rehearsals of *Rienzi* already advanced. The opera was produced with that singular burst of enthusiasm which greets the first appreciation of an important but long-neglected truth, and Wagner, having become the favorite of the Crown Prince, was elected Kapellmeister at Dresden, and found himself for the first time famous. Some might now have rested on their laurels, but to Wagner's imperious development *Rienzi* was already a thing of the past. He had drunk of the crystalline waters of popular myth, and was still thirsty. The *Flying Dutchman* had opened up a new world to him, more real because more exhaustive of human feelings and character than the imperfect types and broken episodes of real history. He seemed to stand where the fresh springs of inspiration welled up from a virgin soil; he listened to the child-like voices of primitive peoples, inspired from the simple heart of Nature, and babbling eternal verities without knowing it.

Legend was the rough ore—the plastic element he could seize and remould, as Æschylus remoulded Prometheus, or Sophocles Œdipus, adding philosophic analysis and the rich adornments of poetic fancy and artistic form.

The legend of *Tannhäuser* now engrossed him. The drama was soon conceived and written. There he summed up, in a few glowing scenes, the opposition between that burst of free sensuous life at the Renaissance, and the hard, narrow ideal of Papal Christianity. Christ not only crowned with thorns, but turned into stone, is all the answer which that Christianity had to give to the stormy impulse which at last poured its long pent-up torrent over Europe. The deep revolt still stares us in the face from the Italian canvases, as we look at the sensuous figures of Raphael or Titian—the free types of fair breathing life, surrounded with the hard aureole of the artificial saint, or limned as in mockery, like the dreams of a pagan world upon the walls of the Vatican.

Tannhäuser, a Thuringian knight, taking refuge with Venus, no longer the beneficent Holda, joy of gods and men, but turned by the excesses of the ascetic spirit into a malign witch, and banished to the bowels of the earth in the Venusberg ; Tannhäuser, with a touch eternally true to nature, bursting the fetters of an unruly sensual life, and sighing for a healthier activity ; Tannhäuser seeing for a moment only, in the pure love of woman, the reconciliation of the senses with the spirit, a reconciliation made forever impossible by the stupid bigotry of a false form of religion, but which is ultimately sealed and accomplished by love and death in heaven—this is the human and sublime parable of the drama, wrought out with the fervor of a religious devotee, and epitomized in that prodigious overture wherein the dirge of the Church mingles with the free and impassioned song of the minstrel knight, and clashes wildly with the voluptuous echoes of the fatal Venusberg.

Wagner's progress was now checked by that storm of invective which burst out all over the art world of Germany—not on account of *Rienzi*, but in consequence of the *Flying Dutchman*, and especially of *Tannhäuser*. The reason is simple. The power of *Rienzi*, the audacity of its sentiment, the simplicity of its outline, and the realism of its *mise en scène*, together with a general respect for the old opera forms, insured it a hearing which resulted in a legitimate triumph. But in *Tannhäuser* the new path was already struck out, which singers, band, audience, critics, and composers, in a body, refused to tread—in short, *aria*, *recitative*, and *ballet* were dethroned, and suddenly found themselves servants where they had been masters.

In 1843 the *Flying Dutchman* was produced at Dresden, and failed. *Rienzi* was still revived with success. Wagner now sent the *Dutchman* and *Tannhäuser* to various theatres. The former was tried at Berlin in 1844, and failed. Spohr had the intelligence to take it up at Cassel, and wrote a friendly and appreciative letter to Wagner; but the MS. scores were, as a rule, returned by the other theatres, and the new operas seemed to react on the earlier success, for at Hamburg *Rienzi* failed.

Meanwhile, failure, together with the close sympathy of a few devoted friends, convincing him that he was more right than ever, Wagner now threw himself into the completion of that work which is perhaps of the whole his most perfect, as it certainly is his most popular creation, *Lohengrin*. The whole of *Lohengrin* is in the prelude. The descent of the Knight of the Swan from the jasper shrines of the sacred palace of Montsalvat, hidden away in a distant forest land—his holy mission to rescue Elsa from her false accusers—his high and chivalric love—his dignified trouble at being urged by her to reveal his name, that insatiable feminine curiosity which wrecks the whole—the darker scenes of treachery by which Elsa is goaded on to press her fatal inquiry—the magnificent climax of the first act—the sense of weird mystery that hangs about the appearance and reappearance of the swan, and the final departure of the glittering Knight of the Sangraal—allegory of heavenly devotion stooping to lift up human love and dashed with earth's bitterness in the attempt;—to those who understand the pathos, delicacy, and full intensity of the *Lohengrin* prelude, this and more will become as vivid as art and emotion can make it. *Lohengrin* in its elevation, alike in its pain, its sacrifice, and its peace, is the necessary reaction from that wreck of sensual passion and religious despair so vividly grasped in the scenes of the Venusberg, in the pilgrim chant and the wayside crucifix of *Tannhäuser*.

Lohengrin was finished in 1847, but the political events of the next few years brought Wagner's career in Germany to an abrupt conclusion. His growing dissatisfaction with society coincided, unconsciously no doubt, with the failure of his operas after that first dawn of success. He now devoted himself to criticism and politics. He read Schopenhauer, whose pessimist philosophy did not tend to soothe his perturbed spirit; and during the next ten years, from 1847 to 1857, he spoke to the world from different places of exile in that series of political and æsthetical pamphlets to which I have before alluded.

In 1855 the Philharmonic Society invited him over to London, and here he conducted eight concerts. He was

not popular; he was surprised to find that the band
thought it unnecessary to rehearse, and the band was
surprised that he should require so much rehearsal. But
he drove the band in spite of itself, and the band hated
him. They said he murdered Beethoven with his *bâton*,
because of the freedom and inspiration of his readings.
Mendelssohn's Scotch symphony had been deliberately
crushed—or it was the only thing that went—according
to which paper you happened to read. He did not care
for the press, and he was not much surprised that the
press did not care for him. The unfailing musical intelligence of the Queen and Prince Albert was the one ray
of sunlight in this his second visit, but the power of the
man could not be hid, even from his enemies; his culture astonished the half-educated musicians by whom he
was surrounded, his brilliant originality impressed even
his own friends, who saw him struggling through an imperfect acquaintance with French and English to make
himself understood. One evening, alone in company
with M. Sainton, Hector Berlioz, and Ferdinand
Praeger, Wagner surprised them all by suddenly launching out on art, music, and philosophy. Berlioz was an
elegant speaker, accustomed to lead easily, but Wagner,
with his torrent of broken French and his rush of molten
ideas, silenced, bewildered, delighted, and astonished
them all. Berlioz is gone, but that night still lives in
the memory of those who were present who survive, and
from whose lips I have the incident.

Thus Wagner passed through England for a second
time, leaving behind him a vague impression of power
and eccentricity, the first of which the musical press did
its best to kill, while fanning the second into a devouring
flame which swallowed up Wagner's reputation. Notwithstanding the exertions of a few devoted believers,

twenty-one years flitted by, and little enough was heard of Richard Wagner in England until, owing to the increasing agitation of a younger school of musicians, the *Flying Dutchman* was at last indifferently produced at Covent Garden.

In 1874 Herr Hans von Bülow, pupil of Liszt and great exponent of Wagner's music, came over, and by his wonderful playing, aided steadily by the periodical Wagnerian and Liszt concerts given by Messrs. Dannreuther and Bache, at which Bülow conducted Wagner's music, brought about the rise of the new Wagner movement in England, which received its development in the interest occasioned by the Bayreuth Festival, and reached its climax in the Wagner Festival actively promoted by Herr Wilhelmj, in 1877, at the Albert Hall.

Mina, Wagner's first wife, was now dead. I cannot here tell at length how Liszt (whose daughter, Cosima von Bülow, became Wagner's second wife in 1870) labored at Weimar with untiring zeal to produce Wagner's works, and how his efforts were at last crowned with success all over Germany in 1849-50. It was a popular triumph. I remember old Cipriani Potter, the friend of Beethoven, saying to me at the time when the English papers teemed with the usual twaddle about Wagner's music being intelligible only to the few, "It is all very well to talk this stuff here, but in Germany it is the people, the common people, who crowd to the theatre when *Tannhäuser* and *Lohengrin* are given." I have noticed the same at the Covent Garden concerts; it was always the pit and gallery who called for the Wagner nights, while the opera which had the great run with Carl Rosa's English company was the *Flying Dutchman*, while *Tannhäuser* and *Lohengrin* at both houses were invariably the crowded nights.

In 1861 the Parisians showed their taste and *chic* by whistling *Tannhäuser* off the stage.

In 1863 Wagner appeared at Vienna, Prague, Leipsic, St. Petersburg, Moscow, Pesth, and conducted concerts with brilliant success. In 1864 his constant friend, the Crown Prince, now Ludwig II. of Bavaria, summoned him to Munich, where the new operas of *Tristan* in 1865, and *Meistersinger* in 1868, *Das Rheingold* in 1869, and *Die Walküre* in 1870, were successively given with ever-increasing appreciation and applause.

The *Meistersinger*, through which there runs a strongly comic vein, deals with the contrast between the old stiff forms of minstrelsy by rule and the spontaneous revolt of a free, musical, and poetical genius, and the work forms a humorous and almost Shakespearian *pendant* to the great and solemn minstrelsy which fills the centre of *Tannhäuser*. In Wagner's opinion it is the opera most likely to find favor with an English audience, a point since established by the German opera performances under Richter.

Tristan and Iseult, in which the drama and analysis of passion—love and death—is wrought up to its highest pitch, was thrown off between the first two and last two great sections of the Tetralogie, and the Tetralogie, itself planned twenty years ago and produced at Bayreuth in 1876, seemed the last most daring and complete manifestation of Wagner's dramatic, poetic, and musical genius, until *Parsifal* revealed still greater heights and depths in 1882.

The purpose and power of that great cycle of Scandinavian and German myths, unrolled in the four colossal dramas of *Rheingold*, *Walküre*, *Siegfried*, and *Gotterdämmerung*, would carry me far beyond the limits of a biographical chapter. Both the *Ring* and the *Parsifal*

I dwell upon at some length in my account of the performances at Bayreuth of 1876, and the memorial performances of 1883.

I will now give a sketch of the general impression that Wagner made upon me and upon others with whom he came in contact, and I shall conclude these biographical pages with a notice of his last days in Venice and his funeral at Bayreuth. Wagner offended a great many people in the course of his life, but then a great many people offended Wagner. Those who hated him lied about him unscrupulously, but not even his worst enemies ever accused Wagner of lying about them. He was an egotist in the sense that he believed in himself; but, then, one must remember that, in his own estimation, for more than forty years, Richard Wagner had been the greatest figure in the musical world, and it took quite thirty years of his life to convince the world of that fact which now, for about a couple of years, we have had proclaimed by all the newspapers of Europe. If in general company his manner was reserved, and even a little acrid, was there not a cause? Such a man, with an immense consciousness of power, meeting with marvellous neglect, and trampled upon, but never crushed, by penury, misfortune, and the bitterest persecution and ridicule, naturally becomes an egotist, and is apt to play the king in disguise, and behave, even in the midst of insult, as if he expected all men to bow down before him; and then as naturally, when at last they do bow down in the most abject of attitudes, he feels a little inclined to kick them.

When I remember that about forty years ago *Rienzi*, and the *Flying Dutchman*, followed by *Tannhäuser* and *Lohengrin*, were finished, that the master—then truly of the future—was patronized here, snubbed there, and supported himself by arranging tunes for the cornet-à-piston and piano ; that he starved a little, was banished for his opinions, nearly shipwrecked, and altogether unable to get anybody except Ferdinand Praeger, Liszt (perhaps M. Sainton and half-a-dozen *intimes*, some of them as unrecognized as himself) to believe in him at all—why, if there ever was a training for egotism, that was ! In fact, for nearly half a century there was no one to believe in Richard Wagner except Richard Wagner. Then, by and by, the crowned heads, and, what was more, the heads of opera-houses, came round, and we had bowing and scraping on all sides ; and connoisseurs arrived, cap in hand, to interview the great man, and tell him to his face, " Richard Wagner, we deem you one of the greatest musicians that ever lived." " Bah !" says Wagner, " I told you that forty years ago ; I can do without you now !" " Oh, fie ! what a vain man !" says your offended aristocrat. I never thought Richard Wagner vain. I knew him to be irritable—so are other people, who only resemble him in that. I knew him to be impatient of interruption—so is your banking-clerk when stopped in the middle of a column of figures. I knew him to be proud—so are many who have nothing to be proud of ; and from the first moment that I heard, now twenty years ago, the prelude to *Lohengrin,* and read a few of his letters on art, I also knew Richard Wagner to be the greatest composer and the most impressive art-personality then in the world.

Wagner's was certainly one of the strongest and most independent natures I ever came across. The ordinary motives which move men had no power with him. He cared neither for money nor for rank, nor for the opinions of his contemporaries. He has been charged with a childish love of display, and it is true that from the simplest and most retiring life he would suddenly pass to the most splendid and imposing scale of living; as when on one occasion he entered Heidelberg in a carriage drawn by four horses with outriders. He was fond of beautiful surroundings, and he would dress expensively; but in these peculiarities any one who understood Wagner would easily see that his excitable and artistic temperament found in these contrasts and accessories the stimulus most favorable to his ceaseless and buoyant productivity, rather than the mere freaks of personal vanity.

Although the most intimate friend of the King of Bavaria, he was not a man whom princes could order about or control. I remember very well his refusing to exhibit himself to order in the box of a certain high personage at the Albert Hall when he was in England, although he readily availed himself of the privilege of visiting Her Majesty at Windsor. Wagner never forgot that the Queen and Prince Albert recognized his genius on the occasion of his first visit to England, and his illustrious patrons were then in a very small minority.

Wagner was adored by his household. He lived for some time at Lucerne in great retirement—he was then working at the *Ring*. A friend who had at that time frequent access to him has given us some charming Wagnerian side-lights. Nervous and intensely impressionable, we are told his sentiments always ran into extremes, but his self-recovery was rapid. He sometimes wounded even his friends by the intense and passionate sincerity of his language; but he atoned so sweetly for a passing heat of temper, that they loved him only the more. "In Wagner," said one of his orchestra at Bayreuth, "it is the second movement that is good."

His life in Switzerland was as regular as it was laborious. He rose at six—bathed—then reclined and read till ten—breakfasted—worked uninterruptedly from eleven till two—dined—rested, always with a book in hand—drove from four till six—worked from six till eight—supped, and spent the evening in the midst of his family.

It was in these evenings that Wagner was most charming. Every cloud was cleared from his brow; his face seemed radiant with a certain light-hearted goodness which diffused a happy atmosphere around him. He had a kind word for every one, he entered into everything, and his conversation scintillated with brilliancy and humor. His boundless liberality sometimes brought him into pecuniary difficulties; he could never bear to see any one in want; he had known too much of it himself.

His poor relatives took advantage of him. His rustic family connections seemed to rise out of the earth wherever he stood, and claim his assistance or protection. They would come on a visit and forget to leave; they would drop in at meal-time; they would use his name, order things of his trades-people and forget to pay travel under his *prestige*, and lodge at his expense.

His heart was larger than his pocket—his generosity far exceeded the discretion of those who traded upon it. A French nobleman, Count Gobineau, said of him, "Herr Wagner will never be perfectly happy, for there will always be some one at his elbow whose suffering or distress he will feel bound to share." As a rule the French spoke no good of Wagner nor Wagner of the French.

I once spent an evening in Paris at Victor Hugo's house. It was not long after the Franco-Prussian War. The talk ran on Wagner. The aged poet at once turned the conversation. Somewhat rashly, perhaps, I ventured to say, "Surely in the great republic of art national or even personal antipathies need not count." Victor Hugo cut me very short. "Monsieur," he said, "il a dit beaucoup de mal de mon pays—il a insulté la France. I cannot hear his music."

In some things Wagner was as simple and tender as a child—so true is it that there is a child-like element in most men of genius. His agility was surprising; he was fond of climbing the trees in his garden. On such occasions Madame Wagner would say to his friends, "I beseech you do not look at him, or encourage him: he will only run greater risks!"

When he was up early he would go round to the other bedroom doors and wake the sleepers by intoning the Marseillaise " (he was a shocking red republican, this bosom friend of the king) to the accompaniment of what has been called the "devil's tattoo."

He was very fond of animals, especially dogs; his favorite dog "Mark" is buried not far from his own grave. The *Meistersinger* was arrested for months in consequence of attentions paid to a poor dog he had met wandering sick and masterless. The ungrateful animal bit his hand, and for months Wagner was unable to hold a pen; but the dog was well cared for.

Like Liszt, he was a strong opponent of vivisection, and was fond of quoting Faust's saying to scientific doctors: "The very dogs wouldn't live in such a world as yours!"

When not absolutely absorbed in his work, he was most thoughtful for others, and was always planning for their comfort and happiness; and, although quick and at times irritable, he could bear suffering calmly. On one occasion a lady remarked that he had been singularly sweet and amiable all day on a pleasure excursion, at a time when he was in actual physical suffering himself. He confessed at the end that he had felt very unwell, but had tried to hide this from those about him for fear of spoiling their enjoyment.

He was naturally adored by his servants, who stayed with him so long that they became like members of the family. He had an extraordinary power of attracting people to his person. There was something irresistibly magnetic about that brilliant eye, that noble, penetrating look, that insatiable and unresting vigor of emotion and intellect.

Liszt, de Bülow, Richter, Wilhelmj, and all his staff of artists, were absolutely devoted to him, and gave him years of willing service which no money could have paid for or secured. The talented painter, Paul Toukowski, left his atelier at Naples to come and live at Bayreuth and paint the *Parsifal* scenery; and what scenery it is! What a dream of summer-land is the moor and woodland in the domain of Montsalvat! What a majestic and gorgeous hall, of more than Eastern magnificence, is that in which the mystery of the Sangrail is enacted! What dim forests, what enchanted caves, what massive walls and battlements, what enchanted bowers, what more than tropical bloom and foliage! It was long before the artist could satisfy Wagner with that magic garden. The master would have the flowers as large as the girls, and he would have the girls exactly like the flowers. It was difficult; but it is enough to say that Wagner willed it, and it was done.

His influence with the actors was supreme; never would they have attempted for another what they did for him. The Rhine girls were terrified at the cages in which they had to be swung up and down in the Rhine depths, singing all the time. They refused at first to face a situation which appeared more fit for acrobats than for dramatic artists. They would not get into their cages at all, until the master, with tears in his eyes, besought them to try, and then all went easily, and more than well.

Madame Titiens had scruples at first about the Wagnerian parts as unsingable, but in her latter days she was quite "fanatisée" about the part of Ortrud, in which she was superb, and she used to declare the Wagner's rôles gave her the fullest and freest scope for her vocalization and acting. The singer Schnor, who was identified with the part of Tristran, when he was told on his death-bed of the preparations for the performance of the *Niebelungen Ring* at Bayreuth, exclaimed—it was his last regret—"Then, after all, I shall never sing Siegfried."

I confess I came fully under Wagner's spell—I spent a delightful evening at his house in 1876. It was at the close of the first Bayreuth festival. All the corps dramatic were present—Richter, the conductor, was chatting with Wilhelmj, the leader of the orchestra, when I went up to him and asked him whether he had recruited his strength well at Nuremberg. There a few nights before I had met him in company with Professor Ella, and in the quiet old city of Albert Dürer—whither he had escaped for a rest between the continued performances of the *Ring*—we had spent an evening over a good bottle of Rhine wine, amid the fumes of those detestable black cheroots which Liszt was so fond of.

Then I caught sight of Walter Bache, who introduced me to Liszt; and presently Richter took me up and presented me to Wagner.

His face beamed with kindness and geniality; he

spoke French, said he had been in England long, long ago, and would perhaps come again. He had great doubts whether the English were sufficiently serious in art ever to appreciate his *Ring*, and seemed pleased when I told him of the great popularity of his music at the Promenade Concerts, and the increasing appreciation of *Lohengrin* and *Tannhäuser*. "Earlier works," he said, shrugging his shoulders.

And Materna, the unique Brünnhilde, was there. Wagner had taken endless trouble in forming her for the *Niebelungen Ring* and the great part she was to play; and master and pupil always entertained the liveliest admiration and affection for each other, which sometimes took an amusing and demonstrative form. That night, when Brünnhilde, an immense woman, arrived *en grande toilette*, and wearing some of her best jewels, she bore directly down upon Wagner—a spare, short, fragile little man. Her enormous bulk seemed to extinguish him for a moment. On reaching him with difficulty in the midst of the glittering crowd she embraced him rapturously—German fashion—with "Ach, Herr Wagner!"

Wagner stood it like a man; but toward the close of the evening I beheld the Materna bearing down upon him again, and as she neared him he held up both his hands energetically repelling a second attack, "Nein, nein, Frau Materna, das will ich gar nicht," and poor Brünnhilde had to put up with a hand-shake instead.

I saw him again in England—it was on that very evening he declined to go with me to be presented to a Royal Princess at the house of a well-known nobleman. If I have cause to regret that circumstance I have also cause to remember that evening with some satisfaction—not only did I hear him read one act of his *Parsifal*, but I received from him a singular token of personal regard. I remember Liszt telling me with some pride how he had received the celebrated "Kiss of Beethoven"—Beethoven was not in the habit, it seems, of embracing people. I now recall with a feeling of singular satisfaction the occasion on which Wagner favored me in the same way, with a kiss.

He advanced toward me as I suddenly entered the room, with "Ach mein lieber Herr Haweis, was haben Sie den über mich schön geschrieben!" and so saying, taking me by both elbows, he saluted me on both cheeks in the orthodox manner.

Wagner's friendship with the king of Bavaria had no doubt contributed largely to the realization of all his plans during his own lifetime. The notion of building a special theatre where the orchestra should be out of sight—the seats arranged tier above tier, with a single row of boxes and a gallery above them—had been long in his mind.

The king was anxious for the theatre to be in Munich; but the opposition of the court, on account of Wagner's political opinions, was then too great. Later on the hotel-keepers offered to build a theatre there on their own account, and to carry out Wagner's plans free of charge as a speculation.

Wagner declined. He chose Bayreuth. He was beholden to none save the king and his own followers. They had stood by him, rehearsed his fame, produced his works, and they built his theatre; but every detail was directed by Wagner, and the perfection which the Bayreuth performances have at last reached is due to the same exhaustive and unremitting personal care.

It was only natural that the master should yield the bâton to a friend like Richter, whose experience, physique, and consummate talent would enable him to perfect the executive part of the work; but it was my privilege in England to see Wagner himself conduct some of his own music at the Albert Hall. Some said he had already lost nerve as a conductor, and, indeed, had never possessed the requisite patience. That may have been to some extent true, but it did not strike me. I went home and wrote the following note, which I see no reason to alter now:

"Wagner's notion is evidently not to rave, but to command, and to deal with his men as one who gives them credit for knowing their own business, instead of treating them like a set of raw recruits, who have to be bullied, shouted at, sworn to, and licked into shape from end to end. The most intense power, concentration, and active energy is often the most silent. Look at the silent, irresistible weight of the fly-wheel that drives the machinery of a large manufactory, or the noiseless swing of the steam-hammer, or the intense, but silent, and apparently motionless vigor of the poised eagle, or the rapt calmness of a Moltke, who watches from the hill-side every evolution of the troops inspired by him. Only occasionally does he raise his telescope, pointing his hand, or sending out scouts and subalterns; and in proportion as all goes well, is fitly inspired, is the embodiment of his will—is he calm. So the 'listless' Wagner sits and orders his band, and they know his mind and obey his look, and heed his smallest gesture, often even quite unperceived by the audience; and this worries the critics. With the best intentions they can't make it out, who are used to their hop, skip, and a jump, and their one, two, three, and away conductors! Doubtless; but the old man wins."

A French critic has since written: "Wagner plays

on the orchestra as though it were a gigantic fiddle, with a firmness of touch which never fails him, and sovereign authority before which all are happy in bowing down. To have an idea of so extraordinary a conductor, one must have seen him." I do not therefore imply that Wagner in his last years was fitted to go through the kind of drudgery which Richter willingly undertook, and which culminated in the triumph of 1876 at Bayreuth.

The close of Wagner's life was crowned by the two great Olympian-like festivals in 1876 and 1882. The Memorial Festival in 1883 was his requiem; while the whole of the city was resounding with his name and fame, the great master's body lay at rest in a funereal bower adjoining the Neue Schloss. The event of 1876 was, I suppose, unprecedented in the annals of Modern Art. I have devoted to it a separate notice. It was my privilege to witness the first unfolding of those four colossal musical dramas of the *Niebelung's Ring* on the Bayreuth stage. People had assembled from all parts of the civilized world; kings, princes, and nobles mingled in that motley throng. The dramas lasted every day from four till ten, with intervals of an hour between the acts. The whole population lived only in the life of that great cycle of tragedies in which gods, demi-gods, and mortals acted out, with more than earthly intensity, the perennially interesting dramas of human life and passion.

It was between the festival of 1876 at Bayreuth, and the performance of *Parsifal* in 1882, that Wagner came to England to assist at the presentation of the *Ring* music at the Albert Hall. He was shaken in health, and exceedingly indisposed to take any exertion not directly bearing upon his work—which was the new

Parsifal drama. He was not satisfied with his reception at the Albert Hall. He was much courted in society, but avoided anything like public receptions, and was considered over-retiring and reticent by casual observers.

Wagner died suddenly on the 13th of February, 1883, at Venice, whither he had come to recruit after the *Parsifal* performances in 1882, and to prepare for their renewal in the following year. He was cut off in the full vigor of his productive genius. Time had not dimmed his eye, nor shaken his hand, nor closed a single channel of thought or emotion. He sank thus suddenly in the spring of the year 1883, not without some warning, yet enjoying life up to its latest hour. "I will bear no longer the gray clouds and wintry skies of Bayreuth," he had said to his friends in the autumn of 1882.

A suite of apartments in the Palace Vendramin at Venice had been secured for him, and his children—Daniel, Eva, Isolde, and Siegfried (now twelve years old)—were already there. Venice was in the greatest excitement on his arrival. Italy had been in the strangest way won over to Wagner at Bologna, under the able and enthusiastic bâton of a lamented maestro ; indeed, Liszt told me he had never heard Wagner's operas more effectively given, except at Bayreuth.

It was Wagner's desire to be left quiet at Venice, and his wishes were sedulously respected ; but he was never inaccessible, and he was often to be found in the Café, surrounded by a group of friends. The first remark of the Venetians who saw that spare, vivid figure, with flashing eye, and who heard the master's eager, eloquent conversation, full of wit and geniality, was, "Why, he is not an old man at all !" It is true, there is something of the eternal child—an *afflatus* of divine youth—about all great genius.

Wagner rose in Italy at Venice between five and six, and worked till ten. In Venice he wrote his last art criticisms; and while the Italian newspapers affirmed that he was already at work upon a drama connected with Buddha and the great Aryan legends, the German prints declared that he had turned his attention toward Greece, and was going to Athens to try and recover on the spot something connected with the ancient Greek music. At the same time he was indefatigable in his efforts to prepare for the repetitions of *Parsifal* in 1883, at which he intended to be present and which were carried out at Bayreuth with such magnificent success—July, 1883—in sad memory of his death.

He was already suffering from heart-disease, and sat usually—the weather being chilly—in his fur coat. A glass of wine was always at hand, and when he suffered pain he would sip cognac.

His rooms, however, before breakfast were sacred, and his wife Cosima scrupulously respected them; but at ten o'clock she went in to bring him his letters, and after a short private chat the family breakfasted together. Wagner would then take his hat and go down the marble steps looking out upon the canal, and ask his gondolier about the weather. If too cold to venture out he would stroll forth, often with his wife, and go into Lavenna's, the pastry-cook's, and buy bonbons for the children.

Between four and six o'clock he might often be seen in the arcades and streets, with all the family, buying little presents for friends, or sipping coffee or the good fresh beer beloved of all true Germans. The military band which played occasionally in the great square had produced a version of the *Lohengrin* overture in his honor, but played it in such fashion that poor Wagner was constrained to take refuge in the pastry-cook's shop and stop his ears with both hands.

On another occasion, however, he went up to the bandmaster, in his great coat and slouched hat, and asked him to play something out of Rossini's *Gazza Ladra.* The conductor, not recognizing Wagner, answered civilly that he had none of the music there, and otherwise could not well derange the programme. On Wagner retiring a musician told the bandmaster who the stranger was. Filled with confusion and regret, the worthy man instantly sent for copies of the *Gazza Ladra* selection, and played it for two consecutive days. Wagner was much pleased, and, again going up to the band, expressed his thanks, and praised especially the solo cornet, who had much distinguished himself.

The master dined early in the afternoon, and usually took a short nap afterward, the faithful Betty Burkel, a confidential family servant, always being at hand in the next room, knitting quietly.

At half-past three the gondolier was usually in attendance, and in fine weather the Lido, the public gardens, the San Lazzaro, and Giudecca were visited.

In the milder autumn days of 1882, Wagner, whose breathing was occasionally oppressed, seemed to inhale new health and vigor out upon the wide lagunes. "Ah!" he would say, drawing a long breath; "no smoke, no dust!" At night his sitting-rooms were a blaze of light with quantities of wax-candles. People used to look up at Byron's quarters when he was in Venice, and wonder what festival could be going on. The waters of the Grand Canal were all aglow, but it was only Byron, alone with the MSS. of *Manfred*, *Parisina*, and *Don Juan*. Wagner's old porter happened to be a brother to Byron's old servant, Fido. "There is something like Byron about this great German," he remarked. "What is that?" they asked. "Why, he has the same marvellous need of wax-candles!" "Where light is, there is joy," Wagner used to say, quoting the Italian proverb.

As the evenings drew on, Wagner used to read aloud to his family—usually from some dramatic author. He sometimes got so excited that the good people in the house knocked at the door to know if anything ailed the master?

When absorbed in thought, he was in the habit of pacing up and down the room, with his hands behind him. He even had pockets made at the back of his coat. Dr. Keppler said this position of the arms allowed him to breathe more freely, and eased the diseased action of the heart.

On November 19th, 1882, Liszt came to see him at Venice. The two old men embraced each other affectionately on the marble stairs. They sat long hours together in deep and friendly converse. Joukovski, the artist, who had painted the *Parsifal* scenery, and for whom the genius of Wagner had an irresistible attraction, was also there. He painted a remarkable portrait of Liszt, and a "Sacred Family" of Jesus, Joseph, and Mary. The guardian angels in the air above were all portraits of Wagner's children.

Liszt was usually up at four o'clock, and both Wagner and Liszt got through a great deal of serious work in those small hours.

Wagner's personal popularity at Venice was extraordinary. In a short time he and every member of his family were known even to the children of the poor. The master was open-handed and sympathetic to all.

He seemed ever about—now with his wife, or with little Eva, his pet daughter, or Siegfried. He mixed with the people, chatted and joked, and was ever ready to relieve the poor. He was worshipped by his gondoliers. "He patted me on the back," said one, "asked me if I was tired, and said, '*Amico mio*, so the Carnival has come to an end.'" The man repeated the incident everywhere, as if it had been the great event of his life. "They say he is greater than a king; isn't it so?" (*Egli e piu di un re, discono non e' vero?*) was the common talk in the streets as he passed.

On December 23d, 1882, Wagner conducted his earliest symphony at the request of a small circle of friends in celebration of Madame Wagner's birthday. On taking the bâton he turned to the musicians and said:

"This is the last time I shall ever conduct."

"Why?" they asked.

"Because I shall soon die."

This was not at all his usual mood; he spoke sometimes of living till ninety—he said that he could hardly finish the work he had in his mind even then. His doctor knew that his heart-disease must one day carry him off, but hoped the end might be delayed for five or six years at least. He was very sanguine himself, but not over-prudent. He took too much tea and coffee and stimulant; he was deaf to all warnings, and joked on the doctors forbidding their patients to indulge in these things without setting them a good example. But there were moments when his words, spoken lightly, were unconsciously prophetic of the coming end. He had taken the utmost delight in the Carnival of 1883 at Venice, and on the first day of Lent said to his gondolier, "And where is it the fashion to go to-day?" "To the new necropolis, my gracious master," replied the man. Arrived at the necropolis, Wagner alighted and walked all over the place, admiring the quiet and reposeful niches and the tastefully laid-out lawns and shrubberies.

"And was my worshipful sir pleased?" asked the gondolier.

"Yes, uncommonly," replied Wagner; "and I shall soon find some such quiet spot for my own last resting-place."

Indeed, there were mornings when he would go out and return breathless in ten minutes. Once at his banker's, and again at the pastry-cook's, he was seized with faintness and put into his gondola. He urgently begged that his family might not be told of this. They had their own misgivings. When alone he had been overheard groaning, and was found sometimes with his hand pressed to his heart; but he would rally and make light of it, and soon seemed quite well again; indeed, on the 12th (he died on the 13th) he said he felt better than he had for weeks—the breathing was freer and the pulse regular.

February 13th came black with clouds. The rain poured in torrents. Wagner rose as usual, and announced his wish not to be disturbed till dinner-time, two o'clock. He had much to do—much to finish— overmuch indeed, and the time was short.

The master did not feel quite well, and Cosima, his wife, bade Betty, the servant, take her work and not leave the ante-room in case her master should call or ring.

The faithful creature seemed to have some presentiment that all was not right. She listened hour after hour—heard the master striding up and down as was his wont.

Wife Cosima came in from time to time. "The

master works ever," said Betty, "and has not called for anything—now he walks to and fro."

At one o'clock Wagner rang his bell and asked: "Is the gondola ordered at four o'clock? Good; then I will take a plate of soup up here, for I don't feel very well."

There was nothing unusual about this, for when absorbed in work he would often thus have his light luncheon alone.

The servant brought in a plate of soup and retired. All seemed quiet for some time. Then suddenly a hurried pacing up and down the room was heard. The footsteps ceased—a sharp cough, checked. Betty threw down her work, walked on tip-toe to the door, and listened with all her ears. She heard one deep groan; she stood for a moment divided between a resolve to call Cosima or break through her master's orders and go into his room at once. The suspense was soon over. "Betty!" It was Wagner's voice, very faint. Betty rushed in. Wagner was leaning back on his sofa, his fur coat was half off, his feet rested on a footstool. His face was fearfully changed—his features cadaverous and drawn down with pain evidently; with the utmost difficulty he contrived to murmur, but almost inaudibly, "Call my wife and the doctor." He never spoke again.

The terrified Betty rushed off to tell wife Cosima. The instant she saw him she cried, "To the doctor, Betty!" Dr. Keppler was sent for three times; at last he was found just finishing an operation. Meanwhile Madame Wagner had sat down by her husband. He immediately laid his head on her shoulder, groaning, but speechless; and she placed her arms about him, and with one hand rubbed his heart, an act which had sometimes eased him when in pain. His breathing grew softer and lighter, and presently he seemed to subside into a quiet, motionless sleep. She thought it a good sign.

About half an hour afterward the doctor came. One glance was enough. He found Madame Wagner still holding her husband in both her arms, with his head resting on her shoulder. "He sleeps," she said—and the good doctor, suppressing his emotion with a great effort, did not tell her that it was the sleep of death, and that now for a long time she had been embracing a corpse.

Dr. Keppler, after feeling for the pulse that was never to beat again, gently took the body of Wagner in both his arms and carried it to his bed. It could not be called his death-bed, for Wagner died as he had lived, working—the table before him was strewn with books and MSS., with the ink scarcely dry upon the last page.

Dr. Keppler then turned to Cosima and said, with irrepressible emotion, "He is dead!" The poor wife, who had been so absolutely one in body, soul, and mind with her husband, fell prostrate with a great cry upon his lifeless body, nor for some time could any persuasion induce her to leave the corpse, which she continued to embrace.

But over the intense sorrow of this true-hearted and affectionate German family I will draw the veil. The servants all seemed to lose their heads. A vast crowd had by this time assembled outside the palace "Vendramin." The bulletin had flown through Venice, "Richard Wagner is very ill—the doctor is at his bedside." No more than this was known in the town at half-past four. At half-past five Dr. Keppler came down the steps and was greeted with shouts of "The doctor! the doctor!" In the dead silence which followed, Dr. Keppler, uncovering his head, said, "Richard Wagner is dead. He died an hour ago from the effects of heart-disease."

No sooner had Dr. Keppler pronounced the words, "Richard Wagner is dead!" from the steps of the "Vendramin Palace," than the vast throng assembled outside to hear the news dispersed with cries of "Dead! dead!" and in a short time there was not a café in Venice without the bulletin, "*Riccardo Wagner, il famoso tedesco, il gran Maestro del Vendramin, è morto.*" It was commonly said that since Garibaldi's death no such sensation had been felt in Venice.

The gondolier who had been ordered by Wagner at four o'clock had been in attendance ever since. Poor Luigi heard the news in speechless astonishment and grief; at last, breaking out in sobs, he exclaimed, "Ah! to think that only yesterday I rowed him in this gondola—the good, noble, great man, who never said an unkind word to any of us, although he was so ill! Here, here is his name;" and he held up his ivory-handled walking-stick with the initials "R. W." "And now he must needs die—*Per Bacco!* Poor dear man! how many people in this world could have been better spared!" Luigi also took care of a little kitten which had become a pet of Wagner's, having been rescued by him from an untimely end in the canal. "See," he would say, "even this kitten he saved from drowning two months ago knows what it has lost. It will hardly move; it lies always here in the gondola, just behind where the master used to sit."

Ill news in these days of telegraphy flies indeed apace. The wires were blocked. In the course of the week no less than five thousand despatches of condolence reached Venice, addressed to the Wagner family, from all parts of the civilized world.

Soon after death Wagner's body was embalmed by his devoted medical attendant, Dr. Keppler, and a cast of his face was taken by Signor Benvenuto.

The bronze coffin which arrived from Vienna was carried upstairs by Hans Richter, the painter Joukovsky, Dr. Keppler, Passini, and Ruben; and the dead master was borne to his funereal gondola by the same devoted friends. The general expressions of sympathy were confined to no class.

The Italian Government had offered the family a public ceremony, which was declined; yet I know not what greater honor could have been paid him than the spontaneous grief of all Venice. The high municipal officers, the chief nobles, and an immense throng accompanied the gondola to the station. The canals were crowded with gondolas draped in crape.

In all the ports through which the coffin passed the flags floated half-mast high. At every town where there was a stoppage the municipalities sent deputations, and the coffin was strewn with fresh flowers.

At the head of the bier there was one enormous wreath, sent by the King of Bavaria, Wagner's close friend, and at Munich the king sent his representative to accompany the funeral *cortège* to Bayreuth.

I will not dwell further upon the honors paid by the way, the processions of musical societies, the numberless wreaths, which by the time the coffin reached Bayreuth amounted to fourteen hundred and filled two large cars.

On the 17th the bier was received at the station by the inhabitants of Bayreuth *en masse*. It was a solemn moment when the widow and her children stepped out of their carriage, and all the people silently uncovered their heads.

A brigade of firemen moved in front of the hearse, which was drawn by four black horses. All the gas lamps were lighted along the road, and black pennons streamed from tall poles to right and left. Midway a fresh wreath arrived from the king with a large inscription, " *To the Deathless One*," and at the same time the burgomaster laid another one on the coffin in the name of the city of Bayreuth.

Arrived at Wagner's house, " Vahnfried "—only a select company were admitted to the garden—the coffin rested for a space at the entrance, but was not taken into the house.

It was Madame Wagner's express wish that no speeches or prayers should be made at the grave—which had long since been dug, by Wagner's orders, in a retired spot of his own garden, surrounded by thick bushes and fir-trees. A simple blessing in the name of the Church was to be given, and the coffin then lowered in silence.

An immense slab of gray polished granite rested above it, and the vault door was to be opened on one side. Hither was the body now brought by a silent and sorrowing throng of attached friends—among them Liszt, Bülow, Richter, Joukovsky, and many more. On either side walked Wagner's children, and when the coffin was about to be slid into the grave, they mounted on the gray slab above it and knelt down.

At this moment Wagner's two favorite dogs burst through the thickets, and sprang toward the children to seek their usual caresses—they, too, had lost a kind master, but they knew it not.

Then Herr Caselmann, in the simplest words, committed the departed, and all his family, to the care of Christ, and blessed the assembly and the grave in the name of the Church. This was all in exact accordance with Madame Wagner's wishes. A few took a leaf or a flower as it fell from the piled-up heap, and the body was lowered silently into its last resting-place—earth to earth—dust to dust!

* * * * * *

I visited Bayreuth on the 24th of July, 1883, and attended two crowded performances of Wagner's last work, *Parsifal*. In the morning I went into the beautiful gardens of the Neue Schloss. On either side of a lake, upon which float a couple of swans and innumerable water-lilies, the long park-like avenues of trees are vocal with wild doves, and the robin is heard in the adjoining thickets. At my approach the sweet song ceases abruptly, and the startled bird flies out, scattering the pale petals of the wild roses upon my path. I follow a stream of people on foot, as they move down the left-hand avenue in the garden of the Neue Schloss, which adjoins Wagner's own grounds.

Some are going—some are coming. Presently I see an opening in the bushes on my left; the path leads me to a clump of evergreens. I follow it, and come suddenly on the great composer's grave. All about the green square mound the trees are thick—laurel, fir, and yew. The shade falls funereally across the immense gray granite slab; but over the dark foliage the sky is bright blue, and straight in front of me, above the low bushes, I can see the bow-windows of the dead master's study—where I spent with him one delightful evening in 1876.

I can see, too, the jet of water that he loved playing high above the hedge of evergreen. It lulls me with its sound. "Vahnfried! Vahnfried!" it seems to murmur. It was the word written above the master's house

—the word he most loved—the word his tireless spirit most believed in. How shall I render it? "Dream-life! dream-life! Earth's illusion of joy!"

Great spirit! thy dream-life here is past, and face to face with truth, "rapt from the fickle and the frail," for thee the illusion has vanished! Mayest thou also know the fulness of joy in the unbroken and serene activities of the eternal Reality!

I visited the grave twice. There is nothing written on the granite slab. There were never present less than twenty persons, and a constant stream of pilgrims kept coming and going.

One gentle token of the master's pitiful and tender regard for the faithful dumb animals he so loved lies but a few feet off in the same garden, and not far from his own grave.

Upon a mossy bank, surrounded with evergreens, is a small marble slab, with this inscription to his favorite dog:

"*Here lies in peace 'Vahnfried's' faithful watcher and friend—the good and beautiful Mark*" (der gute, schöne Mark)!

I returned, too, to Wagner's tomb, plucked a branch of the fir-tree that waved above it, and went back to my room to prepare myself by reading and meditation for the great religious drama which I was to witness at four o'clock in the afternoon—Wagner's latest and highest inspiration—the story of the sacred brotherhood, the knights of San Graal—*Parsifal!*

CHAPTER VI.

PARSIFAL.

THE blood of God!—mystic symbol of divine life—
"for the blood is the life thereof." That is the keynote of *Parsifal*, the Knight of the Sangrail. Wine is the ready symbolical vehicle—the material link between the divine and the human life. In the old religions, that heightened consciousness, that intensity of feeling produced by stimulant, was thought to be the very entering in of the "god"—the union of the divine and human spirit; and in the Eleusinian mysteries, the "sesame"—the bread of Demeter, the earth mother, and the "kykeon," or wine of Dionysos—the vine god —were thus sacramental.

The passionate desire to approach and mingle with Deity is the one mystic bond common to all religions in all lands. It is the "cry of the human;" it traverses the ages, it exhausts many symbols and transcends all forms.

To the Christian it is summed up in the "Lord's Supper."

The mediæval legend of the Sangrail (real or royal blood) is the most poetic and pathetic form of transubstantiation; in it the gross materialism of the Roman Mass almost ceases to be repulsive; it possesses the true legendary power of attraction and assimilation.

As the Knights of the Table Round, with their holy vows, provided mediæval Chivalry with a centre, so did the Lord's table, with its Sangrail, provide mediæval Religion with its central attractive point. And as all marvellous tales of knightly heroism circled round King Arthur's table, so did the great legends embodying the Christian conceptions of sin, punishment, and redemption circle round the Sangrail and the sacrifice of the "Mass."

In the legends of *Parsifal* and *Lohengrin*, the knightly and religious elements are welded together. This is enough. We need approach *Parsifal* with no deep knowledge of the various Sagas made use of by Wagner in his drama. His disciples, while most eager to trace its various elements to their sources, are most emphatic in declaring that the *Parsifal* drama, so intimately true to the spirit of Roman Catholicism, is nevertheless a new creation.

Joseph of Arimathea received in a crystal cup the blood of Christ as it flowed from the spear-wound made by the Roman soldier. The cup and the spear were committed to Titurel, who became a holy knight and head of a sacred brotherhood of knights. They dwelt in the Vizigoth Mountains of Southern Spain, where, amidst impenetrable forests, rose the legendary palace of Montsalvat. Here they guarded the sacred relics, issuing forth at times from their palatial fortress, like Lohengrin, to fight for innocence and right, and always returning to renew their youth and strength by the celestial contemplation of the Sangrail, and by occasional participation in the holy feast.

Time and history count for very little in these narratives. It was allowed, however, that Titurel the Chief had grown extremely aged, but it was not allowed that he could die in the presence of the Sangrail. He seemed to have been laid in a kind of trance, resting in an open tomb beneath the altar of the Grail ; and whenever the cup was uncovered his voice might be heard joining in the celebration. Meanwhile, Amfortis, his son, reigned in his stead.

Montsalvat, with its pure, contemplative, but active brotherhood, and its mystic cup, thus stands out as the poetic symbol of all that is highest and best in mediæval Christianity.

The note of the wicked world—Magic for Devotion—Sensuality for Worship—breaks in upon our vision, as the scene changes from the Halls of Montsalvat to Klingsor's palace. Klingsor, an impure knight, who has been refused admittance to the order of the "Sangrail," enters into a compact with the powers of evil—by magic acquires arts of diabolical fascination—fills his palace and gardens with enchantments, and wages bitter war against the holy knights, with a view of corrupting them, and ultimately, it may be, of acquiring for himself the "Sangrail," in which all power is believed to reside. Many knights have already succumbed to the "insidious arts" of Klingsor ; but the tragical turning point of the *Parsifal* is that Amfortis, himself the son of Titurel, the official guardian of the Grail, in making war upon the magician, took with him the sacred spear, and *lost* it to Klingsor.

It came about in this way. A woman of unearthly loveliness won him in the enchanted bowers, adjoining the evil knight's palace, and Klingsor, seizing the holy spear, thrust it into Amfortis's side, inflicting therewith an incurable wound. The brave knight, Gurnemanz, dragged his master fainting from the garden, his companions of the Sangrail covering their retreat. But, returned to Montsalvat, the unhappy king awakes only to bewail his sin, the loss of the sacred spear, and the ceaseless harrowing smart of an incurable wound. But who is Parsifal?

* * * * * *

The smell of pine-woods in July! The long avenue outside the city of Bayreuth, that leads straight up the hill, crowned by the Wagner Theatre, a noble structure — architecturally admirable — severe, simple, but exactly adapted to its purpose. I join the stream of pilgrims, some in carriages, others on foot. As we approach, a clear blast of trombones and brass from the terrace in front of the grand entrance plays out the Grail "motive." It is the well-known signal—there is no time to be lost. I enter at the prescribed door, and find myself close to my appointed place. Every one— such is the admirable arrangement—seems to do likewise. In a few minutes about one thousand persons are seated without confusion. The theatre is darkened, the foot-lights are lowered, the prelude begins.

Act I.

The waves of sound rise from the shadowy gulf sunken between the audience and the foot-lights. Upon the sound ocean of "wind" the "Take, eat," or "Love-feast" motive floats. Presently the strings pierce through it, the Spear motive follows, and then, full of heavy pain, "Drink ye all of this," followed by the famous Grail motive—an old chorale also used by Mendelssohn in the Reformation Symphony. Then comes the noble Faith and Love theme.

As I sit in the low light, amidst the silent throng, and listen, I need no interpreter, I am being placed in possession of the emotional key-notes of the drama. Every subject is first distinctly enunciated, and then all are wondrously blended together. There is the pain of sacrifice—the mental agony, the bodily torture; there are the alternate pauses of Sorrow and respite from sorrow long drawn out, the sharp ache of Sin, the glimpses of unhallowed Joy, the strain of upward Endeavor, the serene peace of Faith and Love, crowned by the blessed Vision of the Grail. 'Tis past. The prelude melts into the opening recitative.

The eyes have now to play their part. The curtain rises, the story begins. The morning breaks slowly, the gray streaks redden, a lovely summer landscape lies bathed in primrose light. Under the shadow of a noble tree, the aged knight, Gurnemanz, has been resting with two young attendants. From the neighboring halls of Montsalvat the solemn *reveillé*—the Grail motive—rings out, and all three sink on their knees in prayer. The sun bursts forth in splendor, as the hymn rises to mingle with the voices of universal nature. The waves of sound well up and fill the soul with unspeakable thankfulness and praise.

The talk is of Amfortis, the king, and of his incurable wound. A wild gallop, a rush of sound, and a weird woman, with streaming hair, springs toward the startled group. She bears a phial, with rare balsam from the Arabian shores. It is for the king's wound. Who is the wild horsewoman ?—Kundry—strange creation—a being doomed to wander, like the Wandering Jew, the wild Huntsman, or Flying Dutchman, always seeking a deliverance she cannot find—Kundry, who, in ages gone by met the Saviour on the road to Calvary, and derided him. Some said she was Herodias's daughter. Now filled with remorse, yet weighted with sinful longings, she serves by turns the Knights of the Grail, then falls under the spell of Klingsor, the evil knight sorcerer, and, in the guise of an enchantress, is compelled by him to seduce, if possible, the Knights of the Grail.

Eternal symbol of the divided allegiance of a woman's soul! She it was who, under the sensual spell, as an incarnation of loveliness, overcame Amfortis, and she it is now who, in her ardent quest for salvation, changed and squalid in appearance, serves the Knights of the Grail, and seeks to heal Amfortis's wound!

No sooner has she delivered her balsam to the faithful Gurnemanz, and thrown herself exhausted upon the grass—where she lies gnawing her hair morosely—than a change in the sound atmosphere, which never ceases to be generated in the mystic orchestral gulf, presages the approach of Amfortis.

He comes, borne on a litter, to his morning bath in the shining lake hard by. Sharp is the pain of the wound—weary and hopeless is the king. Through the Wound-motive comes the sweet woodland music and the breath of the blessed morning, fragrant with flowers and fresh with dew. It is one of those incomparable bursts of woodland notes, full of bird-song and the happy hum of insect life and rustling of netted branches and waving of long tasselled grass. I know of nothing like it save the forest music in *Siegfried*.

The sick king listens, and remembers words of hope and comfort that fell from a heavenly voice, what time the glory of the Grail passed—

"Durch mitleid Wissend	"Wait for my chosen one,
Der reine Thor,	Guileless and innocent,
Harre sein	
Den ich erkor."	Pity-enlightened."

They hand him the phial of balsam; and presently,

while the lovely forest music again breaks forth, the king is carried on to his bath, and Kundry, Gurnemanz, and the two esquires hold the stage.

As the old knight, who is a complete repertory of facts connected with the Grail tradition, unfolds to the esquires the nature of the king's wound, the sorceries of Klingsor, the hope of deliverance from some unknown "guileless one," a sudden cry breaks up the situation.

A white swan, pierced by an arrow, flutters dying to the ground. It is the swan beloved of the Grail brotherhood, bird of fair omen, symbol of spotless purity. The slayer is brought in between two knights—a stalwart youth, fearless, unabashed, while the death-music of the swan, the slow distilling and stiffening of its life-blood, is marvellously rendered by the orchestra. Conviction of his fault comes over the youth as he listens to the reproaches of Gurnemanz. He hangs his head, ashamed and penitent, and at last with a sudden passion of remorse snaps his bow, and flings it aside. The swan is borne off, and Parsifal (the "guileless one," for he it is), with Gurnemanz and Kundry—who rouses herself and surveys Parsifal with strange, almost savage curiosity—hold the stage.

In this scene Kundry tells the youth more than he cares to hear about himself: how his father, Gamuret, was a great knight killed in battle; how his mother, Herzeleide (Heart's Affliction), fearing a like fate for her son, brought him up in the lonely forest; how he left her to follow a troop of knights that he met one day winding through the forest glade, and being led on and on in pursuit of them, never overtook them and never returned to his mother, Heart's Affliction, who died of grief. At this point the frantic youth seizes Kundry by the throat in an agony of rage and grief, but is held back by Gurnemanz, till, worn out by the violence of his emotion, he faints away, and is gradually revived by Kundry and Gurnemanz.

Suddenly Kundry rises with a wild look, like one under a spell. Her mood of service is over. She staggers across the stage—she can hardly keep awake. "Sleep," she mutters, "I must sleep—sleep!" and falls down in one of those long trances which apparently lasted for months, or years, and formed the transition periods between her mood of Grail service and the Klingsor slavery into which she must next relapse in spite of herself.

And is this the guileless one? This wild youth who slays the fair swan—who knows not his own name nor whence he comes, nor whither he goes, nor what are his destinies? The old knight eyes him curiously—he will put him to the test. This youth had seen the king pass once—he had marked his pain. Was he "enlightened by pity"? Is he the appointed deliverer? The old knight now invites him to the shrine of the Grail. "What is the Grail?" asks the youth. Truly a guileless, innocent one! yet a brave and pure knight, since he has known no evil, and so readily repents of a fault committed in ignorance.

Gurnemanz is strangely drawn to him. He shall see the Grail, and in the Holy Palace, what time the mystic light streams forth and the assembled knights bow themselves in prayer, the voice which comforted Amfortis shall speak to his deliverer and bid him arise and heal the king.

* * * * * *

Gurnemanz and Parsifal have ceased to speak. They stand in the glowing light of the summer-land. The tide of music rolls on continuously, but sounds more strange and dreamy.

* * * * * *

Is it a cloud passing over the sky? There seems to be a shuddering in the branches—the light fades upon yonder sunny woodlands—the foreground darkens apace. The whole scene is moving, but so slowly that it seems to change like a dissolving view. I see the two figures of Gurnemanz and Parsifal moving through the trees—they are lost behind yonder rock. They emerge farther off—higher up. The air grows very dim; the orchestra peals louder and louder. I lose the two in the deepening twilight. The forest is changing, the land is wild and mountainous. Huge galleries and arcades, rock-hewn, loom through the dim forest; but all is growing dark. I listen to the murmurs of the "Grail," the "Spear," the "Pain," the "Love and Faith" motives—hollow murmurs, confused, floating out of the depths of lonely caves. Then I have a feeling of void and darkness, and there comes a sighing as of a soul swooning away in a trance, and a vision of waste places and wild caverns; and then through the confused dream I hear the solemn boom of mighty bells, only muffled. They keep time as to some ghostly march. I strain my eyes into the thick gloom before me. Is it a rock, or forest, or palace?

As the light returns slowly, a hall of more than Alhambra-like splendor opens before me. My eyes are riveted on the shining pillars of variegated marble, the tessellated pavements, the vaulted roof glowing with gold and color; beyond, arcades of agate columns, bathed in a misty moonlight air, and lost in a bewildering perspective of halls and corridors.

I hear the falling of distant water in marble fonts;

the large bells of Montsalvat peal louder and louder, and to music of unimaginable stateliness the knights enter in solemn procession, clad in the blue and red robes of the Grail, and take their seats at two semicircular tables which start like arms to the right and left of the holy shrine. Beneath it lies Titurel entranced, and upon it is presently deposited the sacred treasure of the Grail itself.

As the wounded King Amfortis is borne in, the assembled knights, each standing in his place, a golden cup before him, intone the Grail motive, which is taken up by the entering choruses of servitors and esquires bearing the holy relics.

Gurnemanz is seated among the knights; Parsifal stands aside and looks on in mute astonishment, "a guileless one."

As the Holy Grail is set down on the altar before the wounded king, a burst of heavenly music streams from the high dome—voices of angels intone the celestial phrases, "*Take, eat,*" and "*this is my blood!*" and blend them with the "faith and love" motives. As the choruses die away, the voice of the entranced Titurel is heard from beneath the altar calling upon Amfortis, his son, to uncover the Grail that he may find refreshment and life in the blessed vision.

Then follows a terrible struggle in the breast of Amfortis. *He*, sore stricken in sin, yet Guardian of the Grail, guilty among the guiltless, oppressed with pain, bowed down with shame, craving for restoration, overwhelmed with unworthiness, yet chosen to stand and minister before the Lord on behalf of His saints! Pathetic situation, which must in all times repeat itself in the history of the Church. The unworthiness of the minister affects not the validity of his consecrated acts.

Yet what agony of mind must many a priest have suffered, himself oppressed with sin and doubt, while dispensing the means of grace, and acting as a minister and steward of the mysteries.

The marvellous piece of self-analysis in which the conscience-stricken king bewails his lot as little admits of description here as the music which embodies his emotions.

At the close of it angel voices seem floating in mid-air, sighing the mystic words:

"Durch mitleid Wissend
  Der reine Thor,
  Harre sein
  Den ich erkor."

"Wait for my chosen one,
  Guileless and innocent,
  Pity-enlightened."

And immediately afterward the voice of Titurel, like one turning restlessly in his sleep, comes up from his living tomb beneath the altar, "*Uncover the Grail!*"

With trembling hands the sick king raises himself, and with a great effort staggers toward the shrine—the covering is removed—he takes the crystal cup—he raises it on high—the blood is dark—the light begins to fade in the hall—a mist and dimness come over the scene—we seem to be assisting at a shadowy ceremony in a dream—the big bells are tolling—the heavenly choirs from above the dome, which is now bathed in twilight, are heard: "*Drink ye all of this!*" Amfortis raises on high the crystal vase—the knights fall on their knees in prayer. Suddenly a faint tremor of light quivers in the crystal cup—then the blood grows ruby red for a moment. Amfortis waves it to and fro—the knights gaze in ecstatic adoration. Titurel's voice gathers strength in his tomb:

"Celestial rapture!
How streams the light upon the face of God!"

The light fades slowly out of the crystal cup—the miracle is accomplished. The blood again grows dark—the light of common day returns to the halls of Montsalvat, and the knights resume their seats, to find each one his golden goblet filled with wine.

During the sacred repast which follows, the brotherhood join hands and embrace, singing:

> "Blessed are they that believe;
> Blessed are they that love!"

and the refrain is heard again far up in the heights, re-echoed by the angelic hosts.

* * * * * *

I looked round upon the silent audience while these astonishing scenes were passing before me; the whole assembly was motionless—all seemed to be solemnized by the august spectacle—seemed almost to share in the devout contemplation and trance-like worship of the holy knights. Every thought of the stage had vanished —nothing was further from my own thoughts than play-acting. I was sitting as I should sit at an oratorio, in devout and rapt contemplation. Before my eyes had passed a symbolic vision of prayer and ecstasy, flooding the soul with overpowering thoughts of the divine sacrifice and the mystery of unfathomable love.

* * * * * *

The hall of Montsalvat empties. Gurnemanz strides excitedly up to Parsifal, who stands stupefied with what he has seen—

> "Why standest thou silent?
> Knowest thou what thine eyes have seen?"

The guileless one shakes his head. "Nothing but a fool," exclaims Gurnemanz, angrily; and seizing Parsifal by the shoulder, he pushes him roughly out of the hall, with:

> "Be off! look after thy geese,
> And henceforth leave our swans in peace."

The Grail vision had, then, taught the "guileless one" nothing. He could not see his mission—he was as yet unawakened to the deeper life of the spirit; though blameless and unsullied, he was still the "natural man." Profound truth! that was not first which was spiritual, but that which was natural; before Parsifal wins a spiritual triumph, he must be spiritually tried; his inner life must be deepened and developed, else he can never read aright the message of the Grail.

The life of God in the spirit comes only when the battle for God in the heart has been fought and won.

Fare forth, thou guileless one! thou shalt yet add to the simplicity of the dove the wisdom of the serpent. Thou art innocent because ignorant; but thou shalt be weighed anon in the balance and not be found wanting; and then shalt thou reconquer the holy spear lost in Sin, rewon in Purity and Sacrifice, and be to the frail Amfortis the chosen saviour for whom he waits.

* * * * * *

The foregoing events occupied about an hour and a quarter. When the curtain fell, the vast audience broke up in silence.

The air outside was cool and balmy. In the distance lay the city of Bayreuth, with the tower of the Alte Schloss and the old church standing up gray against the distant Bavarian hills. All around us lay the pine woods, broken by the lawns and avenues that encircle the theatre and embower it in a secluded world of its own —even as the Palace of the Grail was shut off from the profane world. Here, indeed, is truly the Montsalvat of the modern drama—a spot purified and sacred to the highest aims and noblest manifestations of Art.

In about an hour the Spear motive was the signal blown on the wind instruments outside, and I took my seat for the second act.

Act II.

A restless, passion-tossed prelude. The "Grail" subject distorted, the "Spear" motive thrust in discordant, the "Faith and Love" theme fluttering like a wounded dove in pain, fierce bursts of passion, wild shocks of uncontrolled misery, mingling with the "carnal joy" music of Klingsor's magic garden and the shuddering might of his alchemy.

The great magician, Klingsor, is seen alone in his dungeon palace—harsh contrast to the gorgeous halls of Montsalvat. Here all is built of the live rock, an impenetrable fastness, the home of devilish might and terrible spells.

Klingsor is aware of the coming struggle, and he means to be ready for it. He owns the sacred spear wrested from Amfortis; he even aspires to win the Grail; he knows the "guileless one" is on his way to wrest that spear from him. His only hope is in paralyzing the fool by his enchantments as he paralyzed Amfortis, and the same woman will serve his turn.

"Kundry!" The time is come, the spells are woven—blue vapors rise, and in the midst of the blue vapors the figure of the still sleeping Kundry is seen. She wakes, trembling violently; she knows she is again under the spell she abhors—the spell to do evil, the mission to corrupt. With a shuddering scream she stands before her tormentor, denying his power, loathing to return to her vile mission, yet returning, as with a bitter cry she vanishes from his presence.

Parsifal has invaded Klingsor's realm; the evil knights have fled before his prowess, wounded and in disorder. Kundry is commissioned to meet the guileless youth in the enchanted garden and, all other allurements failing, to subdue him by her irresistible fascinations and hand him over to Klingsor.

In a moment the scenery lifts, and a garden of marvellous beauty and extent lies before us. The flowers are all of colossal dimensions—huge roses hang in tangled festoons, the cactus, the lily, the blue-bell, creepers and orchids of enormous size and dazzling color wave in mid-air, and climb the aromatic trees.

On a bright hill appears Parsifal, standing bewildered by the light and loveliness around him. Beautiful girls dressed like flowers, and hardly distinguishable from them at first, rush in, bewailing their wounded and disabled knights, but, on seeing Parsifal, fall upon their new prey, and surrounding him, sing verse after verse of the loveliest ballet music, while trying to embrace him, and quarrelling with each other for the privilege.

About that wonderful chorus of flower-girls there was just a suggestive touch of the Rhine maidens' singing. It belonged to the same school of thought and feeling, but was freer, wilder—more considerable, and altogether more complex and wonderful in its changes and in the marvellous confusion in which it breaks up.

The guileless one resists these charmers, and they are just about to leave him in disgust, when the roses lift on one side, and, stretched on a mossy bank overhung with flowers, appears a woman of unearthly loveliness. It is Kundry transformed, and in the marvellous duet which follows between her and Parsifal, a perfectly new and original type of love duet is struck out—an analysis of character, unique in musical drama—a combination of sentiment and a situation absolutely novel, which could only have been conceived and carried out by a creative genius of the highest order.

First, I note that the once spell-bound Kundry is devoted utterly to her task of winning Parsifal. Into this she throws all the intensity of her wild and desperate nature; but in turn she is strangely affected by the spiritual atmosphere of the "guileless one"—a feeling comes over her in the midst of her witchcraft passion, that he is in some way to be her saviour too; yet, woman-like, she conceives of her salvation as possible only in union with him. Yet was this the very crime to which Klingsor would drive her for the ruin of Parsifal. Strange confusion of thought, feeling, aspiration, longing!—struggle of irreconcilable elements! How shall she reconcile them? Her intuition fails her not, and her tact triumphs. She will win by stealing his love through his mother's love. A mother's love is holy; that love she tells him of. It can never more be his; but she will replace it, her passion shall be sanctified by it; through *that* passion she has sinned, through it she, too, shall be redeemed. She will work out her own salvation by the very spells that are upon her for evil. He is pure—he shall make her pure, can she but win him; both, by the might of such pure love, will surely be delivered from Klingsor the corrupter, the tormentor. Fatuous dream! How, through corruption, win incorruption? How, through indulgence, win peace and freedom from desire? It is the old cheat of the senses —Satan appears as an angel of light. The thought deludes the unhappy Kundry herself; she is no longer consciously working for Klingsor; she really believes that this new turn, this bias given to passion, will purify both her and the guileless, pure fool she seeks to subdue.

Nothing can describe the subtlety of their long interview, the surprising turns of sentiment and contrasts of feeling. Throughout this scene Parsifal's instinct is absolutely true and sure. Everything Kundry says about his mother, Herzeleide, he feels; but every attempt to make him accept her instead he resists. Her desperate declamation is splendid. Her heartrending sense of misery and piteous prayer for salvation, her belief that before her is her saviour could she but win him to her will, the choking fury of baffled passion, the steady and subtle encroachments made while Parsifal is lost in a meditative dream, the burning kiss which recalls him to himself, the fine touch by which this kiss, while arousing in him the stormiest feelings, causes a sharp pain, as of Amfortis's own wound, piercing his very heart—all this is realistic if you will, but it is realism raised to the sublime.

Suddenly Parsifal springs up, hurls the enchantress from him, will forth from Klingsor's realm. She is baffled—she knows it; for a moment she bars his passage, then succumbs; the might of sensuality which lost Amfortis the sacred spear has been met and defeated by the guileless fool. He has passed from innocence to knowledge in his interview with the flower-girt girls, in his long converse with Kundry, in her insidious embrace, in her kiss; but all these are now thrust aside, he steps forth still unconquered, still "guileless," but no more "a fool." The knowledge of good and evil has come, but the struggle is already passed.

"Yes, sinner, I do offer thee Redemption," he can

say to Kundry; "not in thy way, but in thy Lord Christ's way of sacrifice!"

But the desperate creature, wild with passion, will listen to no reason; she shouts aloud to her master, and Klingsor suddenly appears, poising the sacred spear. In another moment he hurls it right across the enchanted garden at Parsifal. It cannot wound the guileless and pure one as it wounded the sinful Amfortis. A miracle! It hangs arrested in air above Parsifal's head; he seizes it—it is the sacred talisman, one touch of which will heal even as it inflicted the king's deadly wound.

With a mighty cry and the shock as of an earthquake, the castle of Klingsor falls shattered to pieces, the garden withers up to a desert, the girls, who have rushed in, lie about among the fading flowers, themselves withered up and dead. Kundry sinks down in a deathly swoon, while Parsifal steps over a ruined wall and disappears, saluting her with the words: "Thou alone knowest when we shall meet again!"

* * * * * *

The long shadows were stealing over the hills when I came out at the second pause. Those whom I met and conversed with were subdued and awed. What a solemn tragedy of human passion we had been assisting at! Not a heart there but could interpret that struggle between the flesh and the spirit from its own experiences. Not one but knew the desperately wicked and deceitful temptations that come like enchantresses in the wizard's garden, to plead the cause of the devil in the language of high-flown sentiment or even religious feeling.

Praise and criticism seemed dumb; we rather walked and spoke of what we had just witnessed like men convinced of judgment, and righteousness, and sin. It was a strange mood in which to come out of a theatre after witnessing what would commonly be called an "Opera." I felt more than ever the impossibility of producing the *Parsifal* in London, at Drury Lane or Covent Garden, before a well-dressed company of loungers, who had well dined, and were on their way to balls and suppers afterward.

I would as soon see the Oberammergau play at a music hall.

No; in *Parsifal* all is solemn, or all is irreverent. At Bayreuth we came on a pilgrimage; it cost us time, and trouble, and money; we were in earnest—so were the actors; the spirit of the great master who had planned every detail seemed still to preside over all; the actors lived in their parts; not a thought of self remained; no one accepted applause or recall; no one aimed at producing a personal effect; the actors were lost in the drama, and it was the drama and not the actors which had impressed and solemnized us. When I came out they asked me who was Amfortis? I did not know. I said "the wounded king."

As the instruments played out the Faith and Love motive for us to re-enter, the mellow sunshine broke once more from the cloud-rack over city, and field, and forest, before sinking behind the long low range of the distant hills.

Act III.

The opening prelude to the third and last act seems to warn me of the lapse of time. The music is full of pain and restlessness—the pain of wretched years of long waiting for a deliverer, who comes not; the restlessness and misery of a hope deferred, the weariness of a life without a single joy. The motives, discolored as it were by grief, work up to a distorted version of the Grail subject, which breaks off as with a cry of despair.

Is the Grail, too, then turned into a mocking spirit to the unhappy Amfortis?

Relief comes to us with the lovely scene upon which the curtain rises. Again the wide summer-land lies stretching away over sunlit moor and woodland. In the foreground wave the forest trees, and I hear the ripple of the woodland streams. Invariably throughout the drama, in the midst of all human pain and passion, great nature is there, peaceful, harmonious in all her loveliest moods, a paradise in which dwell souls who make of her their own purgatory.

In yonder aged figure, clad in the Grail pilgrim robe, I discern Gurnemanz; his hair is white; he stoops with years; a rude hut is hard by. Presently a groan arrests his attention, moaning as of a human thing in distress. He clears away some brushwood, and beneath it finds, waking from her long trance, the strange figure of Kundry. For how many years she has slept, we know not. Why is she now recalled to life? She staggers to her feet; we see that she too is in a pilgrim garb, with a rope girding her dress of coarse brown serge. "Service! service!" she mutters, and seizing a pitcher, moves mechanically to fill it at the well, then totters but half awake into the wooden hut. The forest music breaks forth—the hum of happy insect life, the song of wild birds. All seems to pass as in a vision; when suddenly enters a knight clad in black armor from top to toe.

The two eye him curiously, and Gurnemanz, approaching, bids him lay aside his armor and his weapons. He carries a long spear. In silence the knight unhelms, and sticking the spear into the ground, kneels before it, and remains lost in devotional contemplation. The

"Spear" and "Grail" motives mingle together in the full tide of orchestral sounds carrying on the emotional undercurrent of the drama. The knight is soon recognized by both as the long-lost and discarded Parsifal.

The "guileless one" has learned wisdom, and discovered his mission—he knows now that he bears the spear which is to heal the king's grievous wound, and that he himself is appointed his successor. Through long strife and trial and pain he seems to have grown into something of Christ's own likeness. Not all at once, but at last he has found the path. He returns to bear salvation and pardon both to Kundry and the wretched king, Amfortis.

The full music flows on while Gurnemanz relates how the knights have all grown weak and aged, deprived of the vision and sustenance of the Holy Grail, while the long-entranced Titurel is at last dead.

At this news Parsifal, overcome with grief, swoons away, and Gurnemanz and Kundry loosen his armor, and sprinkle him with water from the holy spring. Underneath his black suit of mail he appears clad in a long white tunic.

The grouping here is admirable. Gurnemanz is in the Templar's red and blue robe. Parsifal in white, his auburn hair parted in front and flowing down in ringlets on either side, recalls Leonardo's favorite conception of the Saviour's head, and, indeed, from this point Parsifal becomes a kind of symbolic reflection of the Lord Himself. Kundry, subdued and awed, lies weeping at his feet; he lifts his hands to bless her with infinite pity. She washes his feet, and dries them with the hairs of her head. It is a bold stroke, but the voices of nature, the murmur of the summer woods, come with an infinite healing tenderness and pity, and the act is seen to be symbolical of the pure devotion of a sinful creature redeemed from sin. Peace has at last entered into that wild and troubled heart, and restless Kundry, delivered from Klingsor's spell, receives the sprinkling of baptismal water at the hands of Parsifal.

* * * * * *

The great spaces of silence in the dialogue, broken now by a few sentences from Parsifal, now from Gurnemanz, are more eloquent than many words. The tidal music flows on in a ceaseless stream of changing harmonies, returning constantly to the sweet and slumbrous sound of the summer-land, full of teeming life and glowing happiness.

Then Gurnemanz takes up his parable. It is the Blessed Good Friday on which our dear Lord suffered. The Love and Faith phrases are chimed forth, the pain-notes of the Cross agony are sounded and pass, the Grail motive seems to swoon away in descending harmonies, sinking into the woodland voices of universal nature— that trespass-pardoned nature that now seems waking to the day of her glory and innocence.

In that solemn moment Parsifal bends over the subdued and humbled Kundry, and kisses her softly on the brow—*her* wild kiss in the garden had kindled in him fierce fire, mingled with the bitter wound-pain; *his* is the seal of her eternal pardon and peace.

In the distance the great bells of Montsalvat are now heard booming solemnly—the air darkens, the light fades out, the slow motion of all the scenery recommences. Again I hear the wild cave music, strange and hollow sounding—the three move on as in a dream, and are soon lost in the deep shadows; and through all, louder and louder, boom the heavy bells of Montsalvat, until the stage brightens, and we find ourselves once more in the vast Alhambra-like hall of the knights.

For the last time Amfortis is borne in, and the brotherhood of the Grail form the procession bearing the sacred relics, which are deposited before him.

The king, in great agony and despair, bewails the death of his father and his own backsliding. With failing but desperate energy he harangues the assembled knights, and, tottering forward, beseeches them to free him from his misery and sin-stained life, and thrust their swords deep into his wounded side. At this moment Gurnemanz, accompanied by Parsifal and Kundry, enter. Parsifal steps forward with the sacred spear, now at length to be restored to the knights. He touches the side of Amfortis, the wound is healed, and as he raises the spear on high the point is seen glowing with the crimson glory of the Grail. Then stepping up to the shrine, Parsifal takes the crystal cup, the dark blood glows bright crimson as he holds it on high, and at that moment, while all fall on their knees, and celestial music ("Drink ye all of this") floats in the upper air, Kundry falls back dying, her eyes fixed on the blessed Grail. A white dove descends and hovers for a moment, poised in mid-air above the glowing cup. A soft chorus of angels seems to die away in the clouds beyond the golden dome—

"Marvellous mercy!
Victorious Saviour!"

* * * * * *

Words can add nothing to the completeness of the drama, and no words can give any idea of the splendor and complexity of that sound ocean upon which the drama floats from beginning to end.

The enemies of the Grail are destroyed or subdued, the wound they have inflicted is healed, the prey they claimed is rescued ; the pure and blameless Parsifal becomes the consecrated head of the holy brotherhood, and the beatific vision of God's eternal love and Real Presence is restored to the Knights of the Sangrail.

* * * * * *

When I came out of the theatre at the end of the third and last act, it was ten o'clock.

The wind was stirring in the fir-trees, the stars gleamed out fitfully through a sky, across which the clouds were hurrying wildly, but the moon rose low and large beyond the shadowy hills, and bathed the misty valleys with a mild and golden radiance as of some celestial dawn.

* * * * * *

When the curtain fell on the last performance of *Parsival*, at Bayreuth, which, on the 30th of July, 1883, brought the celebration month to a close, the enthusiasm of the audience found full vent in applause. The curtain was once lifted, but no calls would induce the performers to appear a second time or receive any individual homage. This is entirely in accordance with the tone of these exceptional representations. On each occasion the only applause permitted was at the end of the drama, and throughout not a single actor answered to a call or received any personal tribute.

Behind the scenes there occurred a touching incident. The banker Gross led Wagner's children up to the assembled actors, and in the name of their dead father thanked the assembly for the care and labor of love expended by each and all in producing the last work of the great dead master. Siegfried, Wagner's son, thirteen years old, then, in a few simple words, stifled with sobs, thanked the actors personally, and all the children shook hands with them. The King of Bavaria charged himself upon Wagner's death with the education of his son.

CHAPTER VII.

THE NIEBELUNG'S RING.

I.—Rheingold.

THE heat at Bayreuth (August, 1876) was intense. The Emperor of Germany, who attended some of the performances, expressed his astonishment at the endurance of the orchestra, who had to work by a great power of gas—sunk in a pit beneath the stage.

"I should just like," said his Imperial Majesty, "to go down below and see where my Kapellmeister Richter sweats"—and he went.

Notwithstanding the excessively sultry weather, a vast company of Art Pilgrims ascended the hill outside the city, and took their seats in Wagner's theatre nearly every day for a month.

Let the reader become with me in imagination one of those pilgrims. If I cannot make the sound of Wagner's music ring in his ears, I will try to make a vision of the first Wagner Festival pass before his eyes. As I contemplate Bayreuth, in that same month of August, 1876, I perceive the whole city to be given over to a kind of idolatry of Wagner. The king appears at times to wave incense before him. Liszt, in some degree, shares the homage. With his venerable white head, he looks like an ancient magician, but with an eye that can still flash fire, and a commanding carriage. The town is hung with wreaths and flags; in the shops nothing but

Wagner portraits, busts, medals of all sorts and sizes, Wagner's works, Wagner's Life and Genius, and an immense German and French literature on the Niebelungen Saga.

The performance of the *Rheingold* will live long in my memory, as the extreme realization of weird beauty steeped in atmosphere such as may be in some other planet, flushed with sunset or moonrise. This music is like a land of dreams, into which the spirit breaks at times, and, hurrying back a million of years, discovers, on the surface of far-off seas, or dim caverns, the light that has long since gone out forever The elemental prelude of deep and slumbrous sound wafts us away from all account of time and space of the present. The vast hall, full of silent human beings, has been touched by the magician's wand. All grows dark, and the dim gray-green depths of the Rhine alone become visible. We strain our eyes into the dimness, and are aware of the deep moving of the Rhine water. The three Rhine daughters grow visible, swimming in midwater, swimming and singing, guardians of the Rheingold. What unearthly, unhuman, magical snatches of sweetest song! There is at last realized the creature of legend, the Undine at once more and less than human.

The hideous King of the Undergrounds, or Niebelungen, sits watching these lovely water-maidens—he courts them in vain. The orchestra weaves on its divine Rhine music, without which we almost feel the scene must vanish. The soft cries and unearthly but musical laughter of the Undines, swimming ceaselessly, begin to give us a strange feeling of limited, monotonous life, pointing subtilely to the difference between such natures and our own. But they, too, are waiting for something. This dim green water is growing oppressive. We feel ourselves immersed in its depths. At first it was a dream scene of exquisite beauty—now it is almost a prison—in another moment we should struggle to be free ; but suddenly the *Rheingold* begins to brighten. A shaft of radiance strikes through the water. The Undines scream with joy. The Underground King, Alberich, blinks with astonishment. Then through the whole depth of the Rhine streams an electric light—glowing upon a distant rock—dimmed to softest yellow only by the water. " Rheingold ! Rheingold !" a wild shout arises—joy of the Rhine daughters ! Haydn has produced the effect of light in the *Creation* by a great burst of sound, " And there was Light ! !" But, sublime as is that one chord on Light, the effect here is far more subtle. We have been kept in dark water for half an hour. The whole system is made to pine and cry out for light. It comes at last—the light of the flashing of the Rheingold ! Every fibre in the body quivers with it. It is as oxygen to the lungs. The eye and whole nervous system drink it in. We could shout like children with the Rhine girls over the joy of the Rheingold !

The whole of this water-scene is of indescribable beauty, and without a trace of vulgar pantomimic effect. A lesser man would have made the Rhine water lighter at first. As it is, for some seconds after the curtain rises we can hardly see anything. Slowly the eye discerns the floating women ; but we still follow them chiefly by their voices. Alberich is hardly visible ; the music itself seems to keep down the light ; but then the dawn of splendor of the Rheingold ! That explains all ; the effect is consummate. Wagner, it is evident, has superintended every detail and every *nuance*. I can understand now his bursting into tears when the Rhine ladies refused to enter the new invisible machines which were to float them about in midwater.

I will here briefly allude to the plot of the *Rheingold*. How Alberich, the King of the Undergrounds, renounces the love of the Rhine girls to clutch the gold. How he leaves the Rhine dark, and flies with his treasure to his own Underground caverns, there to maltreat his wretched hordes of slaves, and compel them to turn the Rheingold into sumptuous vessels, among them a magic helmet and a Ring whose wearer can change himself at will into anything. How the gods meanwhile have been bribing the giants with the promise of the beautiful Freia, their sister, to build them their Walhalla Palace. How the giants on the completion of the palace claim Freia, and only give her up upon the gods extorting the Rheingold from Alberich and his Undergrounds and paying it over to the monstrous architects. How at last the gods, with Freia, go over the Rainbow Bridge into the Walhalla to the sound of heavenly music, while upon the ambrosial air comes from afar the fitful wail of the Rhine Daughters:

> " Rheingold!
> Clear and pure,
> Show thy glory in the depths,
> There alone is Truth and Trust,
> False and faithless all above,
> Who rejoice . . . . . !"

All this the reader may possibly be familiar with. To dwell upon each scene is here impossible. I wish to notice the first employment of what I have called the Color Art of the Future. The eye is prepared for the lurid and horrible interior of the Niebelungen Caves, where the scourged slaves ply, amid shrieks, the ceaseless hammer—by white clouds of steam shot with red light. This is used, with varying intensities, to never-pausing music, simply as a sensuous appeal to the eye, and its effect is a pyschological marvel. All the burden of horror and pain is in the surging, hissing, crimson cloud. It is the terrible bridge over which the spectator passes to the realm Niebelheim, as the gods pass to Walhalla over the rainbow. Steam or any other medium, shot with changing color, and perhaps accompanied by music—the Color Symphony—is still to come ; its raw elements are present in the sunset, as the raw elements of music are in the sounds of nature, and the cries of birds and beasts. Wagner has perhaps unconsciously flashed the first line of the new Art upon us in the *Rheingold*.

Of the spiritual beauty of the "Rainbow scene," which is, pictorially, worthy of Turner, I can hardly speak. Yet even here the fateful curse that hangs over the Rheingold and all who touch it—here, in the hour of joy and godlike splendor—there is a hint of the final overthrow of the Walhalla and the "Dusk of the Gods." It is to be seen in the crimson Niebelheim light upon the mighty ramparts and towers—a light that gives a sober tinge even to the rainbow. It is to be heard in the haunting cry of the Rhine daughters over their lost treasure, which makes even the happy gods pause on the threshold of Walhalla. It is felt in the mingled undertones of the orchestra, breaking forth at last into the strong closing bars of the *Rheingold*. A terrible firmness of purpose, beyond the control even of the gods themselves, is urging forward the course of all things in heaven and earth ; none may go back, none may look behind. The old *Anangke*—or Necessity—of the Greeks is at the bottom of all, and seems to say alike to the Rhine daughters, the dwarfs, the giants, and the gods,

"Go forward; the end must come; what will be, will be."

The *Rheingold* lasts for two hours and a half at a stretch, during which time there is no pause in the music; but there is also no sign of fatigue in the audience, who sit in rapt attention to the close.

II.— Walküre.

With the *Walküre*, or Warrior Daughters of God Wotan (Wodin), begin the famous three days to which the *Rheingold*, described in my last, was the introduction. The God Wotan in his earthly wanderings became the father by a mortal woman of Siegmund and Sieglinde. Upon the interest of one of the Walküre, Brünnhilde, in this couple, and her final sacrifice of Virgin deity in their cause, this next drama in three acts turns. Let us enter the theatre about five o'clock. A *fanfare* of trumpets outside gives the signal. The lights are lowered. In the twilight the whole assembly seems aware that Wagner and the king are approaching. In the royal box I see the two stand for a moment like dark shadows, the king bowing once to the people amid breathless silence, broken only by the woe-burdened chords and unquiet distant thunderings of the orchestra.

The curtain rises. A wild cabin, into which out of the storm enters Siegmund—throws himself, dead with fatigue, before a rude fire, and sleeps. In steals Sieglinde, his sister, the forced wife of Hunding, a savage hunter. Thus brother and sister, separated from the cradle, meet unknown to each other. We are at once completely outside all conventional moralities—in an age and faerie sphere in which human passion has to be contemplated apart from all civilized conditions. We thus follow breathlessly, without shock, the inexorable development of the various phases of recognition, self-abandonment, confession, and ecstasy which follow. The wild music flowing to the wild life of the wandering Siegmund, as he pours it all out to his new friend and protectress, who revives him with a cooling draught, consoles him, and already claims him as her deliverer ; the entrance of Hunding ; the fight between him and Siegmund, which is to take place on the morrow ; the sleeping potion administered to him by Sieglinde ; and the long scene at night, where she steals out all in white, to Siegmund— these are graphic and awe-inspiring situations. The moon spreads through the room, and the fire dies, and through the open door are seen the fair, moonlit woods, and all is peace—this the reader must imagine for himself. Nothing more searching in delineation of passion was ever conceived than this scene between lovers about to risk all, with fate overhanging them, and hearts filled alternately with the pain of dread forebodings and an inextinguishable love.

As the last spark on the hearth dies, the music becomes flowing and deep, like a broadening river. A strange red light—the light of Wotan—falls on the giant oak-tree, showing the hilt of a sword plunged in there by a mysterious stranger. He who could draw it should alone free Sieglinde from her brutal husband. Siegmund rises and draws it, amidst a great burst of triumphant sound. This, on the morrow, should give him victory over the coarse Hunding, for the sword is Wotan's own, hidden there for his son Siegmund. The deep wealth of sound upon which the lovers are now buoyed up as they fall into each other's arms is like the mingling of oceans and rivers and clouds ; and the strong, terrible chords, to which the curtain again falls, are as the might of resistless love, hurrying to its fateful close.

The second act reveals to us the wild Brünnhilde—War Walküre. With spear in hand she scales the rocks; the clouds are about her; she shouts to her companions, and her voice mingles with the winds. As she mounts each crag her notes rise higher and higher—a melody of bewitching, boisterous wildness. How Wotan bids the War Walküre defend his favorite Siegmund in the coming duel with Hunding; how Fricka, his jealous wife, burns for the death of Siegmund, the mortal bastard; how the god gives in weakly, and bids Brünnhilde destroy him; how Brünnhilde, a dear, good creature, protests, and goes at last to her mission, clad in mail and scarlet, with a heavy heart—must be told in few words. From this moment to the end of the act the excitement, without pause, goes on, changing in form, but ever increasing. Now the flying lovers rush on the rocky stage; the sound of Hunding's horn, the cry of his dogs, is in their ears; then all is again ecstasy, until Sieglinde breaks out in a strange scene of passionate remorse at having been the wife of an unloved man. Her intense love for Siegmund makes her past life seem too vile. But hark!—and the sound of dogs and horns, the rushing of wind and crashing of branches, swells in the orchestra, and Sieglinde faints, and is laid resting on a rock. Then a passage of unspeakable solemnity occurs with the re-entrance of Brünnhilde. She stands before Siegmund—come on her fateful errand—and the music grows sweet and solemn, with the majestic Wotan "motif;" she tells the hero that whoever looks on her must shortly die; that she takes the warrior to Walhalla, but that he must fall in fight. Measured and slow as fate, yet strangely full of tenderness, is her terrible message. With knightly calm he listens, and at last, with a burst of love which shakes Brünnhilde's own heart, he declares that he will kill himself and his beloved, but they shall not be divided. The Walküre, at last overcome, and faithless to Wotan's command, promises protection.

But the orchestra resumes the stormy music; the battle hour approaches; clouds hurry restlessly through the sky; Hunding is close at hand among the high crags yonder. With a burning kiss the hero leaves Sieglinde, and hurries to meet the foe. She rises, all is wild, and the air grows stormy and dark around her; she calls Siegmund wildly, and rushes forward; but too late, she never sees him alive again. On the topmost rocks we hear, behind the clouds, the warriors shouting and the arms clashing. It is a fearful moment, and the orchestra is taxed to the uttermost. The clouds part for a moment only—the bright Brünnhilde is seen floating above her hero, clad in shining steel and crimson. In vain! Wotan himself appears, and shatters Siegmund's magic sword with his spear. The hero is slain. The clouds now roll aside; in terrible red smoke and blinding light, the angry god stands out. At a word Hunding, the coarse hunter, falls dead before him; but the god turns upon poor Brünnhilde, and, as the curtain falls, curses her for her disobedience.

The storm music and the thunder roll away; and, after a tension probably unexampled in dramatic art, we issue forth into the now cool and darkened air; eighteen hundred people disperse upon the hill and roadside, and discuss for an hour in the temporary *cafés* their experiences. Liszt I find with his daughter, Madame Wagner, and other ladies, chatting to a group. The prince and poet of the Romantic School has a long cigar in his mouth and a large bock of beer in his hand. People hurry up and are introduced at times—he receives all cordially with "Schön! Schön!" I remember that Wagner was loudly called for at the end of the second act, but did not appear. But, oddly enough, before the last act, when the theatre was half empty, he came on the stage and bowed, and was cheered wildly.

The last act opens with a scenic effect which it was anticipated would tax any theatre to render adequately. The chorus of the Walküre on the rocks, half hidden with clouds, as they wait for Brünnhilde, their Amazon sister, unconscious of her catastrophe, is quite unparalleled in its wild and spontaneous splendor. The cries and shouts are hurled from rock to rock with waving of arms and clashing of spears and shields. The troubled sky is in ceaseless motion, the air is filled with boisterous elemental mirth, and the bursting cries of unbridled animal spirits are, somehow, all woven into a kind of chorus, resting upon such an ocean of orchestral sound as has certainly never before been heard or conceived by mortals. Amid thunder and flashes Brünnhilde, dragging poor rescued Sieglinde, now suddenly appears on the stage, and what follows must be merely summarized: the despair of Sieglinde; the devotion of the tender, reckless Brünnhilde—inconceivably touching symbol of the devotion which good women are capable of for each other; the wild recrudescence of joy which seizes Sieglinde when Brünnhilde hands to her, with fervid song, the fragments of Siegmund's magic sword—all that is left of him now, yet enough for vengeance, enough to win the Rheingold from the Giant Fafner, enough for the hero Sieglinde is about to bear. She is then hurried away to safety, and, with the appropriate recurring strains in the orchestra, the God Wotan at last approaches.

The favorite Walküre, deprived of her arms, comes forth to learn the doom of her disobedience. Some divine necessity compels her banishment from Walhalla, and infinitely subtle and complex are the music and sentiment which follow. Brünnhilde has been drawn earthward by human sympathy—she will become whole woman by and by, who has thus stooped to human affection—but earthly love shall destroy her divinity; and, meanwhile, parted forever from her sisters and her father, who still love her fondly, she shall sleep amid wild and lonely rocks encircled with fire, waiting for the lover who, dauntless, shall find her and wake her there, and make her his earthly bride.

The flight of the sister Walküre in the storm, with a wild chorus full of despairing screams, is followed by a protracted and inconceivably touching parting between the resigned Brünnhilde and the father, Wotan—whose anger has died away as the sunset sky has slowly faded into deeper and deeper gray. Then, to long drawn out and enchanting melody, Brünnhilde's head sinks on her father's breast, and his mind wanders back to the happy time when she, the War Maiden, his pride, brought new warriors, the boldest and best, to fill the Walhalla courts. The poor Walküre can but sob that she has loved her father Wotan and Walhalla, and implore him, if she is to become a mortal's bride, to surround her rock with fire, to bar her from all but the bravest. It is now almost dark; a faint red light lingers on the supple yet lordly form of Brünnhilde. A strange swoon seems to have already seized her; the god lays her gently prostrate on the rock, then waves her into her long sleep. Then, retiring suddenly to the back of the stage, he calls for the Fire God, Loge; a burst of fire breaks out and runs round the stage; in another moment the whole background is an immense wall of rose-colored flame, which gradually creeps round the rock. To the most enchanting and dream-like music of silver bells, harps, and flutes, with an undercurrent of bass strings, the sleep of the Walküre begins ; the god scales the rocks, stands for a moment in the midst of the fire, then passes through it out of sight, as the curtain falls to the silver, peaceful, unearthly cadences, repeated again and again, swelling and falling, and ceasing at last, leaving the heart, after so much fierce storm, at rest.

III.—Siegfried.

The grotesque music given to both Mime and Alberich, like so much of Wagner's misunderstood recitative, aims, no doubt, at following the inflexions of the human voice as it is affected often by very commonplace moods, as well as by the meaner impulses of arrogance, vexation, anger, and spite. What we lose in musical charm we gain in a certain ingenious sense of reality. I think the power of Wagner, the solidity of his work, largely turns upon this. He is never afraid of length, of silence, even of dulness, caused by protracted or delayed action. Like De Balzac, he knew well how to work up slowly and surely to a consummate effect, and his effect never hangs fire, nor is it ever liable to an anticlimax, that bane of second-rate artists.

A cavern rocky—somewhere deep in a forest—lies before us ; and Mime, the misshapen thing, fit brother of Alberich, the lord of Niebelheim, or fog-land, works away at a forge to make a sword fit for—whom ? In he comes, the wild, robust child of the forest—reminding me of the first appearance of that other wild, robust creation Parsifal. In he comes, driving a fierce brown bear bridled in sport. Mime the dwarf shrinks back—Mime, who has been foster-father to this Siegfried, son of Sieglinde and Siegmund. He has brought him up in ignorance of his parentage, knowing well the dash of Deity in his blood, and knowing also that could the fragments of the magic sword, given up by Sieglinde as her most precious legacy, be somehow welded together again, Siegfried, her son, would be able to wield it with resistless might and slay the dragon Fafner who keeps the gold.

This accursed gold-heap—eternal symbol of ill-gotten wealth and the curse of it—forms the magic centre around which all the actors in this cycle of dramas consciously or unconsciously move.

The character-contrast between Mime, the mean, double-dealing, cringing, cowardly creature, who hopes to use the young hero for his purposes, and Siegfried, the free, noble, daring youth, with a presentiment of great destinies before him, is drawn in large outline. There is great distinction of type, great simplicity of conception and straightforwardness of execution; the master is sure of his touches and lays them on with a free, bold hand. Siegfried throughout revolts against Mime—yet Mime holds secrets which he burns to know. Who were his father and mother? What means his wild, secluded, lonely life? He cannot taste broth at Mime's hands without disgust; he cannot talk with him without quarrelling; he can hardly bear the sight of him; will not believe that Mime is his father at all; wants a sword that he cannot break; will have the fragments of the magic sword "Nothung" welded; shatters Mime's welding of them; proceeds to weld them himself.

The welding of Nothung, hammer on anvil in the gloomy cavern, with the regular puffing and blowing of the rude bellows—the protracted song—most tuneful, almost conventional in form—broken off and resumed, and itself, as it were, welded with every blow into the sword Nothung, produces a very singular and "seizing" effect. The actors appear to be entirely lost in their business—the audience have come upon a forge in a very rocky forest cave—difficult work is going on, to very long-winded accompaniment, full of varied realistic detail. If we want to see the work put through we must stop; if not, we may go. But the work cannot be hastened; the welding of that sword is the turning-point of the drama; the wielding of it secures the gold, the ring, and the helmet, and the spell of these secures Brünnhilde for Siegfried; the transfer of these treasures wrecks Brünnhilde and brings on the final catastrophe. The action is delayed, but the welding is thorough, and when with a mighty stroke the anvil is cloven in twain, we know that the young hero is at last fitted with an irresistible weapon, and that the drama has moved through one of its most critical and decisive stages.

The Dragon's Cave—the summer woods—the coming together of the various people interested in the gold—these are the elements of the next act. There is the Wanderer, the god Wotan in disguise, who originally stole the gold from Alberich, who in his turn had filched it from the Rhine girls, and who now thinks he may get it back somehow from Fafner the giant. Fafner, in the form of a great dragon, lies on it day and night. There is Alberich, the first robber, hovering about the Neidhole, or cavern, in the hope of getting back the treasure; there is Mime, who about this time makes sure of the prize in his own mind, as he fancies Siegfried is in his power, and proposes to employ him to kill Fafner.

Then he will poison him with a draught, and clutch both magic sword and treasure.

All these old-world scamps meet and talk and eye each other, and plot and ask riddles and give hints. Siegfried, meanwhile, holds the key of the great enigma—stands completely apart—alone in his strength, simplicity, and might, the holder and wielder of the sword Nothung, with deep scorn in his heart for the pitiful and mean schemers and quacks by whom he is surrounded, and with an innate perception, born of communing with nature, of the snares they are laying for him.

The grimness and hideousness of the cavern and the Worm-dragon seem to resume the spirit of all the unlovely wickedness and avarice of Siegfried's rivals. The glorious sunshine, the glowing foliage of the woodlands, the song of wild birds, symbolize the spirit while providing a *mise-en-scène* for the valor, the victory, and the love-musings of the young hero.

The dragon is no doubt the weak point. I believe Mr. Dannreuther gave three hundred pounds for him in London, and brought him over with the utmost care. His tail, I am told, was worked by one man inside him, and his jaws by another ; but somehow he could not be got to show fight at the right time. He was a poor beast ; the steam came out of his mouth too late ; his tail stuck half-way on the wag, and he had evidently some difficulty in opening his jaws. He was easily slain, and rolled over conveniently enough, leaving the treasure in the hands of Siegfried.

Otherwise the weirdness of the whole scene was indescribable. That enchanting summer-land—that delicious burst of woodland melody—that strong contrast between the blazing sheen of emerald and amber-lighted trees and the gloomy cavern hard by—that sudden poetic, trance-like pause, full of wild birds and love dreams, just before the sharp attack on the Dragon, followed by the repulsive murder of Mime, and the resumption of the same bright love dream immediately afterward : this can never fail to impress the dullest sensibility with its extreme beauty. Vogel's Siegfried, as an impersonation, was on a level with Materna's Brünnhilde. The music to which the curtain falls on the second act, as Siegfried, wild with anticipation, follows the bird that flies before him singing, and showing him the way to Brünnhilde, who lies on her fire-girt rock waiting for him—that ocean of summer woodland music upon which a hero's spirit passes into the consciousness of first love—is beyond these halting words.

The contrasts which follow are dramatically admirable. Old Wotan's gloomy conference with Erda, the mystic partner of his old-world love, in which he takes stock of the situation, views with mixed feelings the rise and progress of Siegfried, and with feelings still more mixed the decay of his own power and the approaching downfall of Walhalla ; then his dubious colloquy with Siegfried, who suddenly confronts him on his way to the fire-girt rock ; his mingled pride and dignity, together with his growing sense of being powerless to hinder the consummation of Brünnhilde's union with the upstart demi-semi-god—follow, scene after scene, with cumulative effect. The striking episode in which Siegfried breaks the old god's spear, when it is thrust between him and the unknown object of his passion ; and finally the terrific ocean of crimson flame through which the hero bursts fearlessly to the side of the sleeping Walküre—truly these be massive and monumental conceptions ! Like great world-types they unroll themselves before us in so many magical scenes of unsurpassed, dramatic, and daring grandeur.

I suppose it will be generally allowed that Wagner is the greatest master of love duets that ever wedded words to music. The absorbing picture of love and jealousy in *Lohengrin*, of pure and impure love subtly contrasted in *Tannhäuser*, passion of love and death in *Tristan and Isolde*, the unique passages between Parsifal and Kundry—passion essentially primeval touched with a certain divine intensity as is fit in demi-gods, like Siegfried and Brünnhilde—these are essential manifestations of dramatic force and profound intention, beside which even the love passages in Gounod's *Faust and Marguerite* seem like mere child's play.

The moment has arrived. The majestic Brünnhilde wakes with all her divine war-maiden instincts still upon her; confronts the hero who is to win her, at first with terror; realizes slowly, painfully, then irresistibly and ecstatically, the might of human passion, and surrenders the old heroism of a crumbling Walhalla, and the dreams of god-like power and independence, at the burning touch of human love. Better that touch of real life than all the flimsy visions of a decaying mythology—nobler the sincerity of human feeling, that seizes its object and concentrates its sympathies, than the vague, restless wanderings of old reprobates like Wotan, or the war-lust of fiery, death-hungry Walküre such as Brünnhilde was — such as the bride Walküre will never be again. Hear her

> " O Siegfried !
> Lightener—world's delight—
> Life on earth—
> And laughing lord,
> Leave, ah ! leave me !"

And Siegfried but replies :

> "Awaken, Brünnhilde!
> Waken, thou maid!
> Live to me, laugh to me,
>   Sweetest delight :
> Be mine! be mine!"

No translation seems to give an adequate vigor or do justice to the strength and passion of the dialogue, which ends in a long pæan of triumph as the curtain falls and Siegfried takes his prize.

> Hail, thou sun
> That shinest around me ;
> Hail, thou morn
> From out the dark ;
> Hail, thou world
> That wakes Brünnhilde.
> She wakes! she lives !
> She laugheth back
> My splendid star,
>
> My Brünnhilde's glow.
> Mine, ever mine,
> All of her mine
> And only mine,
> (*Brünnhilde throws herself into Siegfried's arms*).
> Come, life of me!
> Thou light of love !
> Thou laughing Death!

IV.—*The Götterdämmerung.*

The *Niebelung's Ring* closes with the "Dusk of the Gods." The truly prodigious way in which all the leading subjects are repeated, inverted, and worked up in the music of this last colossal drama cannot be described. The Wotan Melody — perhaps the finest — blown on trumpets outside the theatre, rang out far over hill and dale, and floated like an ominous blast to the town below. At the familiar sound the people flocked to their seats in the theatre. The first melodies of the *Rheingold* break from the orchestra, and the Norns or Fates are seen weaving the last of their ropes ; they see as they weave the story of Siegfried and Brünnhilde— they see the gods growing old—they trace the history of Wotan's earth love—they start with horror as they at last see the flames rising in a vision round Walhalla. The rope breaks; the Norns vanish.

The day dawns to a clear subject worked in skilful counterpoint, and the farewell scene between Brünnhilde and her new mate, Siegfried, as he parts from her to seek knightly adventures, now absorbs us. Her sorrow at parting is almost drowned by her feeling of pride in him and the thought of glorious war; and here the Walküre nature breaks out in her. She would fain follow him, but this may not be; and as she is about to be left again on her fire-girt rock, she scales one height after another, shouting a wild and ecstatic adieu to the hero, who is heard galloping away to a strange mixture of Rhine music and a peculiar, joyous, scampering subject, which, together with his horn-blast, always heralds his coming and going.

But the curse of the Gold is upon him, and death, and worse than death, is brewing for him in the house of Hagen, hateful, bastard son of Dwarf Alberich, by a mortal woman. Hagen lives with his brother on Rhine-banks, when Siegfried, as a wandering knight, appears at his halls. Hagen, Günther, the brother, and the fair sister, Gutrune, are sitting together. Hagen, the instrument of Alberich, is wholly bent on getting back the Rheingold. He tells Günther of the sleeping Brünnhilde, who can be approached by Siegfried only, and inflames his desire to seize her. At this moment Siegfried's horn is heard; he enters, and the plot thickens. He is soon given a drink which makes him forget every woman he has known before, even poor Brünnhilde. Siegfried, thus bewitched, then proceeds to fall in love with Gutrune, and listens to the tale of Brünnhilde on the flame-girt rock with astonishment, swears friendship to Günther, and undertakes to assume his friend's shape by magic, cross the flames, seize his own Brünnhilde, and hand her over to Günther.

From this moment the horrible plot is harrowing in the extreme. No art, no music, no magic can reconcile us to what follows; the horror is piled up. The scene changes. Brünnhilde waits on her rock; hears a horse and Siegfried's horn, but with something jarring and false about it; but she heeds not that, he returns! The fire is crossed, a warrior appears on the height. She flies to throw herself into his arms—the form of Günther is before her! How he coolly hands her over to the real Günther, who is waiting; her horror and bewildering despair; his callous indifference and complete absence of all memory of her, which she cannot revive in him; the meeting of the two couples, Brünnhilde and Günther with Siegfried and his new bride, Gutrune; the terrible scene between Brünnhilde and Siegfried before the household and retainers of Hagen, in which she declares Gutrune's husband to be hers; the jealous frenzy of Günther and the death of Siegfried, which is now plotted and presently carried out by stabbing in the back—all this it is impossible here to do more than summarize.

A brief and exquisite episode between the Rhine-daughters and Siegfried, chiefly a treble trio by the floating nymphs, of sustained and enchanting beauty, relieves the pressure of horror we have just been going through from the despair and fury of Brünnhilde, whose wild cries and heart-rending gestures can never be forgotten.

Then comes, at last, the beginning of the end. Siegfried, seated with Hagen, Günther, and warriors, drinks of a cup which restores his memory, and begins to relate his past life; as he advances in his narrative, full of wondrous declamation and music, he at length nears the Brünnhilde episode ; snatches of the Walküre and the fire-sleep music break out ; a strange fervor seizes him ; he tells of the embrace on the rock, and his mind begins to reel with sudden perplexity. But it is enough ! At this point Hagen stabs him in the back. As he dies his thoughts grow clear. Brünnhilde's love returns—he sees but her, dreams of her in his dying swoon ; although she is not present—she, his first, last love, fills his latest consciousness.

The struggle for the Ring which follows, the suicide of Günther, the sudden apparition of Brünnhilde, introduce the last episode of striking beauty. The scenery from this point becomes indescribable. The moon is full upon the ruffled Rhine-waters ; the tall funeral tapers flash on the steel helms of the retainers ; the body of Siegfried, clad in mail, lies in the middle of the stage ; and the stately form of the Walküre is isolated by his side, as the crowd falls to right and left.

While an immense funeral pyre is being built up in the background beside the Rhine-waters, Brünnhilde makes her last reconciliation with Siegfried. As she gazes on his pallid face she reads that dying recognition. She understands, at last, the magic spell that was on him. Her love towers above everything else — she stands there the embodiment of the sublime trust in love beyond sight, that believes and lasts out against all adverse shocks, and is faithful even unto death. She has known divine might in the halls of Walhalla, she has had the power of the Ring and the power of Gold, and enjoyed all fame of war and victory ; and now, with her latest breath, comes solemnly forth what is the conclusion of the whole drama, " Blessedness, through joy and sorrow, comes to us from Love unquenchable alone !"

With this she moves in the moonlight toward the Rhine. She draws the Ring of the Rheingold—the cause of such grief and manifold pain—from the hero's finger, and flings it back into the Rhine, from whence at the commencement it was snatched by Alberich.

The Walküre's black war-horse has been brought to her; she waves high a flaming torch, and hurls it upon the bier; the fire rises in lurid columns. She mounts her steed and leaps into the flames.

At that moment, in the awful glow of the flaming pyre, the waters, still flashing with moonlight in the background, begin to swell and advance, and the Rhine-daughters, singing the wildest Rhine music, are seen floating to and fro. Beyond, a ruddier light broadens, until the distant sky discloses the courts of the Walhalla in flames. With a crash in the foreground the house of Hagen falls; and while the mighty conflagration flares up in the distance, the Rhine-waters, to rushing music, advance and submerge the whole of the stage.

Thus, with a scene of unequalled dramatic splendor, ends the fourth and last immense drama of the *Niebelung's Ring*. This is not the place for fuller criticism of such a work. At the close of it the pent-up enthusiasm of the public rose to a pitch of frenzy. They stood up, and, turning to the royal box, which Wagner had left, shouted to the king, who remained seated and bowed graciously. The plaudits continuing, His Majesty motioned to the stage. The people turned, and in a moment Wagner, dressed in plain black, with his hat in one hand, stepped out from the middle of the curtain, and stood motionless with his gray head uncovered until repeated cries of "Sit down!" "Sit down!" and "Hush!" had calmed the assembly. Wagner then spoke very quietly, and I regret that not hearing him quite distinctly at moments I am unable to render *verbatim* a speech which has doubtless been elsewhere recorded. I understood him to say he had taken many years in preparing this work ; that he had presented a Saga of the Niebelung in the belief that it dealt with subjects peculiarly congenial to the Germanic races ; that a new and national development of the drama was now within their reach ; he believed that they had been satisfied with what they had listened to, so that it had been to the many assembled there a real *Festspiel*. He then thanked the king for his support and encouragement ; and, the curtain being suddenly lifted, all the crowd of musicians and actors who had taken part in the Festival stood ranged, and Wagner, turning round, thanked them in the warmest terms for their devotion and assistance.

So ended the first great Wagner Festival, held at Bayreuth in 1876.

* * * * * *

As some people seem to have considerable difficulty in mastering the plot of the *Niebelung's Ring*, I venture to offer a rough skeleton account of it, which may profitably be studied before or after witnessing the four dramas.

I.

RHEINGOLD.

SCENE I.—The sun irradiating the depths of the river, becomes in the myth—*mythos*, I ought to say—a concrete treasure—Rheingold. It has marvellous properties, and if stolen and forged into a ring, guides its owner to all the hidden gold-mines of the earth. But he who owns the gold must renounce love. Three Rhine girls guard the gold. Alberich, King of the Undergrounds, a hideous dwarf, makes love to the Underwater girls of the Rhine, is rejected, renounces love, but clutches the gold, and makes off with it to Niebelheim—fog-land—his underground caves.

Scene II.—Wotan, King of Gods, tired of love, has employed giants to build him a majestic palace, and offered them Freia, Goddess of Love, as payment. The other gods refuse to part with Freia when the palace is done, and Wotan has nothing left which the giants will take instead. The clever fire-god Loge hears of the Rhine gold, now in Alberich's possession. Offers it to the giants. Offer accepted, and Loge and Wotan go off to steal it.

Scene III.—Loge and Wotan enter Niebelheim. Alberich displays the gold; also a cap, which enables the wearer to assume any form. At Loge's suggestion, he becomes a toad, just for fun; is captured, and the ring and all his wealth passes over to Wotan, but not before the ring is cursed by Alberich, and destined henceforth to bring misery and disaster to its owner.

Scene IV.—The gold and fatal ring are got rid of to the giants, who take the whole in payment; Freia, who gives youth and joy to the gods, is released, and the gods walk processionally into their new palace, over a beautiful rainbow bridge. Curtain falls.

II.

Walküre.

Scene I.—Opens as Siegmund, a son of earth-woman by god Wotan, staggers into a log hut, breathless, and falls prostrate with fatigue. Flying from his enemies, he has found shelter—but where? In Hunding's hut. Enter Sieglinde, daughter of earth-woman by god Wotan; brother and sister, unknown to each other, converse. Hunding enters, and all three converse. The situation dawns on them, and Hunding, respecting his guest, recognizes his foe, and summons him to mortal combat on the morrow. That night, in a stolen interview, Sieglinde and Siegmund arrange matters; a magic sword left sticking in a big tree by Wotan, is claimed by Siegmund and drawn forth, that being the only provision made by the god for his gallant offspring. The lovers escape together.

Scene II.—Father Wotan parleys with the war-maidens anent the coming duel of Siegmund with Hunding. Father Wotan parleys with his wife Fricka on the same subject. Fricka is mad for the death of the irregular son Siegmund. Wotan, with bleeding heart, at last yields, and Walküre Brünnhilde has commission to get him well slain in the fight. Warlike, but tender, Brünnhilde appears to

Siegmund, and tells him of his fate, but is melted at the spectacle of
the despairing lovers, and goes over in disobedience to their cause,
protects the hero in the duel, but is foiled by Wotan, who comes in
as a most detestable *deus ex machinâ*, and gets his own son killed
after all. Brünnhilde takes care of poor Sieglinde, about to become
the mother of Siegfried, and gives her the fragments of the magic
sword, only shattered by the might of Wotan. Brünnhilde, for her
disobedience, loses her divinity, and is laid to sleep on a fire-encom-
passed rock. Having stooped to love, she is now handed over to the
love of a mortal, only the lover must be brave, and will have to go
through the fire and claim her, which brings us to the threshold of
the third drama, *Siegfried*.

III.

SIEGFRIED.

SCENE I.—Sieglinde has died giving birth to Siegfried. Mime
(Alberich's deformed brother), who lives in a wood, has sheltered her,
and, knowing of the secret of the hero she has given birth to, his
demi-godhood, and the invincible sword he is to wield, the fragments
of which are in Mime's possession, the shrewd dwarf brings him up
with care, and intends to make him by and by slay Fafner, the giant,
who, in the disguise of a dragon, keeps the gold stolen for the giants
by the gods from Alberich. The first scene concludes with the successful mending of the broken sword by the combined efforts of
Siegfried, now grown to manhood, and his foster-father, Mime.

SCENE II.—All parties interested are now found lurking about the
hole where Fafner watches the gold. The old scapegrace of a god
Wotan comes prowling about, partly curious to see his grandson,
Siegfried, who is to wield the magic sword—partly with his eye on
the gold. Alberich turns up at the hole watching the main chance,
and ready to clutch at his lost treasure. Mime makes sure of it when
Siegfried has killed the dragon. He means to bring him a sleep-
drink, slay him, and get the gold. Presently the dragon is slain.
Mime offers the drink; Siegfried sees through him, and slays him too.
Having by chance put his finger, stained with dragon's blood, to his
lips, he suddenly understands the cry of the birds in the branches.
One bird sings out loud and clear, and tells of the maid who lies, fire-
surrounded, on a rock. Siegfried follows the magic bird, who is to
lead him to Brünnhilde.

SCENE III.—On his way he meets Wotan, who opposes his spear, to
test his descendant's prowess and power. Siegfried breaks it with

his magic sword, and with it scatters the might of Walhalla. He reaches the fire-rock, bursts through the flames, and claims Brünnhilde as his bride.

IV.

GÖTTERDÄMMERUNG.

Siegfried having left Brünnhilde in search of knightly adventures, comes to the Rhine castle of Hagen. There he is drugged with a magic potion by Hagen's daughter, Gutrune, who wants to marry him. Said potion causes him to forget his love for Brünnhilde and fall in love with Gutrune. He now promises to go with her brother, Günther, and capture Brünnhilde on her fire-surrounded rock and hand her over to Günther. Arrives with him, seizes Brünnhilde, and hands her over. The frightful situation is then worked out in Hagen's castle by the Rhine. Siegfried appears as Gutrune's lover, Günther as Brünnhilde's; they all four meet. Brünnhilde is puzzled, and falls into despair at not being recognized by Siegfried, who is under a spell. In his lifetime the harrowing mystery is never solved, but before his assassination by Hagen he partially recovers his memory. While reciting the story of his life he is suddenly stabbed. Brünnhilde then comes on the scene to find him dead; but the truth that he has been bewitched dawns upon her. She proclaims him tender and true in death. They heap up logs; he is hoisted on to the pile, but not before Brünnhilde has taken the fatal ring from the hero's finger, and cast it back into the Rhine. The Rhine-girls appear on the surface singing. The air darkens, the flames rise. Brünnhilde's war-horse is led out for the last time, horse and Walküre leap into the flames. The Rhine swells up to the footlights, washing over everything, and extinguishing the funeral pile; and the house of Hagen—pillars, doors, and lintel—falls into ruin.

CHAPTER VIII.

LISZT.

The greatest phenomenal players of their age have undoubtedly been Liszt and Paganini. They were great not merely because they could play better than others, but because they created what they played. It is quite possible to maintain that Rubinstein and Bülow play quite as well as Liszt, or that Ernst and Joachim are as good as Paganini ; but it is nevertheless an absurdity and impertinence to argue the point. They were not the first—they came afterward. A man who takes gold out of a mine may be as good as the man who discovered the mine, but he is not that man. He does excellent work, but he was not the first on the ground—he came afterward.

A thing once discovered cannot be rediscovered, and an aureole shines round the head of the pioneer to which no subsequent traveller may lay claim. But quite apart from what is new and original in their respective contributions to Art, it is doubtful whether two such extraordinary personalities as those of Paganini and Liszt have ever appeared in the world of virtuosity. In some respects Liszt is even more extraordinary than Paganini ; for, in the first place, he electrified a world still under the spell of the weird Italian's Cremona ; and, in the second place, his demands have achieved for the piano what no demands of Paganini ever could for the violin—a profound modification and re-creation of the instrument to enable him to realize his prodigious feats of sonority and execution. The modifications introduced by violin repairers—strengthening bars, ribs, gluing cracks, etc.—are trifling compared to the changes which separate the pianoforte of 1820 from that of 1880. Paganini is the creator of the modern violin school; but Liszt has not only created the modern pianoforte school, but in some sort the modern pianoforte.

Great heart, great brain, daring originality, electric organization, iron nerve, and a soul vibrating to sound like an Æolian harp to the wind—there you have the personality, phenomenal and unique, of Franz Liszt.

Who has not heard of Liszt? Who has heard Liszt? I suppose to most of us he is personally a great tradition and nothing more; his compositions, indeed, form the chief *pièces de résistance* of our annual crop of pianoforte recitals; but the man and his playing are alike unknown. He has already become historical during his lifetime. Only by a happy chance can I reckon myself among the few who have lately heard Liszt play.

I happened to be staying in Rome, and Liszt kindly invited me over to the Villa d'Este twice.

There at Tivoli, alone with him, he conversed with me of the times long gone by—of Mendelssohn, of Paganini, of Chopin.

There in the warm light of an Italian autumn, subdued by the dark-red curtains that hung in his study, with an old-world silence around us, he sat at his piano once more; and as he played to me the clock of time went back, and Chopin entered with his pale, refined face, his slight aristocratic figure; Heine sat restlessly in a dark corner; Madame Sand reclined in the deep window-niche overlooking the desolate Campagna, with Rome in the distance; De Lammenais stood at the foot of the piano—a delicate, yet sinewy and mobile frame—with his noble, eager face all aglow, his eloquent tongue silent, listening to the inspiration of another believer in another *evangelium*—the evangelium of the emotions, the Gospel of Art.

Shadows all of you, yet to me for an hour, in the deep solitude of the great Cardinal's palace alone with Liszt, more real than the men and women of our lesser day.

One thousand eight hundred and eleven was the year of the great comet—a year which, we are told, re-echoed with the sounds of the lyre and the sword, and announced so many pioneering spirits of the future.

In 1811 was Franz Liszt born. He had the hot Hungarian blood of his father, the fervid German spirit of his mother, and he inherited the lofty independence, with none of the class prejudices, of the old Hungarian nobility from which he sprang.

Liszt's father, Adam, earned a modest livelihood as agent and accountant in the house of Count Esterhazy. In that great musical family inseparably associated with the names of Haydn and Schubert, Adam Liszt had frequent opportunities of meeting distinguished musicians. The Prince's private band had risen to public fame under the instruction of the venerable Haydn himself. The Liszts, father and son, often went to Eisenstadt, where the count lived; there they rubbed elbows with Cherubini and Hummel, a pupil of Mozart.

Franz took to music from his earliest childhood. When about five years old, he was asked what he would like to do. "Learn the piano," said the little fellow. Soon afterward his father asked him what he would like to be; the child pointed to a print of Beethoven hanging on the wall, and said, "Like him." Long before his feet could reach the pedals or his fingers stretch an octave, the boy spent all his spare time strumming, making what he called "clangs," chords, and modulations. He mastered scales and exercises without difficulty.

But there was a certain intensity in all he did which seemed to wear him out. He was attacked with fever, but would hardly be persuaded to lie down until completely exhausted; then he lay and prayed aloud to God to make him well, and vowed that on his recovery he would only make hymns and play music which pleased God and his parents. The strong lines of his character early asserted themselves—religious ardor, open sincerity, a certain nobleness of soul that scorned a lie and generously confessed to a fault, quick affections, ready sympathies, a mind singularly without prejudices or antipathies, except in music. Liszt's musical antipathies are matters of world-wide notoriety—his hatred of "Conservatorium" dogma, his contempt for the musical doctrinaire, his aversion to the shallow and frivolous, his abhorrence of mere sensationalism.

The boy's decided bent soon banished all thought of anything but a musical vocation, but the *res angustæ domi* stood in the way. How was he to be taught? how was he to be heard? how to earn money? That personal fascination, from which no one who has ever come in contact with Liszt has quite escaped, helped him thus early. When eight years old, he played before Count Esterhazy in the presence of six noblemen, among them Counts Amadee, Apponyi, and Szapary— eternal honor to their names! They at once subscribed for him an annuity of six hundred gulden for six years. This was to help the little prodigy to a musical education.

His parents felt the whole importance of the crisis. If the boy was to prosper, the father's present retired life with a fixed income must be changed for an unsettled wandering and precarious existence. "When the six years are over, and your hopes prove vain, what will become of us?" said his mother, who heard, with tears in her eyes, that father was going to give up the agency and settle down wherever the boy might need instruction, protection, and a home. "Mother," said the impetuous child, "what God wills!" and he added, prophetically enough, "God will help me to repay you for all your anxieties and for what you do for me." And with what results he labored in this faith, years afterward in Paris, we shall see.

The agency was thrown up; the humble family, mother, father, son, went out alone from the little Hungarian village into an unknown and untried world, simply trusting to the genius, the will, the word of an obscure child of eight: "I will be a musician, and nothing else!"

As the child knelt at his farewell mass in the little village church of Raiding, many wept, others shook their heads, but some even then seemed to have a presentiment of his future greatness, and said, "That boy will one day come back in a glass coach." This modest symbol represented to them the idea of boundless wealth.

Hummel would only teach for a golden louis a lesson, and then picked his pupils; but at Vienna the father and son fell in with Czerny, Beethoven's pupil, and the famous Salieri, now seventy years old. Czerny at once took to Liszt, but refused to take anything for his instruction. Salieri was also fascinated, and instructed him in harmony; and fortunate it was that Liszt began his course under two such strict mentors.

He soon began to resent Czerny's method, thought he knew better and needed not those dry studies of Clementi and that irksome fingering by rule; he could finger everything in half-a-dozen different ways. There was a moment when it seemed that master and pupil would have to part; but timely concessions to genius paved the way to dutiful submission, and years afterward the great master dedicated to the rigid disciplinarian of his boyhood his *Vingt-quatre Grandes Études* in affectionate remembrance.

Young talent often splits upon the rock of self-sufficiency. Many a clever artist has failed because in the pride of youthful facility he has declined the method and drudgery of a correct technique.

Such a light as Liszt's could not be long hid; all Vienna in 1822 was talking of the wonderful boy. "Est deus in nobis," wrote the papers rather profanely. The "little Hercules," the "young giant," the boy "virtuoso from the clouds," were among the epithets coined to celebrate his marvellous rendering of Hummel's "Concerto in A" and a free "Fantasia" of his own.

The Vienna Concert Hall was crowded to hear him; and the other illustrious artists then—as indeed they have been ever since forced to do wherever Liszt appeared—effaced themselves with as good a grace as they could.

It is a remarkable tribute to the generous nature as well as to the consummate ability of Liszt, that, while opposing partisans have fought bitterly over him—Thalbergites, Herzites, Mendelssohnites *versus* Lisztites—yet few of the great artists who have, one after another, had to yield to him in popularity have denied to him their admiration, while most of them have given him their friendship.

Liszt early wooed and early won Vienna. He spoke ever of his dear Viennese and their "resounding city."

When I saw Liszt at Tivoli in 1880, I remember his saying to me, "J'ai reçu le célèbre baiser de Beethoven." I found that Beethoven's secretary, Schindler, wrote, in 1823, to Beethoven : "You will be present at little Liszt's concert, will you not? It will encourage the boy. Promise me that you will go." And Beethoven went. When the "little Liszt" stepped on to the platform, he saw Beethoven in the front row; it nerved instead of staggering him — he played with an *abandon* and inspiration which defied criticism. Amidst the storm of applause which followed, Beethoven was observed to step up on the platform, take the young virtuoso in his arms, and salute him, as Liszt assured me, " on both cheeks." This was an event not to be lightly forgotten, and hardly after fifty-seven years to be alluded to without a certain awe ; indeed, Lizst's voice quite betrayed his sense of the seriousness of the occasion as he repeated, with a certain conscious pride and gravity, " Oui, j'ai reçu le baiser de Beethoven."

A concert tour on his way to Paris brought him before the critical public of Stuttgardt and Munich. Hummel, an old man, and Moscheles, then in his prime, heard him, and declared that his playing was equal to theirs. But Liszt was bent upon completing his studies in the celebrated school of the French capital, and at the feet of the old musical dictator Cherubini.

The Erards, who were destined to owe so much to Liszt, and to whom Liszt throughout his career has owed so much, at once provided him with a magnificent piano; but Cherubini put in force a certain by-law of the Conservatoire excluding foreigners, and excluded Franz Liszt.

This was a bitter pill to the eager student. He hardly knew how little he required such patronage. In a very short time "*le petit Liszt*" was the great Paris sensation. The old *noblesse* tried to spoil him with flattery, the Duchess de Berri drugged him with bonbons, the Duke of Orleans called him the "little Mozart." He gave private concerts at which Herz, Moscheles, Lafont, and De Beriot assisted. Rossini would sit by his side at the piano and applaud. He was a "miracle." The company never tired of extolling his "verve, fougue et originalité," while the ladies, who petted and caressed him after each performance, were delighted at his simple and graceful carriage, the elegance of his language, and the perfect breeding and propriety of his demeanor.

He was only twelve when he played for the first time at the Italian Opera, and one of those singular incidents which remind one of Paganini's triumphs occurred.

At the close of a *bravura cadenza* the band forgot to come in, so absorbed were the musicians in watching the young prodigy. Their failure was worth a dozen successes to Liszt. The ball of the marvellous was fairly set rolling.

Gall, the inventor of phrenology, took a cast of the little Liszt's skull; Talma, the tragedian, embraced him publicly with effusion; and the misanthropic Marquis de Noailles became his mentor, and initiated him into the art of painting.

In 1824 Liszt, then thirteen years old, came with his father to England; his mother returned to Austria.

He went down to Windsor to see George IV., who was delighted with him, and Liszt, speaking of him to me, said: "I was very young at the time, but I remember the king very well—a fine, pompous-looking gentleman."

In London he met Clementi, whose exercises he had so objected to, Cipriani Potter, Cramer, also of exercise celebrity, Kalkbrenner, Neate, then a fashionable pianist, once a great favorite of George III., and whom I remember about thirty years ago in extreme old age at Brighton. He described to me the poor old king's delight at hearing him play some simple English melodies. "I assure you, Mr. Neate," said George III., "I have had more pleasure in hearing you play those simple airs than in all the variations and tricks your fine players affect."

George IV. went to Drury Lane on purpose to hear the boy, and commanded an encore. Liszt was also heard in the theatre at Manchester, and in several private houses.

On his return to France people noticed a change in him. He was now fourteen, grave, serious, often preoccupied, already a little tired of praise, and excessively tired of being called "le petit Liszt." His vision began to take a wider sweep. The relation between art and religion exercised him. His mind was naturally devout. Thomas à Kempis was his constant companion. "Rejoice in nothing but a good deed;" "Through labor to rest, through combat to victory;" "The glory which men give and take is transitory" — these and like phrases were already deeply engraven on the fleshly tablets of his heart. Amidst all his glowing triumphs he was developing a curious disinclination to appear in public; he seemed to yearn for solitude and meditation.

In 1827 he now again hurried to England for a short time, but his father's sudden illness drove them to Boulogne, where, in his forty-seventh year, died Adam Liszt, leaving the young Franz for the first time in his life, at the early age of sixteen, unprotected and alone.

Rousing himself from the bodily prostration and torpor of grief into which he had been thrown by the death of his father, Franz, with admirable energy and that high sense of honor which has always distinguished him, began to set his house in order. He called in all his debts, sold his magnificent grand Erard, and left Boulogne for Paris with a heavy heart and a light pocket, but not owing a sou.

He sent for his mother, and for the next twelve years, 1828–1840, the two lived together, chiefly in Paris. There, as a child, he had been a nine-days' wonder, but the solidity of his reputation was now destined to go hand in hand with his stormy and interrupted mental and moral development.

Such a plant could not come to maturity all at once. No drawing-room or concert-room success satisfied a heart for which the world of human emotion seemed too small, and an intellect piercing with intuitive intelligence into the "clear-obscure" depths of religion and philosophy.

But Franz was young, and Franz was poor, and his mother had to be supported. She was his first care. Systematically, he labored to put by a sum which would assure her of a competency, and often with his tender, genial smile he would remind her of his own childish words, "God will help me to repay you for all that you have done for me." Still he labored often wofully against the grain.

"Poverty," he writes, "that old mediator between man and evil, tore me from my solitude devoted to meditation, and placed me before a public on whom not only my own but my own mother's existence depended. Young and overstrained, I suffered painfully under the contact with external things which my vocation as a musician brought with it, and which wounded me all the more intensely that my heart at this time was filled entirely with the mystical feelings of love and religion."

Of course the gifted young pianist's connection grew rapidly. He got his twenty francs a lesson at the best houses; he was naturally a welcome guest, and from the first seemed to have the run of high Parisian society. His life was feverish, his activity irregular, his health far from strong; but the vulgar temptations of the gay capital seemed to have little attraction for his noble nature. His heart remained unspoiled. He was most generous to those who could not afford to pay for his lessons, most pitiful to the poor, most dutiful and affectionate to his mother. Coming home late from some grand entertainment, he would sit outside on the staircase till morning sooner than awaken, or perhaps alarm, her by letting himself in. But in losing his father he seemed to have lost certain method and order. His meals were irregular, so were his lessons; more so were the hours devoted to sleep.

At this time he was hardly twenty; we are not surprised anon to hear in his own words of "a female form chaste and pure as the alabaster of holy vessel;" but he adds: "Such was the sacrifice which I offered with tears to the God of Christians!"

I will explain.

Mdlle. Caroline St. Cricq was just seventeen, lithe, slender, and of "angelic" beauty, and a complexion like a lily flushed with roses, "impressionable to beauty, to the world, to religion, to God." The Countess, her mother, appears to have been a charming woman, very partial to Liszt, whom she engaged to instruct Mademoiselle in music.

The lessons were not by time, but by inclination. The young man's eloquence, varied knowledge, ardent love of literature, and flashing genius won both the mother and daughter. Not one of them seemed to suspect the whirlpool of grief and death to which they were hurrying. The countess fell ill and died, but not before she had recommended Liszt to the Count St. Cricq as a possible suitor for the hand of Mademoiselle.

The haughty diplomat St. Cricq at once put his foot down. The funeral over, Liszt's movements were watched. They were innocent enough. He was already an *enfant de la maison*, but one night he lingered reading aloud some favorite author to Mademoiselle a little too late. He was reported by the servants, and received his polite dismissal as music master.

In an interview with the count his own pride was deeply wounded. "Difference of rank!" said the count. That was quite enough for Liszt. He rose, pale as death, with quivering lip, but uttered not a word.

As a man of honor he had but one course. He and Caroline parted forever. She contracted later an uncongenial marriage; he seems to have turned with intense ardor to religion. His good mother used to complain to those who came to inquire for him that he was all day long in church, and had ceased to occupy himself, as he should, with music.

Love, grief, religion, all struggling together for victory in that young and fervid spirit, at last seemed fairly to exhaust him. His old haunts knew him not; his pupils were neglected; he saw no friends; shut himself up in his room; and at last would only see his mother at meals. He never appeared in the streets, and not unnaturally ended by falling dangerously ill.

It was during this period of severe sickness that Paris

was one morning startled with a newspaper announcement which was worded as follows:

"DEATH OF YOUNG LISZT.

"Young Liszt died at Paris—the event is painful—at an age when most children are at school. He had conquered the public," etc.

So wrote the *Étoile*. In fact, he was seriously ill. M. von Lenz, Beethoven's biographer, went to visit him. He was lying pale, haggard, and apathetic; could hardly be roused to converse except occasionally when music cropped up. Then his eye brightened for a moment like the "flashing of a dagger in the sun."

In 1830 the Revolution burst on Paris. This, it seems, was needed to arouse Liszt. The inner life was suddenly to be exchanged for the outer. Self was to be merged in the larger interests, some of them delusions, which now began to pose again under the cunning watchwords of "Liberté, Égalité, Fraternité." Generous souls saw in the quarrel of Charles X. with his people the hope of a new national life. They proposed to exchange the old and effete "Divine right" for the legitimate "sovereignty of the people." "C'est le canon qui l'a guéri!" his mother used to say. Liszt was hardly restrained by her tears and entreaties from rushing to the barricades. The cure threatened to be worse than the disease. The heroic deeds of the "great week" inflamed him, and he shouted with the rest for the silver-haired General Lafayette, "genius of the liberties of two worlds."

The republican enthusiasm, so happily restrained from action out of affection for his dependent mother, found a more wholesome vent in a vigorous return to his neglected art. Just as he was busy revolving great battle symphonies, his whole artistic nature received a decisive and startling impulse from the sudden apparition of

Paganini in Paris. Preceded by revolution and cholera, this weird man had come upon the bright city that had sinned and suffered so much, and found her shaken and demoralized, but still seething with a strange ferment of new life in which Saint-Simonianism, communism, and scepticism, side by side with fanaticism, piety, and romance, struggled to make confusion worse confounded. Into the depths of what has been called the Romantic movement of 1830–40 it is not my purpose here to enter. There was war alike with the artificial humdrum of the old French world and the still more artificial revival of the classical world of Greece and Rome.

The human spirit was at length to be liberated; no one, it was held, need believe anything that did not happen to commend itself to his fancy or passion. As Heine put it: "The great God, it appeared, was not at all the being in whom our grandmothers had trusted; he was, in fact, none other than you yourself." No one need be bound by the morals of an effete civilization. In Love the world of sentiment alone must decide our actions. Every one must be true to nature. All men were brothers, and women should have equal and independent rights. The social contract, most free and variable, must be substituted for marriage, community of goods for hereditary possessions, philosophy for law, and romance for religion. The beautiful and pregnant seeds of truth that lay imbedded in the teeming soil of this great movement have since fully germinated; its extravagances have already, to a great extent, been outgrown.

In spite of theories disastrous to political and social order, the genius of Madame Sand, Victor Hugo, and A. de Musset, sceptic and sensualist as he was, have rescued the movement from the despair of raw materialism, and produced works of immortal beauty.

They helped the European spirit to recover its independence, they reacted against the levelling tyranny of the first Napoleon, and were largely instrumental in undermining the third Napoleon's throne of gilded lead. Stained with license and full of waywardness, it was, nevertheless, an age of great and strong feelings—an age volcanic, vivid, electric. Such an age eagerly welcomed the magicians who set the language of emotion free, and gave to music its myriad wings and million voices.

Paganini appeared. The violin was no more the violin. A new transcendent *technique* made it the absolute minister of an emancipated and fantastic will. The extraordinary power exercised by the Italian violinist throughout Europe was quickened by the electric air which he breathed. The times were ripe. He stood before kings and people as the very emotional embodiment of the *Zeitgeist*. He was the emanicipated demon of the epoch, with power to wield the sceptre of sound, and marshal in strange and frenzied legions the troubled spirits of the time.

When Liszt heard Paganini, it seemed to him to be the message for which he had been waiting. From him he doubtless received that passion for "transcendent execution," that absolute perfection of *technique*, which enabled him to create the modern pianoforte school, and win for Erard and Broadwood what Paganini won for Stradivarius and Joseph Guarnerius. His transcriptions of Paganini's studies, the *arpeggio*, the *fioriture*, the prodigious *attaque* and *élan* that took audiences by storm, the meetings of extremes which abolished the spaces on the pianoforte key-board by making the hands ubiquitous — these and other "developments" were doubtless inspired by the prodigious feats of Paganini.

Liszt now suddenly retired from the concert-room.

He was no longer heard in public; he seemed disinclined, except in the presence of his intimates, to exhibit his wondrous talent; but he retired to perfect himself, to work up and work out the new impulses which he had received from Paganini.

He thus early laid deep the foundations of his unique virtuosity; and when he reappeared in public, he seemed to mount at once to that solitary pinnacle of fame and surpassing excellence to which the greatest pianists then and ever since have looked up in admiring and despairing wonder. Tausig said, "We are all blockheads by the side of Liszt." Rubinstein has often declared Liszt's perfection of art and wealth of resource to be simply unrivalled.

For a short time in his absence at Paris, it was thought that Thalberg would prove a formidable opponent. But Liszt had only to reappear, and Thalberg himself was forced to join in the general applause. When between the various schools there was war, it was carried on by the partisans of the great men. Although they freely criticised one another, nothing is more remarkable than the kindly personal feeling which obtained between Liszt and his natural enemies, the great pianists of the age, Moscheles, Chopin, Mendelssohn, Thalberg.

There were no doubt cabals, and at one time in Paris he met with much detraction; but he seemed to move in a region of lofty courtesy in which squabbling for precedence was out of place; and his generosity of heart and genial recognition of others' talent disarmed criticism and silenced malice.

With the outburst of the Revolution, with the appearance of Paganini, came also to Liszt a violent reaction against the current religious ideas and the whole of the Catholic teaching. Reading had opened his eyes; the

Catholic system seemed to him not only inadequate, but false. He required a freer atmosphere, one rather more interpretative of human facts and human nature; he thought he found it in the doctrines of the Saint-Simonians. The "Nouveau Christianisme," by far the best of St. Simon's lucubrations, seemed to show that the Church had misrepresented and outraged the religion of Christ. It failed to take due account of art and science, had no sympathy with progress, refused altogether to assimilate the *Zeitgeist*, and had evidently ceased to lead the thinkers or purify the masses.

About this time Liszt came across the eloquent and gifted Abbé de Lamennais. This man it was who, more than any other, saved Liszt from drifting into the prevailing whirlpool of atheism. The heterodox Abbé, who himself had broken with the retrograde religion of Rome, re-formulated his system, and discovered for him what at that time he most craved for—a link between his religion and his art.

"Art," said De Lamennais, "is in man what creative power is in God." Art is the embodiment of eternal types. Nature suggests a beauty she never completely realizes. Only *in the soul of man* is the supernal beauty mirrored as it exists *in the mind of God*. Art is the soul's formula for the expression of its inner life. "Art, therefore, is an expression of God; her works are an infinite manifold reflection of Him."

The mission of art to reveal the secrets of the inner life, to lift the souls of others into high communion with itself, to express its joy in possession, its hope of attainment, its insatiable and divine longings, its dreams of the infinite—these seemed to Liszt high functions, enriching, fertilizing, and consoling all life, and leading the spirit forth into that weird border land of the emotions, where voices come to it from the Unseen, and radiant flashes from behind the Veil.

It was toward the close of 1831 that Liszt met Chopin in Paris. From the first, these two men, so different, became fast friends. Chopin's delicate, retiring soul found a singular delight in Liszt's strong and imposing personality. Liszt's exquisite perception enabled him perfectly to live in the strange dreamland of Chopin's fancies, while his own vigor inspired Chopin with nerve to conceive those mighty Polonaises that he could never properly play himself, and which he so gladly committed to the keeping of his prodigious friend. Liszt undertook the task of interpreting Chopin to the mixed crowds which he revelled in subduing, but from which his fastidious and delicately-strung friend shrank with something like aversion.

From Chopin, Liszt and all the world after him got that *tempo rubato*, that playing with the duration of notes without breaking the time, and those arabesque ornaments which are woven like fine embroidery all about the pages of Chopin's nocturnes, and which lift what in others are mere casual flourishes into the dignity of interpretative phrases and poetic commentaries on the text.

People were fond of comparing the two young men who so often appeared in the same salons together—Liszt with his finely-shaped, long, oval head and *profile d'ivoire*, set proudly on his shoulders, his stiff hair of dark blonde thrown back from the forehead without a parting, and cut in a straight line, his *aplomb*, his magnificent and courtly bearing, his ready tongue, his flashing wit and fine irony, his genial *bonhomie* and irresistibly winning smile ; and Chopin, also with dark blonde hair, but soft as silk, parted on one side, to use Liszt's own words, "an angel of fair countenance with brown eyes, from which intellect beamed rather than burned, a gentle, refined smile, slightly aquiline nose, a delicious, clear, almost diaphonous complexion, all bearing witness to the harmony of a soul which required no commentary beyond itself."

Nothing can be more generous or more true than Liszt's recognition of Chopin's independent support. "To our endeavors," he says, "to our struggles, just then so much needing certainty, he lent us the support of a calm, unshakable conviction, equally armed against apathy and cajolery." There was only one picture on the walls of Chopin's room; it hung just above his piano. It was a head of Liszt.

The over-intensity of Liszt's powerful nature may have occasionally led him into extravagances of virtuosity, which laid him open to some just criticism. Robert Schumann observed acutely: "It appears as if the sight of Chopin brought him again to his senses."

It is no part of my present scheme to describe the battle which romanticism in music waged against the prevalent conventionalities. We known the general outcome of the struggle culminating, after the most prodigious artistic convulsions, in the musical supremacy of Richard Wagner, who certainly marks firmly and broadly enough the greatest stride in musical development made since Beethoven.

That Hector Berlioz emancipated the orchestra from all previous trammels, and dealt with sound at first-hand as the elemental and expressional breath of the soul; that he was thus the immediate precursor of Wagner, who said with more modesty than truth, "I have invented nothing," this is now admitted. That Schumann was afraid of the excesses into which the romantic musicians threatened to plunge, and, having started well and cheered them on, showed some tendency to relapse into old form at the moment when his ingenious and passionate soul sank into final and premature gloom — that has been whispered. That Mendelssohn was over-wedded to classical tradition and a certain passion for neatness and precision which prevented him from sounding the heights and depths of the revolutionary epoch in the midst of which he moved, and by which his sunny spirit was so little affected—this I am now able to see. That Spohr was too doctrinaire and mannered, Meyerbeer a great deal too fond of melodrama and sensation for its own sake ; that Rossini and Auber, exclusively bent on amusing the public, were scarcely enough *hommes sérieux* to influence the deeper development of harmony, or effect any revolution in musical form — most musicians will allow. And that Liszt by his unique virtuosity has made it difficult for the world to accept him in any other capacity, is the constant grievance paraded by his admirers. From all which reflections it may be inferred that many workers have contributed to the wealth, resource, and emancipation of modern music from those trammels which sought to confine its spirit or limit its freedom. Through past form, it has at length learned to use instead of being used by form. The modern orchestra has won the unity and spontaneity of an independent living organism. Like the body, it is a complex mechanism, but it is to the mind of the composer as the human body is to the soul. It has grown so perfect an instrument, and deals with so perfectly mastered an art, that a prelude like *Lohengrin* or the opening of *Parsifal* sounds like the actual expression of the inner moods of the spirit rendered outwardly with automatic unconscious fidelity. The rule, the *tech-*

nique, are lost, hidden, forgotten, because completely efficacious, and subordinated to the free movements of the composer's spirit.

To this latest triumph of the musical art three men since Beethoven have mainly contributed; their names are certainly Hector Berlioz, Wagner, and Liszt.

The darling of the aristocracy, accustomed from his earliest youth to mix freely with the *haute noblesse* of Germany and France, Liszt was a republican at heart. He felt acutely for the miseries of the people, and he was always a great player for the masses. "When I play," he once said, "I always play for the people in the top gallery, so that those who can pay but five groschen for their seats may also get something for their money." He was ever foremost in alleviating the sufferings of the poor, the sick, and the helpless. He seems, indeed, to have been unable to pass a beggar, and the beggars soon found that out; they would even intrude upon his privacy and waylay him in his garden.

Once, when at the height of his popularity in Paris, a friend found him holding a crossing-sweeper's broom at the corner of the street. "The fact is," said Liszt simply, "I had no small change for the boy, so I told him to change me five francs, and he asked me to hold his broom for him till he returned." I forgot to ask Liszt whether the lad ever came back.

I was walking with him one day in the private gardens of the Villa d'Este at Tivoli when some little ruffians, who had clambered over the wall, rushed up to him with a few trumpery weeds, which they termed "bouquets." The benevolent Maestro took the gift good-humoredly, and, fumbling in his pocket, produced several small coins, which he gave to the urchins, turning to me apologetically: "They expect it, you know. In fact," he added, with a little shrug, "whenever I appear they *do* expect it." His gifts were not always small. He could command large sums of money at a moment's notice. The proceeds of many a splendid concert went to manufacturing committees, widows, orphans, sick and blind. He founded pensions and provided funds for poor musicians; he set up monuments to great artists. A pecuniary difficulty arising about Beethoven's statue at Bonn, Liszt immediately guaranteed the whole sum. In the great commercial crisis of 1834 at Lyons Liszt gave concerts for the artisans out of work; and in Hungary, not long after, when the overflow of the Danube rendered hundreds homeless, Liszt was again to the fore with his brilliant performances for charity.

All through his life he was an ardent pamphleteer, and he fought not only for the poor, but in the highest interests of his art, and above all for the dignity of his own class. In this he was supported by such musical royalties as Mendelssohn, Rossini, Paganini, and Lablache. We have heard how in past days the musicians were not expected to mix with the company, a rope being laid down on the carpet, showing the boundary line between the sacred and profane in social rank.

On one occasion Lablache, entering the music saloon at a certain great house, observed the usual rope laid down in front of him when he came on to sing in a duet. He quietly stooped down and tossed it aside. It was never replaced, and the offensive practice dropped out of London society from that day.

Liszt refused to play at the court of Queen Isabella in Spain because the court etiquette forbade the introduction of musicians to royalty. In his opinion even crowned heads owed a certain deference and homage to the sovereignties of art, and he determined it should be paid.

He met Czar Nicholas I., who had very little notion of the respect due to any one but himself, with an angry look and a defiant word ; he tossed Frederick William IV.'s diamonds into the side scenes ; and broke a lance with Louis Philippe, which cost him a decoration.

He never forgave that thrifty king for abolishing certain musical pensions and otherwise snubbing art. He refused on every occasion to play at the Tuileries. One day the king and his suite paid a "private view" visit to a pianoforte exhibition of Erard's. Liszt happened to be in the room, and was trying a piano just as His Majesty entered. The king advanced genially toward him and began a conversation ; but Liszt merely bowed with a polished but icy reserve.

"Do you still remember," said the king, "that you played at my house when you were but a boy and I Duke of Orleans ? Much has changed since then."

"Yes, Sire," replied Liszt dryly, "but not for the better."

The king showed his royal appreciation of the repartee by striking the great musician's name off the list of those who were about to receive the cross of the Legion of Honor.

The idol of Parisian drawing-rooms at a most susceptible age, with his convictions profoundly shaken in Catholicism and Church discipline, surrounded by wits and philosophers who were equally sceptical about marriage and the very foundations of society as then constituted, Liszt's views of life not unnaturally underwent a considerable change.

He had no doubt frankly and sincerely imbibed Mme. Sand's early philosophy, and his witty saying, which reminds me of something of the kind in Rasselas, that "whether a man marries or not, he will sooner or later be sure to repent it," belongs to this period. His relations with Mme. Sand have been much misrepresented. He was far more attracted by her genius than by her person, and although for long years he entertained for her feelings of admiration and esteem, she never exercised over him the despotic influence which drove poor Chopin to despair.

Of the misguided countess who threw herself upon his protection, and whom he treated with the utmost consideration and forbearance for several years, I shall not have much to say; but it must be remembered that he was considerably her junior, that he did his best to prevent her from taking the rash course which separated her from her family and made her his travelling companion, and that years afterward her own husband, as well as her brother, when affairs came to be arranged and the whole facts of the case were canvassed in a *conseil de famille* at Paris, confessed of their own accord that throughout Liszt had acted "like a man of honor."

It was during his years of travel with the Countess d'Agoult in Italy and Germany that Liszt composed the great bulk of his celebrated transcriptions of songs and operatic pieces, as well as the renowned *Études d'Exécution Transcendante.*

Liszt's attempt to preserve his *incognito* in Italy conspicuously failed. He entered Ricordi's music-shop at Milan, and, sitting down at a grand piano, began to improvise. "'Tis Liszt or the devil!" he heard Ricordi whisper to a clerk, and in another moment the great Italian *entrepreneur* had welcomed the Hungarian *virtuoso* and placed his villa, his box at the opera, his carriage and horses at his disposal. Of course Ricordi very soon organized a concert, in which the Milanese were invited to judge the "pianist of the future," as he was then styled. The Milanese were better pleased with Liszt than was Liszt with the Milanese. He could not make them take to Beethoven. They even kicked at certain favorite studies of his own, but he won them by his marvellous improvisations on fragments of their darling Rossini, and afterward wrote a smart article in the Paris *Gazette Musicale*, expressing his dissatisfaction with the frivolity of Italian musical culture, quoting in scorn a voice from the pit which greeted one of his own "Preludes Etudes"— it was the word "étude" at which the pit stuck — "Vengo al teatro per divertirmi e non per studiare," a sentiment which I think I have heard repeated in more northern latitudes.

Of course Liszt's free criticism got back to Milan. Milan was furious. Liszt was at Venice. The papers denounced him. Everybody proposed to fight duels with him. He was told that he could not play the piano, and they handed him over to the devil. Liszt wrote pacifying letters in the Milanese papers, but the uproar only increased. What would happen if he ever dared to show himself in Milan again, no one dared to speculate. He was a monstrous ingrate ; he had insulted every one down to the decorators and chorographers of La Scala, and he must be chastised summarily for his insolent presumption.

When the disturbance was at its height, Liszt wrote to the Milanese journals to say that he declined a paper war ; that he had never intended to insult the Milanese ; that he would arrive shortly in Milan and hold himself in readiness to receive all aggrieved persons, and give them every explanation and satisfaction they might require.

On a hot summer's day he drove quietly through Milan

in an open carriage, and, taking up his abode at a fashionable hotel, awaited the arrival of the belligerents. But as not one of them turned up or made the least sign, Liszt went back to Venice.

When, however, in fulfilment of a promise, he returned in September, he met with a characteristic snub, for his concert was poorly attended, and then only by the upper classes. He had mortally wounded the people. He did not consider Mercadante and Bellini so great as Beethoven, and he said so. This was indeed a crime, and proved clearly that he could not play the piano!

Toward the year 1840 the relations between Liszt and the Countess d'Agoult had become rather strained. The inevitable dissolution which awaits such alliances was evidently at hand. For a brief period on the shores of the Lake of Como the cup of his happiness had indeed seemed full; but *es war ein Traum*. "When the ideal form of a woman," so he wrote to a friend, "floats before your entranced soul—a woman whose heaven-born charms bear no allurements for the senses, but only wing the soul to devotion—if you see at her side a youth sincere and faithful in heart, weave these forms into a moving story of love, and give it the title, *On the Shores of the Lake of Como.*"

He wrote, we may be sure, as he then felt. He was sometimes mistaken, but he was always perfectly open, upright, and sincere.

A little daughter was born to him at Bellaggio, on the shores of that enchanted lake. He called her Cosima in memory of Como. She became afterward the wife of Von Bülow, then the wife and widow of Richard Wagner.

But in 1840 the change came. The countess and her children went off to Paris, and the roving spirit of the great musician, after being absorbed for some time in composition, found its restless rest in a new series of triumphs. After passing through Florence, Bologna, and Rome, he went to Bonn, then to Vienna, and entered upon the last great phase of his career as a virtuoso, which lasted from 1840 to between 1850-60.

In 1842 Liszt visited Weimar, Berlin, and then went to Paris. He was meditating a tour in Russia. Pressing invitations reached him from St. Petersburg and Moscow. The most fabulous accounts of his virtuosity had raised expectation to its highest pitch. He was as legendary even among the common people as Paganini.

His first concert at St. Petersburg realized the then unheard-of sum of £2000. The roads were crowded to see him pass, and the corridors and approaches to the Grand Opera blocked to catch a glimpse of him.

The same scenes were repeated at Moscow, where he gave six concerts without exhausting the popular excitement.

On his return to Weimar he accepted the post of Kapellmeister to the Grand Duke. It provided him with that settled abode, and above all with an orchestra, which he now felt so indispensable to meet his growing passion for orchestral composition. But the time of rest had not yet come.

In 1844 and 1845 he was received in Spain and Portugal with incredible enthusiasm, after which he returned to Bonn to assist at the inauguration of Beethoven's statue. With boundless liberality he had subscribed more money than all the princes and people of Germany put together to make the statue worthy of the occasion and the occasion worthy of the statue.

The golden river which poured into him from all the capitals of Europe now freely found a new vent in boundless generosity. Hospitals, poor and needy, patriotic celebrations, the dignity and interests of art, were all subsidized from his private purse.

His transcendent virtuosity was only equalled by his splendid munificence; but he found what others have so often experienced—that great personal gifts and prodigious *éclat* cannot possibly escape the poison of envy and detraction. He was attacked by calumny, his very gifts denied and ridiculed, his munificence ascribed to vainglory, and his charity to pride and ostentation; yet none will ever know the extent of his private charities, and no one who knows anything of Liszt can be ignorant of the simple, unaffected goodness of heart which prompts them. Still he was wounded by ingratitude and abuse. It seemed to check and paralyze for the moment his generous nature.

Fétis saw him at Coblenz soon after the Bonn festival, at which he had expended such vast sums. He was sitting alone, dejected and out of health. He said he was sick of everything, tired of life, and nearly ruined. But that mood never lasted long with Liszt; he soon arose and shook himself like a lion. His detractors slunk away into their holes, and he walked forth victorious to refill his empty purse and reap new laurels. His career was interrupted by the stormy events of 1848. He settled down for a time at Weimar, and it was then that he began to take that warm interest in Richard Wagner which ended in the closest and most enduring of friendships.

He labored incessantly to get a hearing for the *Lohengrin* and *Tannhäuser*. He forced Wagner's compositions on the band, on the Grand Duke; he breasted public opposition and fought nobly for the eccentric and obscure person who was chiefly known as a political outlaw and an inventor of extravagant compositions which it was impossible to play or sing, and odiously unpleasant to listen to.

But years of faithful service, mainly the service and immense *prestige* and authority of Liszt, procured Wagner a hearing, and paved the way for his glorious triumphs at Bayreuth in 1876, 1882, and 1883.

At the age of seventy-two Liszt retained the wit and vivacity of forty. He passed from Weimar to Rome, to Pesth, to Berlin, to Vienna, but objected to crossing the sea, and told me that he would never again visit England. Latterly he seldom touched the piano, but loved to be surrounded by young aspirants to fame. To them he was prodigal of hints, and ever ready to lavish all sorts of kindness upon people who were *sympathique* to him.

At unexpected moments, in the presence of some timid young girl overpowered with the honor of an introduction, or alone with a friend when old days were spoken of, would Liszt sit down for a few minutes and recall a phrase of Chopin or a quaint passage from Scarlatti, and then, forgetting himself, wander on until a flash of the old fire came back to his eyes as he struck a few grand octaves, and then, just as you were lost in contemplation of that noble head with its grand profile and its cascade of white hair, and those hands that still seemed to be the absolutely unconscious and effortless ministers of his fitful and despotic will, the master would turn away—break off, like one suddenly *blasé*, in the middle of a bar, with "Come, let us take a little walk; it will be cool under the trees;" and he would have been a bold man who ventured in that moment to allude to the piano or music.

I saw Liszt but six times, and then only between the years 1876 and 1881. I have heard him play upon two occasions only, then he played certain pieces of Chopin at my request and a new composition by himself. I have heard Mme. Schumann, Bülow, Rubinstein, Menter, and Essipoff, but I can understand that saying of Tausig, himself one of the greatest masters of *technique* whom Germany has ever produced: "No mortal can measure himself with Liszt. He dwells alone upon a solitary height."

THE END.

INDEX.

A.
ACCOMPANISTS, 36.
ALBERT, Prince, 173.
ALPS, 144.
AESCHYLUS, 150, 153.
AMADEE, Count, 254.
AMATI, 97.
APPONYEE, Count, 254.
AMSTERDAM, 64.
ART, Gospel of, 253; nature of, 267; power of, 148; study of, 151; unity of, 144, 154.
ATHENS, 151.
AUBER, 160, 167, 270.
AUDITORY nerve, 67.

B.
BALLADS, 57.
BALZAC, 236.
BAVARIA, King of, 178, 184, 196, 246.
BAYREUTH, 164, 184, 225.
BEETHOVEN, 141, 144, 146, 153, 157, 159 seq., 163, 184, 253, 255, 257, 269, 271, 275.
BEGGARS, 271.
BENNETT, Sterndale, 42.
BERGONZI violin, 25.
BERLIOZ, 163, 269, 271.
BIRDS, Paganini silencing, 118.
BLINDNESS, Deafness and, 49.
BLOOD of Christ, 200 seq.
BOWING, violin, 24, 139.
BRIDGE, violin, 46, 92.
BRIGHTON, 27.
BRODIE, Sir Benjamin, M.D., 26.
BROWNING, 157.
BÜLOW, Hans von, 174, 181, 251, 276.
BULWER, 160.
BYRON, 157, 163, 189.

C.
CALCAGNO, Catherine, 111.
CAMBRIDGE Musical Society, 41.
CANTABILE-PLAYING, 24.
CARNIVAL de Venise, 23, 140.
CATHOLICISM, 143, 266.
CHERUBINI, 253, 257.
CHOPIN, 59, 159, 163, 252, 266, 268, 274.
CHORUS, Greek, 152.
CHURCH, taking orders in, 47.
COLERIDGE, 30.
COLOR art of the future, 228.
COMET, the great, 253.

COMO, Lake, 276.
CONCERTS, private, 54.
CONDUCTORS, musical, 185.
CONSERVATORIUM, 254, 257.
COSIMA, wife of Wagner, 174, 276.
CREMONA, 85, 97.
CZERNY, 255.

D.
D'AGOULT, Countess, 274.
DANNREUTHER, 157, 239.
DEAFNESS and blindness, 49.
DE BERIOT, 21, 258.
DE LAMMENAIS, 163, 252, 267.
DE MUSSET, Alfred, 163, 264.
DE PERKYNS, Mrs., 54.
DEVONPORT, 17.
DEVRIENT, Madame Schröder, 159.
DRAMA, 148 seq.

E.
EAR, musical, 52.
EGOTISM, Wagner's, 177.
ELIZA, Princess, 112, 125.
EMOTION, ill-regulated, 74 seq.; in the abstract, 80; parallel trains of, 77; power of music over, 65 seq.
ENGLAND, 164.
ERARD, 257.
ERNST, 15 seq., 251.
ESTERHAZY, Count, 253 seq.
EURIPIDES, 150.
EXHIBITION of 1851, 8.
EXILE, Wagner's, 172.
EXPRESSION, 147.

F.
FARRINGFORD, 29.
FERRARA, 114.
FETIS, Monsieur, 133, 136, 278.
FIESOLE, 116.
FINGER-BOARDS, 12.
FINGERS, exercising the, 19, 28.
FLORENCE, 116.
FLYING Dutchman, 167 seq.
FRESHWATER, 29.

G.
GARDNER, Mr., of Leicester, 138.
GEORGE III., 259.
GEORGE IV., 258 seq.
GERMANY, Emperor of, 225.
GEYER, Louis, 145.

INDEX.

GLUCK, 156.
GOETHE, 146, 157, 159.
GÖTTERDÄMMERUNG, 242, 250.
GOUNOD, 241.
GRAIL, the Holy, 200 seq.
GREEK drama, 150.
GREEKS, music of the, 75.
GRINDERS, 23.
GUARNERIUS, Andrew, 98.
GUARNERIUS, Joseph, 102 seq.
GUARNERIUS violins, 110.
GUHR, Prof., 139.
GUITAR, 111, 119.

H.

HARMONICS, 40, 139.
HARP, 16
HAYDN, 45, 227, 253
HEALER, musical, 72.
HEINE, 264.
HELMHOLTZ, 52.
HENZ, 258.
HERZITES, 256.
HUGO, Victor, 163, 179, 264.
HUMMEL, 253, 255, 257.
HUNGARIAN Airs, 14.

I.

IFFLAND, 146.
IMAGINATION, 148.
IN MEMORIAM, Tennyson's, 30.
INSPIRATION, musical, 38
INTERVALS on violins, 12, 53.
ISABELLA, Queen, 272.
ITALY, 64.

J.

JAELL, 20.
JOACHIM, 187, 251.

K.

KEPPLER, Dr., 193.
KEMPIS, Thomas à, 259.
KERMESS, feast of the, 64.
KOTZEBUE, 146
KREUTZER's Exercises, 28.

L.

LABLACHE, 272.
LACORDAIRE, 163.
LAFAYETTE, 263.
LAFONT, 126, 258.
LAPINSKI, 18
LAPRINSKI, 127.
LAST Rose of Summer, 82.
LEGEND, 169 seq.
LIED ohne Worte, 77.
LIGHT, 227.
LISZT, 14, 17, 163, 174, 180, 181, 184, 190, 225, 233, 251 seq.
LISZTITES, 256.
LOCATELLI, 112.
LOHENGRIN, 160, 171, 177, 241, 270.
LOUIS PHILIPPE, 273.
LOVE, 123, 245, 264.
LOVE Duets, 241.

M.

MAGDEBURG, 160, 164.
MARK, Wagner's dog, 180, 199.
MATERNA, 183.
MAZZINI, 163.
MEHUL, 160.
MEISTERSINGER, 175, 180.
MENDELSSOHN, 9, 29, 61, 157, 163, 165, 266, 270, 272.
MENDELSSOHNITES, 256.
MESMERISM, 117.
MESSIAH, Oratorio of, 81.
METTERNICH, 128
MEYERBEER, 159, 164 seq., 270.
MIDSUMMER Night's Dream, 10.
MILAN, 275.
MONTSALVAT, 181, 202.
MOSCHELES, 257 seq., 266.
MOZART, 45, 142, 159, 253.
MUNICH, 184.
MUSICAL Healer, 72.
MUSIC, an ear for, 40 ; as a restorative, 71 seq ; conversation and, 55 ; defects in the art of, 148 ; discipline of the emotions by, 74 seq. ; for the masses, 81 seq.; future of, 70, 269 ; in large halls, 67 seq.; national impressions from, 64 ; of the Greeks, 75 ; power of over emotion, 65.

N.

NAPOLEON, 265.
NEATE, 259.
NECESSITY, 229.
NEUE Schloss, 198.
NICHOLAS I., Czar, 273.
NIEBELHEIM, 229
NIBELUNG's Ring, 178, 186, 225 seq., 247 seq.
NOVELS, 27.

O.

OPERA, 155.
ORCHESTRA, 270.
ORCHESTRAL work, 26.
OURY, 20.

P.

PAGANINI, 15, 21 seq., 41, 105 seq., 251, 263, 265, 272.
PAGANINI, Theresa, 128.
PAINTING, 148.
PARIS, 136.
PARSIFAL, 175, 181, 200 seq., 270.
PIANO, 251.
POETRY, 28, 148, 154 seq.
POTTER, Cipriani, 174.
PUBLIC singers and players, 67.

R.

REVOLUTION, 162 seq., 263.
RHEINGOLD 225 seq., 245.
RHINE girls, 226.
RICHTER, 181, 184.
RICORDI, 274.
RIENZI, 160 seq., 169.
RIOS, 164.
RODE's Air in G, 24, 42.

INDEX.

ROLLA, 108.
ROMANTICISM, 163, 264, 269.
ROSSINI, 126, 164, 189, 253, 270, 272, 275.
RUBINSTEIN, 17, 163, 251, 266.
RULE Britannia, 164.

S.

ST. CRICQ, Caroline, 261.
ST. SIMONIANISM, 207.
SALIERI, 255.
SAND, Madame, 163, 252, 264, 273.
SANGRAIL, legend of, 200.
SCHILLER, 146, 157, 159.
SCHLESINGER, 166.
SCHNOR, 182.
SCHUBERT, 59, 150, 253.
SCHUMANN, 157, 163, 269.
SCULPTURE, 148.
SHAKESPEARE, 146, 149, 153, 159.
SHELLEY, 163.
SIEGFRIED, 236 seq, 249.
SIMPLICITY, 58.
SIVORI, 16.
SOLITUDE, 28.
SONG without words, 77.
SOPHOCLES, 150, 153.
SOUND-FILTERING, 69.
SOUND-POST, 46, 88.
SPOHR, 159, 171, 270.
SPONTINI, 160.
STRADIVARIUS, 98 seq.
STRADIVARIUS violins, 25, 93, 100.
STRINGS, violin, 94; breaking, 114; plucking, 140.
SWINBURNE, 157.
SZAPARY, Count, 254.

T.

TANNHAUSER, 170, 241.

TARISIO, 6.
TAUSIG, 266, 280.
TEACHING, 19.
TECHNIQUE, 256, 270, 280.
TENNYSON, 29, 157, 163; visit to, 31 seq.
TENNYSON, Mrs., 31 seq.
THALBERG, 266.
THALBERGITES, 256.
THUNDER-STORM, 68.
TITIENS, Madame, 182.
TOUKOWSKI, Paul, 181.
TRANCE, 9.
TRINITY College, 39.
TRISTAN and Iseult, 160, 175, 241.
TUNING the violin, 139.

V.

VARNISH, 91.
VENICE, 187, 190.
VENUA, 43.
VICTORIA, Queen, 173.
VIOL, 95.
VIOLIN-COLLECTING, 7.
VIOLIN, the, anatomy of, 87; grace of, 96; holding, 23; learning to play, 11; material of, 91; power of, 96; varnish of, 91.

W.

WAGNER, 144 seq., 225, 246, 269, 271, 278
WALKÜRE, 230, 248.
WEBER, 159 seq.
WEDDING March, 9.
WHEWELL, 39.
WILHELMJ, 174, 181.
WILLIAM IV., of Germany, 273.
WORDSWORTH, 30.
WOTAN, 230.

www.ingramcontent.com/pod-product-compliance
Lightning Source LLC
Chambersburg PA
CBHW032117230426
43672CB00009B/1765